Also by Danielle J. Lindemann

Commuter Spouses: New Families in a Changing World

Dominatrix: Gender, Eroticism, and Control in the Dungeon

True Story

Farrar, Straus and Giroux
New York

True Story

What Reality TV Says About Us

Danielle J. Lindemann

Farrar, Straus and Giroux
120 Broadway, New York 10271

Library of Congress Cataloging-in-Publication Data
Names: Lindemann, Danielle J., author.
Title: True story : what reality TV says about us / Danielle J.
    Lindemann.
Description: First edition. | New York : Farrar, Straus and Giroux,
    2022. | Includes bibliographical references and index.
Identifiers: LCCN 2021021366 | ISBN 9780374279028 (hardcover)
Subjects: LCSH: Reality television programs—United States—
    History and criticism. | Television programs—Social aspects—
    United States.
Classification: LCC PN1992.8.R43 L56 2022 | DDC 791.45/6—dc23
LC record available at https://lccn.loc.gov/2021021366

Our books may be purchased in bulk for promotional,
educational, or business use. Please contact your local
bookseller or the Macmillan Corporate and Premium Sales
Department at 1-800-221-7945, extension 5442, or by email at
MacmillanSpecialMarkets@macmillan.com.

www.fsgbooks.com
www.twitter.com/fsgbooks • www.facebook.com/fsgbooks

10 9 8 7 6 5 4 3 2 1

For Fiona

Contents

True Story

Introduction

Make two lists.

In column A, write down as many current U.S. Supreme Court justices as you can name, just off the top of your head. In column B, do the same but with Kardashians.

I recently assigned this exercise in my Introduction to Sociology class. Among the nearly two hundred undergraduates, only three could name all nine justices, and only one student had a longer column A. I don't point this out to throw my students under the bus. In fact, I have difficulty remembering all of the justices. And, to be fair, there are more Kardashians than justices (particularly if you include the Jenners) and the family keeps replicating. Still, when more students at an elite university can name Kim Kardashian's *children* than can name Sonia Sotomayor, it's time to start taking reality TV seriously.

The Real World, arguably the first reality TV show, debuted on MTV more than a quarter century ago. Since then, the genre has exploded, with twenty-three million people watching Darva Conger and Rick Rockwell get hitched on *Who Wants to Marry a Multi-Millionaire?*[1] and upward of fifty-one million tuning in for *Survivor*'s season one finale in 2000.[2] In 2010, *American Idol* was drawing more than twenty-five million viewers per episode, a number "equal to the entire populations of Missouri, Maryland, Wisconsin, Minnesota, and Colorado combined, and more than the entire population of Australia."[3] Of the top four hundred shows to air on US television in 2017, 188 of them were reality TV.[4]

You may call it a "guilty pleasure" or, if you're feeling less charitable, "trash" or "train-wreck TV," or perhaps, like Ted Koppel, you may wonder aloud if the genre marks "the end of civilization."[5] The truth is that vastly more of us are watching reality TV than not,[6] and those who avert their eyes are still haunted by its apparitions. One study found that college students who claimed not to watch reality TV, or who said they watched very little, still knew specific details about these shows.[7] Anecdotally, my own encounters with strangers, colleagues, and friends support these findings. A new acquaintance, for instance, declared that he doesn't watch reality TV—moments later clarifying that he had "only" seen *The Anna Nicole Show*, Logo's *Fire Island*, "and all of *RuPaul's Drag Race*, obviously." I have this kind of conversation a lot.

But even for those who *really* don't watch, knowledge of these programs has become part of the cultural ether. It reaches us in unavoidable fragments: product lines, Instagram posts, advertisements, snippets of conversation, referents in scripted media, and intersections with news and politics. It infuses our own personal realities, leaving even highbrow consumers and skeptics with the hazy mental images of a New Jersey housewife flipping a table and a man extending an index finger to punctuate the words "You're fired!"

WHY SHOULD WE CARE ABOUT REALITY TV?

An often ridiculed form of entertainment, seemingly marginal to the serious business of life, reality TV is in fact a pop-cultural touchstone that illuminates our everyday experiences and can help us to make sense of complex social forces. The genre is a fun-house mirror, to be sure, but one that powerfully reflects the contours of our social world. It takes the elements that are central to our culture—our collective preferences, our norms and taboos, and the jagged edges of our social inequalities—and beams them out to us in frenetic detail.

The idea that pop culture can teach us about ourselves is nothing new. Media researchers have long suggested that television reflects our values as a culture.[8] More than any other medium, they have argued, TV is our collective storyteller.[9] While other forms of media are also shaped by public tastes, mainstream television programs must appeal to vast swaths of society or risk cancellation. Their content is indicative of our broadest social patterns and values.[10]

And reality TV is particularly primed to reveal these patterns.[11] Because it is not overtly scripted, much of its drama, intrigue, and conflict relies on casting people who are *dissimilar* to one another, exposing the categories of difference that are patchworked into our society. This was apparent from the first season of the show *The Real World*, which grappled with broad issues of inequality by race, class, gender, and sexuality. The genre also rivets us with cultural contradictions: Amish folks ambling through Times Square, Snoop Dogg and Martha Stewart cooking dinner together, rich ladies attacking each other with their Gucci bags. These unusual combinations often magnify real-life disparities and tensions.

The genre confronts us with the same social dynamics that exist, in muted form, in our own lives. Social critic Judith Butler has argued that drag queens, by presenting gender in an exaggerated way, expose our taken-for-granted gender norms.[12] In the same way, by showing us extreme versions of everyday situations, reality TV magnifies the contours of our cultural landscape. *The Real Housewives of Atlanta* and *Here Comes Honey Boo Boo*, for instance, are not just entertaining to watch; through their exaggerated caricatures, they reveal the social fictions of race and class that we falsely assume to be natural and fixed.

It may seem counterintuitive that a genre focused on zany personalities and extreme cases has so much to teach us about our own ordinary lives. Yet scholars have long argued that we can learn about core features of society by looking at the extremes.[13] The same behaviors that make reality TV participants cultural sideshows are also diffuse within our culture. These people are larger-than-life embodiments, for instance, of our own materialism, our obsessions with our bodies, and the steps we take to mold our children in our own images. The people on reality shows are people who are willing to eat bugs and take pregnancy tests on TV, but they're parodies of ourselves. They dwell in the blurry space between the mundane and the disreputable, and they show us how we all do the same.

In showcasing all of these interesting people, the reality genre turns over stones that scripted programming leaves undisturbed. From debutantes to doomsday preppers, and from homemakers to hoarders, these programs cast a searchlight on the center as well as the nooks and crannies of society. Its perimeter is not all-encompassing, but even its absences help us understand which types of people we grant legitimacy as a culture.

Finally, it's important to understand reality TV because watching it is not a passive experience. It changes us. There are direct links between the material on these shows and the ways people think about and move around in the world. As evidenced by Koppel's remark about "the end of civilization," this genre has long been a source of our cultural anxieties. And some research suggests that this concern may be warranted. In one experiment, for instance, participants who were exposed to an episode of the weight-loss show *The Biggest Loser*, versus an episode of a nature show, walked away with a significantly greater dislike of overweight individuals.[14] But these shows have arguably more constructive outcomes as well. Another study, published in *The American Economic Review*, found strong evidence that the show *16 and Pregnant* had reduced births by teens.[15] Reality TV is important to understand, not only because of what it can tell us about our lives but because of what it does *to us*. The experience of watching these shows, like looking in any mirror, is interactive. We see ourselves, and then we groom ourselves accordingly.

WHERE IT CAME FROM, AND WHAT IT IS

Before getting into the nitty-gritty of what reality TV can teach us about ourselves, it's important to pin down how this genre emerged and where its boundaries lie. Unfortunately, the answers to "What is reality TV?" and "Where did it come from?" are perhaps unsatisfyingly hazy. "Reality TV" is a social construction—and like all social constructions, as we'll see throughout this book, it's slippery.

There's some question about when or where, exactly, reality TV began. Some media historians locate its beginnings in the quiz shows of the 1950s or the romance-oriented game shows that sprang up in the 1960s (e.g., ABC's *The Dating Game* and *The Newlywed Game*). (While some suggest that the genre is a member of a documentary lineage that began

far before that, others have drawn a thick line between reality TV and documentaries.)[16] Another important forerunner
was *Queen for a Day* (1956–1964), in which female contestants vied for the best sob story, ranked by audience applause;
the winner took away a series of prizes, ranging from a new
refrigerator to a hearing aid. Yet another key player was *Candid Camera*, which was first broadcast as the radio show *The
Candid Microphone* in 1947, before coming to TV in 1948 and
airing on and off in various formats until 2014. *An American Family* (1973), a PBS documentary chronicling the dissolution of a family by the last name of Loud, is also a fine
contender for the title of first reality TV program. It wasn't
until *The Real World*, though, that many of the characteristics
of reality TV, as we know it today, emerged—for instance, a
house filled with cameras, its "serial structure," and casting
procedures "intended to ignite conflict and dramatic narrative development."[17] While it's fruitless to try to establish a
singular starting point for the genre, needless to say: reality
TV was not a flash storm that arose suddenly on a sunny day.
It had been brewing for quite some time.

While those chronicling the rise of the genre may dispute
exactly when it began, most agree that *Survivor*, first airing
in 2000, changed everything.[18] Though the premise of the
show, which featured cast members competing in challenges
and voting one another off a literal island, was initially a
difficult sell, what sealed the deal at CBS was the potential
for brand integration.[19] *Survivor* paid for itself in advertising
revenue before it even aired and was the first real indication
of what a gold mine reality TV could be.[20] Today, decades
later, contestants on the show are still meeting at tribal
councils and forming alliances. And profit-wise and ratings-
wise—if not, perhaps, respectability-wise—the reality genre

has moved out of the shadows of popular culture and onto its central stage.[21]

Survivor's executive producer Mark Burnett had a solid profit model, but we can't lay the success of the genre completely at his feet—especially since, in true reality TV style, he recycled the *Survivor* format from the Swedish show *Expedition Robinson*, which had aired three years earlier. There were various historical reasons why reality TV gained momentum when it did. At a moment when cable TV had fully arrived, networks were duking it out for advertising dollars, and the salaries of high-profile actors were ballooning, reality programs were able to incorporate promotional tie-ins while keeping operating costs relatively low. The producers of these shows didn't have to pay their contestants, writers, or crews union wages or offer them health insurance.[22] They didn't have to build expensive soundstages.[23] Technological advances, such as the rise of relatively cheap handheld cameras, facilitated the production of these shows. And the repeal of the so-called fin-syn (financial interest and syndication) rules in the mid-1990s, which returned the rights of syndication back to the major television networks themselves, was also an important catalyst for reality TV. In sum, the death of fin-syn newly incentivized networks to air these cheaply made programs, even if they did not garner the ratings or acclaim of their scripted counterparts.[24]

Then, beginning in late 2007, with scripted shows on hiatus and networks scrambling for content during the hundred-day Writers Guild of America strike, it was time for reality programming's moment in the sun. The writers' strike wasn't the cause of the genre's explosion, but it was certainly one catalyst, with more than one hundred reality shows either emerging or returning during that 2007–2008 TV season.[25]

The extreme proliferation of the genre as it spreads to new markets, covers new ground, and assumes shifting guises makes its boundaries tricky to discern.[26] We can narrow it down, though:

Generally, we can think of reality TV as a set of programs that feature non-actors (though they may *also* feature actors in reenactments) and make a claim to reality (whether or not there is any sort of "scripting" actually taking place) but are intended mainly to entertain rather than inform.[27] Finally, most reality shows use the same elements pioneered by *The Real World*. For example, they feature the "talking head," "testimonial," or "ITM" ("in the moment") convention in which participants are interviewed regarding the action on the show. This definition encompasses a variety of subgenres, including competition shows, dating shows, docusoaps, makeover/self-help programs, programs that purport to show distinct subcultures or lifestyles, crime and punishment shows, and celebrity shows as well as celebrity variations on many of these other themes. These umbrella categories, though large, may fail to cover some borderline cases, and some programs straddle multiple categories. Again: slippery.

WHY WE WATCH

We know why reality TV shows keep getting produced. They're relatively quick and cheap to make, and they're potential cash cows. From the supply side, it's a no-brainer. But why do we keep tuning in?

Research has suggested that people get several different "gratifications" from these programs. One of these is voyeuristic pleasure.[28] We're excited and curious to watch people in their unguarded moments, particularly when we suspect there might be a train wreck on the horizon.[29] And, paradoxically, even though our viewing of these shows is frowned upon, another reason people tune in is for social connection.[30] This connection happens when fans hold viewing parties, chat with their friends about developments on the shows, and even discuss the content with strangers; it also happens online, through interactive websites, social media feeds, and message boards.[31]

There are other things we could be watching. But one unique appeal of this genre is that it involves real people ostensibly reacting to real-world stimuli, which facilitates our putting ourselves in the participants' shoes. (Would *I* have told Shannon that Vicki was talking behind her back? What protein would *I* have selected for the barbecue challenge?) Reality television places its viewers in the driver's seat in ways that scripted TV does not. As we'll see, this is related to the genre's multiplatform approach. We can participate in these shows through various forms of consumption and via social media engagement with their stars—and, in some cases, we literally get to vote on the outcomes. Perhaps unsurprisingly, research has found that, even controlling for age and gender, reality TV viewers spend more time on, and make more extensive use of, social-networking sites than do nonviewers.[32]

Archetypes, the lifeblood of reality TV, further help us to make connections with these characters.[33] Going back to *The Real World*, disparate personalities who fit into broad, easily identifiable social categories form the vertebrae of many of these shows. As a former producer of *The Bachelor* told the journalist Amy Kaufman, for instance, "We studied [the contestants] ad nauseam before they arrived. . . . You'd pre-categorize everyone and have some shorthand as to who they were. Mom. Southern Belle. The cheerleader. The bitch.

We all called them by ridiculous names. The fat one, the hot one, the crier."[34] Further, as we'll see, it's not just the show's creators who craft these archetypes but the performers themselves who grab hold of these broad categories and sway with them.[35]

We take the ride as well. Psychiatric research has explained how viewers form "parasocial relationships"—that is, quasi face-to-face relationships—with TV characters; they feel especially connected to television personalities who are like people they know.[36] Scholarship also suggests that we're particularly likely to experience these "relationships" with reality TV personas.[37]

One might argue that we identify with broad character types within other forms of entertainment, and that's true. When you read *Little Women* as a girl and decided that you were "a Jo," or when you watched *Sex and the City* and fancied yourself "a Samantha," only to have your friends break the news that you were definitely "a Miranda" (um, hypothetically), you were doing something similar. The difference, however, is that with reality TV you're reacting to someone who is ostensibly being herself. Along these lines, one study observed that people who watch reality TV are particularly apt to connect elements of these programs with pieces of their own lives, creating "a form of self-referential hyperauthenticity."[38] That is, viewers are able to bind together elements of their own histories and the stars' histories, and their own personalities and the stars' personalities, and place themselves in the aspirational, imaginative situations that occur on the shows. So, you're not just imagining yourself in the shoes of the "smart one," you're imagining yourself in the shoes of the "smart one" sailing over Tuscany in a hot-air balloon as two men vie for your hand in marriage. You no longer just identify with a character but actively fantasize about the various dramatic scenarios in which this character finds herself; it's easier to do this when, ostensibly, the artifice of scripting has been stripped away.

Indeed, many reality stars are able to capitalize on the fact that we feel particularly close to them, whipping those imagined connections into their bread and butter. As we saw with *Survivor*, reality TV has been a rich venue for "advertainment," or "the merging of advertising and entertainment programming."[39] As the media scholar June Deery has explained, reality programs "tend to normalize the embedding of commercial agenda into experience."[40] That "commercial agenda" spills off the screen and into the stars' awards-show appearances, book tours, and Twitter feeds. It emerges as particularly salient at certain moments, as in 2017 when we learned that Kendall Jenner had reportedly been paid $250,000 for a single Instagram post promoting the Fyre Fest,[41] a disaster of such epic proportions that it spawned two documentaries and multiple lawsuits. The Kardashian/Jenners are not the only reality TV personalities doing these endorsements, though they are arguably some of the most successful. There are *Bachelor* alumni, for instance, who now make a living off this sponsored content, or "SponCon."[42] The tabloid industry, too, has drawn sustenance from reality TV—the genre's stars now dominating the pages of *OK!* and *Us Weekly*. Reality shows and the people on them, Deery notes, help to promote the idea that "virtually all forms of social interplay are ultimately about selling, about sponsorship, about spin."[43] This notion may resonate with you if you've ever gotten a Facebook message from an old high school friend who wants to reconnect— only to try to sell you leggings or green smoothies.

Reality TV is couch-potato fodder. Part of its allure, for

many of us, is that we can switch off our brains and let the content rush over us in a relaxing and anesthetic wave. Yet, paradoxically, in some ways, we can *more* actively consume these shows than we can scripted TV. Their characters, often, are heightened versions of ourselves placed in more intriguing scenarios than we will typically encounter. We want to peek into the lives of these interesting people, but it's their similarity to us that keeps us riveted. We're voyeurs, but part of what tantalizes us about these freak shows is that the freaks are ourselves.

IN THIS BOOK . . .

One of the reasons the genre is so apt to teach us about our social world is that it contains these "hyper" versions of ourselves. In following the contours of our own caricatures, we come to a greater understanding of the forces that society exerts on us—how we organize our lives around beliefs that stem from and reinforce entrenched social hierarchies.

And, illogically, for all of its extreme personalities and outlandish premises, reality TV reflects *how regressive we truly are*. It shows us how we tend to perceive our social world in linear and crystallized ways that reflect the persistent tug of history. The fist-pumping partiers and three-year-old beauty queens who swarm on our screens demonstrate how conservative we remain—about everything from how we think about race and gender to where we draw the boundaries of acceptable style. And when I say "conservative" here, I don't mean in the sense of conservative politics—though the conservatism I am discussing sometimes aligns with those political values. I mean "conservative" in the sense of interpreting the world in narrow and unyielding ways, whether those interpretations are relatively contemporary or more historically entrenched. (As we'll see, in some cases, we confuse the former with the latter—for instance, identifying notions about motherhood that are relatively contemporary as "traditional.")

For all of its carnivalesque aspects, the genre reflects how steadfastly we cling to simplistic, collective notions about who and what is legitimate and "real." It spotlights the categories and meanings that we take for granted as essential, biological, and unshakable. But in doing so, it allows us to poke at these assumptions, revealing the socially constructed natures of what we consider to be "true," "normal," "healthy," "legitimate," and "good"—in areas ranging from what constitutes a "real" marriage to which pants we should buy. The genre exposes our conservative reality, but it also exposes *reality itself* to be a social fiction.

To be clear, to point out that many of our everyday distinctions are social figments is not to suggest they are unimportant. Just the opposite: these fictions shape our experiences of the world in crucial ways. As the sociologists W. I. Thomas and Dorothy Swaine Thomas have pointed out, "If men define situations as real, they are real in their consequences."[44] Many of the categories we use to organize our worlds are at once "unreal" in that they are socially manufactured and "real" in that they impact our lives. The programs covered in this book, while seemingly over the top in some ways, have much to teach us about those unreal realities.

The two parts of the book have loosely different but overlapping aims. In part 1 (chapters 1–5), I lay down a baseline for how to view these shows through a sociological lens, while part 2 (chapters 6–10) builds on that foundation. When sociology shows us the world, it may take us to spots that are familiar. Sociology offers us new insights, but part of its value lies in confirming what we may have already suspected. Consequently, this book sometimes does the same. Some of the material here will surprise you, exposing elements of society that you might not have already noticed, helping you think not only about reality TV but also about your own life in new ways. Other conclusions—for instance, that families are still important to us, racism and sexism are alive and well, the class system shapes all of our lives—are equally important but may be less astonishing. What *is* surprising, perhaps, is that these often outrageous programs would serve as beacons of our retrograde values. A polygamist who gets catfished into sending a photo of herself seductively licking a banana, for instance, shows us how rigidly we think about family. In some ways, these shows with unusual premises—sister wives, a marriage competition, "survive" on an island—are the least wacky content on television.

This book spans a wide array of these shows. Some shows are cultural tidal waves and others mere ripples across the back channels of basic cable, quietly appearing for a season or two before receding from view. *I Didn't Know I Was Pregnant* and *My Strange Addiction* have not had the same cultural impact as *The Real World* or *Survivor*. The programs discussed in this book have varying aims and intended audiences, and some are arguably more "art" than others.

However, they *all* teach us about ourselves.

In each chapter, I balance more mainstream shows with shows that are more fringe. It is particularly important to attend to the latter, because often they are simultaneously the most outlandish *and* the most retrograde. At the same time, as we'll see, the fringe programs can hold the richest potential for liberation from our fusty, well-worn ideals. While there may never be a gay *Bachelor*, less watched shows on cable networks have been showing us queer possibilities for decades. Reality TV confirms that our feet are stuck in the past, but it can also demonstrate that *it does not have to be that way*.

I begin the book by focusing on the smallest unit of society and then gradually widen the lens to include larger and larger social structures. Each chapter focuses on a sociological theme or principle that reality TV illuminates: the self, couples, groups, families, childhood, class, race, gender, sexuality, and deviance. At the same time, I highlight how these categories are intertwined. Other sociological topics—economics, education, immigration, consumerism, sports, and so forth—populate these pages as well, and various scholars and their theories emerge as key players. What follows is a story that begins with each of us, funnels out to encompass all of us, and teaches us about ourselves as individuals, as groups, and—it turns out—as a country.

NOT IN THIS BOOK . . .

Bearing in mind the imperfect definition of "reality TV," there are some types of shows that do not appear in the chapters that follow. While reality TV is a global phenomenon, I focus primarily on shows produced in the United States. Though some "crime and punishment"-type shows appear briefly, the book generally sidesteps both court TV and the "true crime" docuseries genre, popularized by programs such as *Making a Murderer* (Netflix, 2015, 2018), in which a single case unfolds over a number of episodes. In addition, it generally ignores news programs, documentaries, talk shows (which sociologists have analyzed previously),[45] sports, and traditional-format game shows such as *Wheel of Fortune*—as opposed to documentary-style game shows, or "gamedocs," such as *Survivor*. The book does not discuss every reality show ever made (sorry, *My Big Fat Obnoxious Boss*!), though it explores nearly all of the subgenres mentioned above.

Finally, I do not draw distinctions between shows that have more and shows that have less producer intervention, scripting, manipulation, and editing. While social constructions of "the real" are an important theme in this book, it doesn't resolve the thorny issue of whether these programs themselves are "really real," whatever that might mean. Nothing shaped by humans into a cultural product is ever going to offer a pure reality. Specific participants are selected for reality shows; they are sometimes put into artificial and extreme environments; and their footage is cut and reconfigured, occasionally through a process known as "frankenbiting," in which different strands of dialogue are spliced together to manufacture a story.[46] Reports of scenes being scripted, of participants being asked to reenact scenes, and of manufactured story lines have dogged shows like *The Hills* for years.[47] And then there is producer intervention. The contestants on *The Bachelor*, for instance, are psychologically manipulated by physical isolation, removal of all forms of entertainment, shrewd interview tactics, and a steady flow of alcohol.[48]

Yet we don't have to believe that reality TV is 100 percent unadulterated reality in order to want to watch it or even to like it—though believing it's real may aid in our enjoyment of it, one study suggests.[49] We also don't need to buy into the idea that it's fully unscripted and organic in order to accept that disassembling it, dusting it off, and analyzing the pieces can teach us something significant about ourselves. And indeed, these programs speak to our everyday interactions as well as the social structures and cultural understandings that influence the way we move through the world. They hold the capacity to swing the door wide and reveal the major circuits of power that shape all of our daily lives. It's time to get real.

DISCLAIMER: I'M A FAN

I was three days shy of my twelfth birthday when the first episode of *The Real World* aired. The premiere didn't register for me and I didn't watch it at the time, though it hung gauzily in the background of my late childhood. It was the fourth season, set in London, that drew me into the show. I was a freshman in high school, we had just gotten cable, and I was hooked! Interestingly, *Real World* cocreator Jonathan Murray has listed that season among his disappointments. It was purportedly so boring that the producers took the roommates' TV out of the house after that season and gave the subsequent casts a collective job or project to do.[50] Maybe for that reason, you'll seldom see *London* airing in reruns, but I found so much to love about it, from Kat and Neil's sexual tension to Jay's playwriting aspirations. I stayed up late devouring episodes I'd recorded on VHS tapes, periodically stopping and rewinding, neglecting my homework.

These shows are old friends that have followed me through the major plotlines and turning points of my own life. When I first encountered *The Real World*, I was hurting; the show was a strange balm then. After graduating from college and moving to New York, I met up weekly with my friends to watch Kahlen and Naima square off on *America's Next Top Model*, the show briefly taking the edge off our anxiety about how to move through the world as adults. When I discovered *The Real Housewives of Orange County*, my boyfriend and I had just broken up, I'd moved out of our shared apartment, and Vicki Gunvalson falling off the stage while receiving a fake award was everything I needed in my life at that moment. (She was fine.) In graduate school, another student and I would secretly bask in the lowbrow glow of Speidi and Justin Bobby from *The Hills* before tunneling back into the dark world of sustained, soul-crushing critique. After my second miscarriage, I stumbled across old episodes of the MTV show *Meet the Barkers* (about a rock drummer and his beauty-queen wife) on YouTube; for days, I was numbly transfixed by their liberating frivolity.

If many reality programs have appeared in my life during low times or pressure points, I'm not alone in that experience. In her autobiography, former First Lady Michelle Obama has recalled how she turned to these shows to allay the stress of her husband's campaign. "At the end of a busy day," she writes, "I will tell you, there is nothing better than watching a young couple find their dream home in Nashville or some young bride-to-be saying yes to the dress."[51] On a related note, the religion scholar Kathryn Lofton has questioned whether binge-watching these shows may be perceived as a "meditative" act.[52] Indeed, bingeing reality TV, at least for me, can have kind of an anesthetic effect.

So, to be clear: I'm a fan. I have an emotional attachment to some of these shows. Whenever they flash into view again, it's like hearing the familiar echoes in the house where I grew up. I am someone who wakes up in the middle of the night, idly wondering whether Pam and Judd from *The Real World: San Francisco* are still together. (They are! They have two kids!) I gave shout-outs to both *Project Runway* and *Bad Girls Club* in my wedding vows. But while I personally like reality TV, this book is not a love letter to the genre. And while I recognize that many of these programs are deeply problematic, neither is it a critique. As Georg Simmel wrote in 1903, the sociologist's task is "not to complain or condone but only to understand."[53] If anything, the chapters that follow are a love letter to sociology—to its capacity to show us how a form of pop culture often belittled as lowbrow, frivolous, and nonredeeming can so vividly illuminate our own social worlds.

Because reality TV is now ubiquitous—and because some of its participants have become cultural icons—we might be tempted to conclude that the genre has ascended from "guilty pleasure" status and has earned the mantle of legitimacy. But ubiquity is not the same as social acceptance. As someone who teaches and writes about reality TV, and who enjoys it and is bursting to talk about it, I have a good vantage point for observing its continued stigmatization. True, I'm often around academics, and academics are probably snootier about this sort of thing than the average person. But across social contexts, from ivied halls to family functions and from post office lines to back-to-school nights, I notice that the distaste for these shows hasn't quite gone away. At a children's birthday party, for instance, I chatted with a father about the topic of this book. Excitedly, he called over his wife and introduced her as a gigantic *Bachelor* fan. "Yeah, but nobody *knows* that," she sputtered back, flushed and flustered. Though I have spoken to this woman multiple times since, we never discussed reality TV again. This sort of thing happens to me a lot.

As we'll see, there's a hierarchy of acceptance when it comes to reality TV—from screaming, conflict-driven affairs to the HGTV home improvement programs that play innocuously in dental waiting rooms across America. And reality shows may be "guiltier" for people in some social groups (such as professors) than others (their students). Still, my hunch is

that many people today—the same people who would not
think twice about tuning in to a football game or an old episode of *Friends*—would still feel self-conscious about flipping
over to a *Kardashians* rerun on the elliptical at the gym.

But we don't have to rely on my hunch. Research shows us
that all these years after the first *Real World* cast piled into
a New York loft, these programs are still wildly popular yet
can't quite escape the whiff of the seedy. They're still "guilty
pleasure" TV, and viewers feel some remorse about tuning
in.[54] And, yes, watching an entire season of *Teen Mom OG* in
one sitting may feel like the shameful intellectual analogue to
binge-eating a sleeve of fudge-stripe cookies (to use two completely hypothetical examples not taken from my own life).
But this genre is not without nutritional value. It's watched by
millions, it's known by nearly everyone, and it generates cultural references that we can draw upon to connect with one
another. Its participants are often framed as trashy, freaky,
slutty, sloppy, violent, and extreme. At the same time, one
reason we just can't quit reality TV is that we see flashes of
ourselves in the images on our screens. It is this same duality
that makes it possible for us to dismiss the genre as nonsense
while simultaneously installing a reality show host in the Oval
Office.

Speaking of that elephant in the room, Donald Trump's
campaign and subsequent presidency often drew upon the
tropes and conventions of reality TV—in particular, capitalizing on our collective uncertainty about where the boundary
lies between the factual and the fake. While this book is not
a retrospective on the Trump presidency, he is an important data point for helping us to understand how reality TV
both reflects and molds culture. I return to this point in the
conclusion.

These programs show us the ugly places we've been and the ugly places where we still are; they illuminate the inequalities that cut our culture deeply, leaving ruts we may never repair. They showcase elements of our culture in drag form, bold and garish. At the same time, the genre holds the potential to explore new possibilities, diversities, and creativities. By looking at reality TV, we gain insight not only into this genre but also into interpersonal dynamics, large and small—ultimately, better comprehending our own lives within the context of broader forces. When we gaze into the fun-house mirror, the reflection may not be pretty, but we gain a keener understanding of ourselves.

Part I

1

"Don't Be All, Like, Uncool" (The Self)

Seven strangers are sitting around a table, making introductions.

Heather explains that she went to an all-Black high school. "Maybe . . ." She pauses and adds, "No, it was just a Black high school." The others laugh. "You know, I can't even say, 'Maybe [one white person].' It was just a Black high school."

Eric's neighborhood, on the other hand, was populated with white middle- and upper-class families. "But then you can go jog like two miles and you get into Asbury Park. And that's like predominantly Black."

"I was way out in the country," Becky explains. "This was, like, as white as can be—one culture there."

Kevin's eyes widen at the "one culture" comment.

There's no better place to start exploring what reality TV teaches us about ourselves than the premiere episode[1] of *The Real World*. First airing on MTV in 1992, as explained in its original opening sequence, the show is "the true story of seven strangers picked to live in a loft and have their lives taped." Not only was *The Real World* arguably the "first" reality show, but it also shows us, very clearly, what it means to think sociologically.

At its core, sociology is concerned with understanding collective human experience. It is the study of how we do things in groups, how those groups work, and how they change over time. But that doesn't mean we neglect the individual; the discipline has always explored the tricky tango between our individual selves and the social contexts that shape, and are shaped by, them. One classic sociological topic, for instance, has been unemployment—which is at once a personal issue and a collective problem, subject to broad cultural and economic patterns.[2]

Widely considered to be one of the founding fathers of sociology, French sociologist Émile Durkheim (1858–1917) promoted the idea that our lives are shaped by social forces, which can be analyzed in a systematic, scientific way. Durkheim broke with existing fields (such as psychology) that had focused on individual experience, as well as fields (such as philosophy) that had analyzed the social world from a more humanistic perspective. In his bid to legitimate sociology as a discipline, he drew comparisons to the more established, "hard" sciences—arguing, for instance, that we can study the different elements of society in the same way that a biologist might examine the components of a cell. Not only was society a worthy object of study, Durkheim claimed, but by investigating it, we could extract quantifiable truths and make future predictions.

Society, Durkheim contended, isn't simply a collection of individuals; rather, it is its own entity and demands its own analysis. Specifically, our lives are governed by "social facts," which "consist of manners of acting, thinking and feeling external to the individual, which are invested with a coercive power by virtue of which they exercise control over him."[3] If suicide, for instance, were just about the individual decision to commit the act, that wouldn't explain why suicide *rates* vary among countries or why they change within a country as characteristics of the economy change.[4]

Further ruminating on the relationship between the individual and broader society, the modern sociologist C. Wright Mills (1916–1962) defined what he called the "sociological imagination" as "the capacity to range from the most impersonal and remote transformations to the most intimate features of the human self—and to see the relations between the two."[5] Both Durkheim and Mills, in slightly different ways, were concerned with a core sociological issue: How can we understand our own lives as a part of something larger?

"We're all influenced by our social environments" may not seem like a revolutionary premise, but in Durkheim's time, Mills's time, and even today, many of us scarcely realize the extent to which this is true. Often when we have troubles in our lives, Mills wrote, we lack a sociological imagination. We tend to see things as the result of individual failures rather than as the products of large-scale sociohistorical forces. To be clear, this imagination doesn't absolve people from making bad choices, but it demonstrates how we always make those choices within particular social constraints. Going back to unemployment, for instance, it's objectively true that I lost my high school job as a bank teller because I was slow and unmotivated. But it's also objectively true that the economy was tanking and the branch needed to fire someone. As the newest, youngest, and worst employee, I was the lowest-hanging fruit.

At first blush, reality TV might seem like an inapt candidate to teach us about the social forces that influence our lives. In some ways, the genre is hyperfocused on the individual, showcasing humans with interesting traits or quirks (drag queens! celebrities! people who eat their couches!) and underscoring the importance of personal responsibility.[6] Yet reality programs also expose how these personalities are cultivated within the patches of social life they happen to inhabit. When diverse individuals socialized in different ways come into contact, sparks may fly, illuminating the fact that our understandings of the world are *learned* rather than innate.

WELCOME TO *THE REAL WORLD*

Magnification of social difference is at the heart of *The Real World*. The first season's cast members were all in their late teens to mid-twenties and individually compelling in some way. You may remember Julie, who, attempting to break free from her southern conservative upbringing, rode on the back of a stranger's motorcycle and spent time with the homeless. Heather (aka "Heather B.") had already established a career as part of a rap group and was trying to make it as a solo artist. Becky and Andre were also musicians. Eric was a model. Kevin was a poet. Norman, the token queer character (and the first of many on that series), was a painter and gave his testimonials in a bathtub for no apparent reason.

Though *The Real World* is ostensibly about these unique individuals, it's fairly easy to view it with a sociological imagination, because the show does much of the work for us. Julie's fish-out-of-water trajectory highlights how, despite her zeal for exploration, her upbringing has in many ways molded her outlook on the world. In one iconic scene, Heather's beeper goes off, and Julie asks whether Heather sells drugs. While the comment is punctuated by a dramatic guitar riff, nobody on the show calls it out as racist. In fact, Kevin, who is also Black, tells the cameras that Julie seems "very open."

But in another scene, race is the explicit topic of dinner-time conversation, when Kevin comments that racism "is alive and well." He goes on to discuss his experience with the n-word and people's assumption that he's good at basketball, while Heather describes how she's treated like a potential shoplifter when she visits stores. It's not a stretch to understand how collective, historical understandings of race and gender have impacted these three housemates' perceptions of and interactions with the world. And if we can't make that leap ourselves, Kevin, Heather, and Julie help us over the hurdle, by explicitly pointing out that the US has a shared history that disparately impacts members of its various groups. "At some point in my life," Kevin says, "I recognized that a large part of my history was denied from me."

"Your history is my history," Julie objects.

"I agree," says Kevin. "You just don't realize it."

It's Sociology 101, and it's gorgeous.

In more recent seasons, *Real World* (it dropped the *The* in 2014) evolved into, basically, conventionally attractive people making out in hot tubs. One might argue that this change was culturally illuminating in its own way, but it wasn't really illuminating anymore in the sense of people sitting around tables and discussing how race, class, and gender have shaped their lives. Yet *reality TV still teaches us about these things*. We may have to work a little harder these days to get the sociological meat off the bone, but it's still there in abundance.

THE MAN WITH THE CAT ON HIS HEAD

Today, reality TV continues to be a rich context for understanding how we become selves within social contexts. The contrast between people from small-town and urban environments, for instance, is a recurring theme within the genre. On that first episode of *The Real World*, Julie is traveling on

a subway train that stalls; when she attempts to get her token refunded, her roommates laugh at her naivete, and Kevin
comments that she's obviously not a New Yorker.

Early sociologists, writing during a time of rapid indus-
trialization, were quite interested in these types of individual
differences. The burgeoning city changed our experiences as
social beings in concrete and observable ways, creating new
behavioral norms. In his 1903 book, *On Individuality and
Social Forms*, for instance, Georg Simmel argued that life in
these environs creates a particular "type" of individual. Because urbanites are constantly being bombarded with sights
and sounds, they become relatively immune to these sensa-
tions. Unlike people in small towns, Simmel observed, the
"metropolitan type" develops a "blasé outlook," which is an
"incapacity to react to new stimulations with the required
amount of energy."[7] Hand in hand with this, there's a greater
acceptance of diversity and uniqueness in the city—or at
least an indifference to it.

In sum, the metropolis and the small town create very
different kinds of individuals—in terms of how they respond
to their surroundings, how they feel internally, and how they
treat others. And various reality shows have touched on these
differences. *Breaking Amish* (TLC, 2012–2014), for example,
follows a group of young adults, raised in Amish and Menno-
nite communities, who move to New York City and experience
the new environment together. The show often highlights
these characters' sensory overload in the city. In one episode
at the beginning of the series, for instance, the group visits
Times Square for the first time.[8] They recall that the experience was "overwhelming" and that the streets were noisy and
"it didn't feel safe." Strangers rush past them, adopting Simmel's "blasé" attitude—toward not only the Amish in their

midst but also the TV cameras. Yet the sound of a loud whistle frightens the Amish. Various sights that might not stop the average New Yorker in his tracks, such as a man casually standing on the sidewalk with a cat on his head, fascinate these newcomers. "It's a little crazy," a cabbie advises them at one point, "but that's what New York is all about."

These characters' fish-out-of-water experiences, while augmented by the fact that they come from cultures that reject modern technologies, are likely familiar to many of us. Anecdotally, when I first moved to New York in my early twenties, I shared the subway one morning with an elderly man dressed in a bumblebee costume who elicited zero reaction from anybody else in the car. Later, as an experienced subway-goer, I learned to plop headphones over my ears, to stare at a book or a crossword puzzle—to wrap myself in a "protective shell," as Simmel puts it.[9] Beyond the specific culture shock of the urban experience, many of us have needed to adjust to new behavioral expectations—moving between different socioeconomic contexts, across racial boundaries, or through international space. It's telling that both Becky and Heather from *The Real World* talk about how entering the world beyond their single-race high schools required an adjustment. What becomes apparent in these moments is the extreme role of our socialization in shaping who we are—our attitudes and preferences, our behaviors, and our overall orientations toward the world.

CARDI B AND THE SOCIAL SELF

So, society shapes the self. But it would be too simple to leave things there, because we're active participants in this, too. One major tension often explored in sociology is between *structure*, on the one hand, and *agency* on the other. *Structure* is how society is organized (in ways that may constrain or empower us as individuals), and *agency* is our individual free will to move within that system of organization and sometimes transcend it. In nearly all situations, to varying degrees, both elements are at play.

While that first season of *The Real World*, for instance, was focused on social difference, it did not leave agency behind. At the same time that these roommates showed us how social forces constrain our lives and shape our senses of self, they also demonstrated our ability to transcend these forces. As Durkheim noted, because society is more than just a bunch of individuals, social facts don't need to apply to everyone in order for them to *be* social facts.[10] Even during times when the suicide rate is skyrocketing, clearly not everybody is committing suicide. And we can also break free from social facts, though often not without struggle. Julie's story line, for instance, concentrates on her choice to step outside of her previous experience by coming to New York. In many ways she *is* "open"—propelling herself into different adventures, meeting new people, testing out different frames for understanding the world. And in its early seasons especially, *The Real World* highlighted moments when its participants drew close to one another despite their differences. It's perhaps telling that Heather B. has said she still keeps in touch with most of the original housemates all these years later.[11]

As both classical sociologists and *Real World* cast members show us, to say that our selves are shaped by society is to tell only half the story. Individuals also work actively to shape and present their selves to others, within social contexts. Charles Horton Cooley (1864–1929), for instance, developed the concept of a "looking glass self." Just as we might examine ourselves in a mirror and be happy or unhappy based on how we look, he argued, we see ourselves reflected in other people's reactions to us, and that helps to shape not only how we act but who we think we are.[12] Erving Goffman (1922–1982), too, has suggested that we actively reason and operate in the world based on how we think others perceive us. Arguably one of the most influential modern sociologists, Goffman engaged in *dramaturgical analysis*—explaining the social world using terms and ideas from the theater. For Goffman, we were all actors, mobilizing props and costumes and reciting lines for others. While there is a "backstage" area— when we're away from other people and we can sprawl on the couch and do socially unacceptable things like watching *Real Housewives*—even then we don't fully cut our cord with the public. We're able to relax somewhat backstage, but we're also busy rehearsing and putting together props for future social performances.[13] (True story about Goffman: his sister played Adam Sandler's grandmother in *Happy Gilmore*.)

Across reality programs, we see individuals interacting with the broader social world, crafting selves in concert with their social surroundings. While, as Goffman and Cooley point out, we *all* do this, reality TV participants do it in a heightened, public way. In fact, reality TV as a genre is particularly poised to reveal this process. As the media and culture scholars Susan Murray and Laurie Ouellette have pointed out, unscripted television has long been at the vanguard when it comes to the use of new and interactive technologies, going back to *Big Brother* (CBS, 2000–present), a show with twenty-four-hour web streams. The genre "continues to serve as the principal testing ground for emerging convergence strategies such as podcasting, user-generated content, and greater viewer involvement in television."[14] Along with capitalizing on new technologies that engage viewers in unique ways, the genre has always functioned on multiple platforms simultaneously: TV, web, social media, books, video games, music, and more. These two, interrelated aspects of reality TV—its interactive qualities and its multiplatform approach—uniquely converge to show us people who are crafting, assessing, and revising their self-presentations in response to highly engaged publics, across various social stages.

Perhaps no one exemplifies this reciprocal process between self and society more than Cardi B. A former teenage gang member who was raised in the Bronx, Cardi B first ascended into public view when she posted messages and videos on social media discussing her career as a stripper and her musical aspirations. Then, from 2015 to 2017, she was a cast member on *Love & Hip Hop: New York* (VH1)—a reality show following several women with connections to the hip-hop music scene. Since her appearance on the show as an aspiring artist, she has continued to pull herself up the celebrity pipeline, ultimately emerging as a Grammy-winning rapper. By 2019, she had received two Guinness World Records for her music[15] and was being followed by 42.5 million people on Instagram.

Cardi B personifies Graeme Turner's notion of the contemporary "DIY," or "do-it-yourself," celebrity, who propels herself into the public arena through the internet or reality TV.[16] But she not only reflects our new parameters and pathways for celebrity. She also shows us, more broadly, how one can use the social pulleys and levers that are available in order to craft and present a self. Her career trajectory illuminates how one can move within social constraints—new technological frameworks, new modes of work—to create an image for public consumption. For instance, *Love & Hip Hop*, a show featuring mainly women of color, often dips into the well of race and gender stereotypes. The central characters are regularly portrayed as sexually irresponsible, materialistic, and quick to anger. (We'll further explore these stereotypes later in the book.) But Cardi B, who is Afro-Latina and Afro-Caribbean, has also been able to work within the confines of these collective meanings to serve her own ends. As one article in *The Cut* points out, the rapper has "taken the concept of 'ratchet'—a southern rap term, first used as an insult akin to 'ghetto,' that evolved over the years to mean 'raw'—and played with it to her advantage. She's an adroit creature of the media she's been saturated by growing up. . . ."[17]

I want to pause for a moment here on "ratchet," which is a term for a subcategory of reality TV characterized by explosive conflicts and ostensibly uncouth behavior—not always but often featuring people of color. Because the term can have derogatory, racist (and often sexist) connotations, I use it in quotation marks throughout the book. I still do use it, however, because the *concept* of "ratchet" is analytically useful for thinking about the relative value we assign to different types of reality TV shows and how that value links up with broader social hierarchies. Further, it is important to note that, as Cardi B illustrates, some people of color on these shows and scholars who write about them have reappropriated the term as a form of resistance. The African American literature and culture scholar Therí A. Pickens, for example, has argued that "ratchet" can function "as a performative strategy that secures a liberatory space for black women."[18] Again, more on this later in the book.

In sum, Cardi B takes the cultural mechanisms available to her—for instance, the social meanings connected to her gender and racial categories—and she manipulates these materials to craft an image that is not only palatable to others but immensely lucrative for herself. And Cardi B is far from the only reality star who seemingly gazes into the looking glass and creates a persona around the expectations she sees reflected. As Amy Kaufman has pointed out, it's not just the show's creators who construct the broad archetypes on *The Bachelor* but the performers themselves who also play along; many contestants "cop to their part in the creation of those roles."[19] And it makes sense that they do this. They, like Cardi B, are potentially able to benefit by transitioning their reality TV personalities to other contexts, such as the business world, talk shows, and scripted TV.[20] So while reality TV has always demonstrated the weight of society as it pushes individuals into particular molds, it also shows us how people move around under that weight, shifting it and imagining new possibilities for themselves.

WILL THE REAL COUNTESS PLEASE STAND UP?

So far, we've seen how individuals are shaped by their surroundings and how those individuals engage in this process, too, actively changing in response to social feedback. But ultimately, reality TV teaches us that we can't understand either of the two players in this drama—the self and society—without understanding the other.

This brings us to "Countess" LuAnn de Lesseps.

The Countess has been a fixture on *The Real Housewives of New York City* (Bravo, 2008–present)—a show following a revolving group of five to eight wealthy-ish New York women—since its inception. We've been able to watch LuAnn mold her on-air persona over the course of multiple seasons in response to real-world interactions and viewer responses.

In her first appearance on the show's "Meet the Wives" episode, she uttered the tagline "I never feel guilty about being privileged." She explained that she was married to an actual count and also had two kids and a housekeeper, whom she enlisted to pack up the family for the Hamptons. "Everybody wants me to come to their events so I really have to pick and choose what I do over the summer," LuAnn told the camera, throwing up her hands and adding, "But I manage."[21] In another notable scene from that same episode, when Bethenny introduced LuAnn to her driver by her first name, LuAnn corrected her. "If you introduce me to, like, a driver, it's, like, 'Mrs. de Lesseps,'" she explained.

"It's, like, get over yourself," Bethenny commented in a testimonial.

Later we'd find out LuAnn's life until that point had been a rich tapestry. She'd been a licensed nurse, a Wilhelmina model, a beauty queen, and an Italian TV show host, and she'd once impersonated Sharon Stone on an Italian awards show.

Despite the fact that she came into public consciousness as a caricature of a New York snob, and still retains elements of that persona, LuAnn has remained compelling enough to keep her spot on the show for over a decade. (Technically, she was a "friend of" the Housewives and not billed as one of the leads in season six.) She accomplishes this by clinging to the "Countess" persona—even though she has divorced and remarried and divorced again—as an amorphous archetype that she slides from seriousness to satire as it suits her. In 2009, for instance, she took the public's association (whether "real" or ironical) between her name and the concept of sophistication and spun it into a book, *Class with the Countess: How to Live with Elegance and Flair*, as well as a highly auto-tuned single, "Money Can't Buy You Class" (2010). In 2015, during a confrontation between some cast members on the beach, LuAnn sauntered over in full Countess mode and calmly offered them plates of "eggs à la française."[22] Fans debated whether there is indeed such a dish or if it's just a snobby name for scrambled eggs; LuAnn shared the recipe in *Glamour* magazine.[23] A subsequent profile of the Countess in *The New York Times* mentioned that she was "sipping espresso out of a mug emblazoned with the phrase."[24] On that same cast trip, LuAnn's castmate Heather rebuked her for bringing home a male stranger, who had fallen asleep upstairs in their shared house. LuAnn told Heather, "Be cool. Don't be all, like, uncool."[25] Bravo played the line repeatedly in previews, and when it aired, it was splashed across the internet, with *People* calling it "the moment fans have been waiting for all season."[26] That year, LuAnn recorded a new song, "Girl Code: Don't Be So Uncool." The tagline was featured on various merchandise.

In perhaps her most un-"Countess" move to date, in December 2017 LuAnn was arrested in Palm Beach, Florida, after drunkenly trespassing in a hotel room and assaulting a police officer. A grainy video appeared, on the internet and various news media, of her in the back of a police car, shouting, "Don't touch me! I will kill you!" at the cops. She entered an alcohol treatment program and addressed the incident on the show, seemingly approaching it with the self-awareness and humility she lacked in season one. In the 2018 season finale, she then rose as a phoenix from the ashes of her incarceration by headlining a sold-out cabaret act, #CountessAndFriends.[27] The act, in which she poked fun at her Countess image and her arrest, was profiled in that *Times* piece, which called

LuAnn "a woman for whom art and life have always been deeply intertwined."[28]

Some might view LuAnn's shifting selfhood as evidence of her own phoniness or perhaps the unreality of reality TV. Indeed, Bethenny has repeatedly questioned the Countess's authenticity, pointing out incongruities in LuAnn's personality over the years. "Keeping it real" is a common rhetorical weapon on reality TV, generally wielded by someone who is making an unkind pronouncement about another cast member ("But I kept it real!"). Reality TV personalities also use it as a charge that castmates are being inauthentic. Bethenny aligns herself squarely with this mantra. In Bethenny's eyes, LuAnn appears to contradict herself at every turn—at once classy and classless, prim and licentious, judgmental yet seemingly such a prime target for judgment. We have seen different sides of LuAnn as the seasons progress, and even within single seasons, single episodes, and single scenes.

So who is the "real" LuAnn? Is it the woman who shows her daughter the proper fork to use for shrimp, the cabaret headliner, or the woman who ends up in the back of a squad car on Christmas Eve? Cooley and Goffman would suggest that LuAnn, like all of us, shifts her performances based on audience response. Central to the definition of the sociological term "role" is its context-specificity—the notion that we act as different selves on the various stages of our lives.[29] We have watched LuAnn peer into the looking glass for more than a decade, shifting her on-air personality to become more likable, capitalizing on well-received one-liners, and branding herself in accordance with public tastes. She shows us how we all build selves in concert with society, changing in response to compliments and critiques, capitalizing on well-received moments, and adopting seemingly incongruous roles in different social contexts. By looking at her, we can better understand how each of us responds to feedback on our own smaller scale.

It's not hard to understand where Bethenny is coming from here. (For me, perhaps it helps that my *Real Housewives* archetype is "a Bethenny.") She's right that LuAnn sometimes puts on airs and misrepresents the circumstances of her life, and that is understandably frustrating. But if we've learned anything from Goffman, it's that we're all acting. While LuAnn's fellow Housewives, and we viewers, might find it maddening that LuAnn, for instance, rhapsodizes about romantic relationships that are demonstrably imperfect, who among us has never feigned confidence or contentment? This is even more obvious now that we have social media: a glittering "frontstage" on which we can perform our perfect worlds. In fact, research shows that people who spend more time on social-networking sites tend to be less happy in their marriages and more likely to be thinking about divorce.[30] We've even invented the term "realbooking" to denote those unusual moments on Facebook when we consciously bring our backstage failures and insecurities to the front.

We all engage in Goffman's "presentation of self,"[31] and social media is the jumbotron of this presentation. It is a vehicle through which we transmit curated and digestible information about ourselves. We brag about our kids, express our love for our partners, promote our professional endeavors, and share snapshots of our fancy dinners. People like LuAnn, who are paid to perform their private lives publicly, are no different from all of us in this way; they simply highlight the unstable dichotomy between our frontstage and our backstage selves.

But ultimately, the key thing we can learn from watching LuAnn is that there *is no* "authentic" self. Bethenny's comments aside, there is no singular, "real" LuAnn. George Herbert Mead (1863–1931) has argued that everyone in society has an "I" and a "me" that work in tandem.[32] The "I" is our acting self that has needs and desires, while the "me" is our ability to grasp the roles and perceptions of others (somewhat analogous to Cooley's looking glass). For instance, we learn to take into account others' perspectives as we progress from playing imaginatively with dolls and trucks to participating in organized games where we must understand everyone else's roles as well as our own. However, Mead makes the key point that, past infancy, *nobody is purely an "I."* We are all concurrently individual and social. So, at the same time that we might wish for more authenticity from LuAnn, she demonstrates that for none of us is it possible to extract a completely natural persona, unadulterated by social context. LuAnn is a composite reaction to interactions with friends and family members, relationships with the other women on the show, and feedback from viewers. Countess. Mother. Entertainer. Criminal.

Bethenny often wryly characterizes her own traumatic childhood by saying she was "raised by wolves." But the truth is that none of us were. Though we are born with innate preferences and abilities, and we have animal instincts, we learn about and express them within social contexts. In this way, *there is no self without society.* Looking at how the dynamic between self and society plays out on reality TV shows us the muddiness of this dichotomy—the fallacy of the concept of some sort of virgin self, untouched by social forces.

Finally, when reality TV demonstrates how every self is a social self, it simultaneously shows us our preoccupation with rooting out authenticity. The Housewives, for example, are often presented as silly women who use malapropisms, get drunk, and ruin the serenity of elegant restaurants with their loud fights. But these seemingly outlandish people highlight something fundamental about ourselves: our obsession with "the real." This preoccupation extends past reality stars like Bethenny, who demand that others reveal their true personalities. Moving forward, we'll see how the reality genre illuminates and complicates the notion of "realness" on a variety of levels beyond the individual. It shows us how in groups, through institutions, and as a society, we construct notions about legitimacy that are historically specific, that change with context, and that feed into and reinforce existing power structures.

So, although we're preoccupied with identifying and defining pure, uncut reality, it eludes our grasp. We, like reality stars, create our own "true stories" that, because they are connected to broader social dynamics, demand constant revision. Like Kevin and Julie, Cardi B, and the Countess, we're all inexorably social creatures. In that sense, none of us can truly "keep it real."

2

"Here for the Right Reasons" (Couples)

The women, wearing bikinis, are racing tractors down a Los Angeles street.

Tara is convinced she's going to win. "I'm, like, in my element," she tells the camera. "It's game over." A chyron appears on the screen, reminding us that she is twenty-six years old and a "sportfishing enthusiast."

"These girls are looking smokin' hot on these tractors. It's incredible," Chris says, adding that he's the "luckiest dude with two thumbs."

"I have to win it," Ashley I. explains. "And I've got the need for speed."

Ashley I. gets her wish.

"I feel so good. It's so crazy," she gasps after crossing the finish line. At this point, the chyron reveals that she's also twenty-six and a freelance journalist. "Getting alone time with Chris is the best prize," she says, fluttering her hands in excitement.

Later, at the rose ceremony, Chris thanks the women for being there. "I know this is not easy, and it's definitely going to be filled with ups and downs." As the music swells, he begins passing out red roses to the women who will remain in the running to win his affections.

Ashley I. again appears in a talking head: "Tonight is the most important night. I want it really bad."

Then we hear from Tara: "It's hard to stand out when we have twenty-two other amazingly gorgeous girls. Maybe I'm wrong but I feel like he wants, you know, someone who's a natural beauty. Not caked-on makeup with fake lashes."

Cut to a shot of Ashley I.'s fake lashes.

Chris calls Ashley I.'s name.

"But, you know," Tara tells us, "I could be wrong."

Ashley I. smiles with relief, sighs, and steps forward to receive her rose.[1]

The idea that *The Bachelor* can teach us anything about everyday life may seem laughable. The participants are placed in abnormal situations, the women's eyelashes stretch out to eternity, and nobody ever eats when they go to dinner. On the season finale, the protagonist is supposed to make his final pick and propose to her, having known her only a few weeks; relatively few of these couples remain together for the long haul.[2] *The Bachelor* and its counterpart, *The Bachelorette* (where a female lead chooses from among male hopefuls), don't even seem to take *themselves* all that seriously, as evidenced by the cheeky way they sometimes list their contestants' "jobs": "sportfishing enthusiast," "social media participant," "tickle monster."

Still, *The Bachelor* has remained immensely popular since its inception. More than five million people watched its *three-hour* season premiere in 2019, for instance, and it was the most watched show that night among adults under thirty-five.[3] The show does something for a lot us. And like it or not, it tells us something about ourselves. We've seen how reality TV highlights the relationship between the individual and society—showing us that there are no "pure" selves, inseparable from their social surroundings. Shows like *The Bachelor*, which focus on dating and marriage, reveal how our *twosomes* are shaped by and reflect broader society as well.

Two is the magic number in popular culture and in life. Even television shows such as *Friends* and *Sex and the City*, which glorify non-romantic relationships and no-strings sex, often conclude with their characters neatly paired. If the monogamous, romantic couple were not the basic building block of our society, our lives would look markedly different. We live with the expectation that we all will participate in these duos—an expectation that gets translated into everything from marriage certificates and insurance policies to bed sizing and the content of reality dating shows. We also give side-eye to those who don't conform; we stigmatize people who are consensually non-monogamous,[4] as well as those who remain single.[5]

The creation of a (heterosexual, and we'll get to that) monogamous twosome is the central premise of *The Bachelor*. The contestants are all women, the bachelor has never chosen more than one in the end, and it's rare that he leaves the show without a mate. And the show amplifies the social forces that are at work when we create these duos. It reveals that we don't simply link up with our mates in a random way; our choice of our mates is strongly shaped by the roles and divisions that exist within our broader culture. Despite all our talk about social progress, *The Bachelor* shows us how long-standing ideas about gender and relationships still powerfully influence the way we think and behave.

EYELASHES, ABS, AND EVENING GOWNS

On *The Bachelor*, gender roles are stark, binary, and conventional. Men have Ken-doll abs, and women twinkle in bedazzled gowns. Sometimes, the gender presentations on the show are so extreme that they might appear terribly antiquated. But while the couples on *The Bachelor* may seem like throwbacks to the 1950s, they show us how those old ideas about gender and sexuality still powerfully influence our dating culture.

Looking at advice books written in the mid-twentieth century, the historian Beth Bailey has observed a particular "etiquette" for gender roles in heterosexual courtship.[6] These roles sharply aligned with existing ideas about "natural" masculinity and femininity. We thought about "masculine men" as "powerful, dominant, aggressive, and ambitious," while "feminine women" were "dependent, submissive, [and] nurturing."[7] Consequently, men were supposed to ask out women, plan and pay for the dates, hold the door for the women and help them out of the car, and order for the women at restaurants.

The Bachelor closely mirrors these gendered expectations for courtship. The man ostensibly plans the date and selects the woman or women he'd like to take on it, offers roses, and makes a final selection. (While it's likely that the producers are involved in these decisions, within the narrative of the show these are the Bachelor's choices.) Even on *The Bachelorette*, while the woman selects her mate, he's still the one to propose. And on *The Bachelor*, though arguably not *The Bachelorette*, it's taken for granted that the women want the final prize, which places them in a submissive position from the get-go. This expectation comes into particularly sharp focus in the rare instances when it's disrupted. On season eighteen, for instance, Andi called out Bachelor Juan Pablo for smugly assuming her interest in him without exerting any effort of his own.[8] "You don't even really know who I am," she told him. "And I feel like every time I've tried to explain things, all your response is [sic] 'It's okay,' 'It's okay.' Everything's always, 'It's okay.'" She added that she felt he was never trying to get to know her: "Do you have any idea, like, what religion I practice? How I want to raise my kids?"

"I have no idea about any of that," he replied. Then he challenged her: "What's my religion?"

"Catholic," she responded correctly.

Zing. Merely by suggesting she didn't want what a man had to offer, Andi went off script. In doing that, she highlighted the script itself—both the scripted premise of *The Bachelor* and the gendered script for the courtship process more generally.

While some elements of 1950s courtship, like men ordering dinner for their dates, may have fallen by the wayside, other gendered expectations for heterosexual dating remain firmly intact. In one 2017 survey, for instance, 78 percent of respondents said they thought men should pay on the first (heterosexual) date.[9] In heterosexual relationships on *The Bachelor*, *The Bachelorette*, most wedding-themed reality shows, and real life, men—not women—are still charged with the task of proposing marriage. The ideas of "masculine men" as "powerful, dominant, aggressive, and ambitious" and "feminine women" as "dependent, submissive, [and] nurturing" still permeate our dating practices. Asked about their preferences in mates, heterosexual men still value physical attractiveness more than women do, while heterosexual women are more likely to value earning potential in their mates.[10] As we'll see later, these specific ideas about gender also extend past the courtship process and infuse these couples' family lives. For instance, women are more likely than men to be stay-at-home parents, and they do more housework than their husbands even when both spouses are employed.[11] These notions about gender are not passé but remain with us, molding our relationships today. In between its eyelash flutters and bikini tractor races, *The Bachelor* is telling us something powerful about ourselves—not just who we *were*, but who we still *are*.

"I'M JEALOUS THAT YOU'RE A VIRGIN RIGHT NOW"

One might argue that when it comes to gender roles in dating, at least our ideas about women and sex have loosened up a bit since the 1950s. Bailey discusses the "sexual economy" that existed on college campuses back then: "If a woman maintained her virtue (making sex a scarce commodity) her value to men would rise, and she would realize a long-term gain greatly exceeding her 'cheap' sisters' one-time bonanza."[12] The gender double standard for chastity wasn't new in the 1950s, nor did it fizzle after midcentury. For example, this same philosophy about a woman's value lying in sexual restraint was the foundation for *The Rules*, the massively popular mid-1990s self-help book for women,[13] and is the basis for the adage "Why buy the cow when you can get the milk for free?" Women's liberation, the advent of the Pill, #metoo—all of these tides appear to have swept us away from the gender dynamics that permeated the 1950s malt shop. But while some things have changed, much remains the same.

While *The Bachelor* is not a show about abstinence (see below), it does reflect the continued sexual double standard in its treatment of male and female virginity. In the same episode with the tractor race, for instance, Ashley I. reveals to some of the other women that she's a virgin and questions whether Chris is "gonna like it or not." Her castmate Mackenzie assures her that he will, as "every guy likes it. . . . I swear to God, I'm jealous that you're a virgin right now." Mackenzie adds, "It's gonna make you stay here so much longer." Contrast this with Colton—who initially appeared as a contestant on *The Bachelorette* and, upon rejection, got a *Bachelor* season of his own—whose virginity was treated as, at best, a curiosity and at worst a problem. Seldom did anyone discuss how desirable it was.

While sexual economy is present on *The Bachelor*, perhaps nowhere on reality TV is this concept as blatant as on *The Millionaire Matchmaker* (Bravo, 2008–2015). On the show, the eponymous matchmaker Patti Stanger fixes up her millionaire clients. In each episode, she gathers potential dates for two different millionaires—who are typically, but not always, male and interested in women. One of her favorite lines is, "The penis does the picking," which suggests that men think with their anatomy and select dates that way. She emphasizes the sexual value of women, evaluating them based on their individual parts. In the pilot episode,[14] for instance, one of her clients tells her, "I'm not into the big stripper double D's," and she reasons, "Okay, he's an ass guy." She regularly reminds all clients, but especially women, that being sexual too early will hurt their chances for a long-term relationship. In fact, her business has specific rules about this. There should be "no sex without monogamy," which means "no *in*, no *in*, and no *in*," she often says, punctuating each *in* by pointing a finger at her mouth, vagina, and anus, respectively.

These shows aren't just telling us how we've felt about sex, gender, and dating in the past. They're showing us—in over-the-top ways that involve gesturing to body parts—how we feel about those things *right now*. Sure, post–sexual liberation, post–*Sex and the City*, post–Miley Cyrus straddling a wrecking ball, and post–J. Lo pole dancing at the Super Bowl, overt female sexuality is more culturally acceptable than it was in the mid-twentieth century—even if all of these examples have also stirred controversy. But we haven't completely moved past rigid ideas about women, men, and sex. The 1950s notion of women as the "controllers of sex," with the responsibility to "enforce sexual limits," for instance, is still sharply reflected in the way that we respond to sexual assault.[15] I'm far from the first to point out the proliferation of educational programs, with their groin kicks and their rape whistles, devoted to teaching women how to prevent assault and the relative sparsity of those that seek to curb potential male assailants.

When it comes to consensual casual sex—yes, that has become more widespread and normalized, for both men and women. In recent years, for instance, sociologists have observed that "hookup culture" has begun to supplant conventional dating on college campuses. Couples may go out on dates, but typically *after* they're already an item, which now tends to happen *after* they've been hooking up for a while.[16] (If you're not a college student or someone who spends time with them, you may need to know that "hooking up" is an umbrella term that encompasses a wide range of activities, from kissing to intercourse.)

The hookup is alive and well on *The Bachelor*, too. The contestants frequently make out with the protagonist (particularly if he's season twenty-two's "kissing bandit," Arie), and other sexual activities can happen in the "fantasy suite" episodes toward the end of each season. The very fact of Ashley I.'s virginity being noteworthy speaks to how times have changed. But, as we've also seen with Ashley I. and Colton, conventional gender expectations can persist, even in a context where a lot of people are making out. Hookup culture is not a gender-norm free-for-all. Indeed, sociologists have observed that the hookup, while potentially liberating for women, can also reinforce such norms.[17] One study of college students, for instance, found that a double standard exists for those who engage in frequent hookups: women are more likely than men to be stigmatized as slutty, whereas men are more likely to gain status from multiple conquests. The researchers also reported a gender gap in sexual pleasure, with only 14 percent of women reporting having orgasmed during their last hookup, compared with 40 percent of males.[18] While the women on *The Bachelor* might enjoy hooking up with these men, and may potentially experience these make-out sessions as empowering, the show also demonstrates how sexual liberation can exist within a power structure that disadvantages women. Ultimately, regardless of how sexually empowered they are, their time on the show revolves around pleasing and snagging a man. *His* desires are always central to the narrative. *The Bachelor* may have a lot of tongue action, but it doesn't really shake up our ideas about what it means to be a man or a woman on the dating scene.

Indeed, it is significant that stereotypical markers of female appearance—such as *The Bachelor*'s eyelashes and evening gowns—often coexist with female sexual liberation on reality TV. Along these lines, the Kardashian/Jenners—for all of their nude mirror selfies—show us a form of femininity that's comforting in its familiarity. This is evident in the products that they shill. One 2016 listicle titled "Things Built Under the Kardashian/Jenner Empire" featured fifty-six bullet points, including a shoe subscription service, fragrances, a cookbook, hair extensions, nail polish, jewelry, a tanning product, and various clothing, makeup, and beauty product lines.[19] The connection between the family's success and feminine physicality is so solid that Rob, the only male sibling, has complained on the show that his gender has held him back from cashing in. Exploiting this connection, too, is Caitlyn (formerly Kris's husband), who came out as transgender in 2015 on the cover of *Vanity Fair*, sporting flowing, highlighted hair and a white silken bodice, her arms stuck behind her back in a pinup pose. She has now collaborated with MAC cosmetics on a lipstick collection.[20]

The Kardashian/Jenner women are able to use their sexuality to remain intriguing to fans while, in many ways, performing a femininity that is not threatening to the status quo. Indeed, Kim has explicitly said that she does not identify with the f-word: "My personality has never been, 'I'm such a feminist and follow me and be naked!'" she told a podcast in 2016.[21] For most of the women in this family, their personas are also solidly linked to *heterosexual* femininity—to the men in their lives and to their own ability to reproduce. Heterosexual romantic coupling is central to their lives, to their show, and to their brand. Programs like the *Kardashians* suggest that if women look the way they "should" look, and if they behave in stereotypically feminine ways in other domains of their lives, we may be more willing to give them a hall pass on their overt sexuality.

We may even like it. Indeed, the specific combination of conventional gender roles/presentations and sexual liberation could be one of the things that draws us to reality shows. An analysis of *The Girls Next Door* (E!, 2005–2010)—a show focusing on the three live-in girlfriends of *Playboy* founder Hugh Hefner—found that "reality television preferences relate to greater endorsement of sexual empowerment and traditional feminine roles."[22] This suggests that viewers may find it appealing to watch sexually liberated women, as long as they conform to our expectations for women in other, key ways. Indeed, the women on *The Girls Next Door* are all white blondes with taut bodies who live in their boyfriend's mansion, and, ostensibly, each remains monogamous with Hef while he has relationships with all three of them. So, while women's sexual liberation potentially offers us new possibilities for gender roles (e.g., the potential to be the sexual aggressor), every rose has its thorn. The rising acceptance of casual sex in courtship doesn't necessarily shake the overarching dynamics of gender and power, either on reality TV or in real life.

"I'M BLACK AND I HAVE SHORT HAIR SO I JUST WANT TO SAY, 'GOODBYE' "

Just as our notions about gender influence our mating rituals, so, too, do our ideas about race and class. For example, the lack of Black women as serious competitors on *The Bachelor* has become so well known it's been parodied on *Saturday Night Live*. In the 2019 *SNL* skit "Virgin Hunk," the contestants introduce themselves to the male lead; one woman tells him, "I'm Black and I have short hair so I just want to say, 'Goodbye.'"[23] In 2012, *The Bachelor* was even hit with a class-action lawsuit alleging that it violated racial discrimination laws by failing to include people of color.[24]

Within popular culture, *The Bachelor* is far from unique in its sparsity of nonwhite participants. Multiple studies, for instance, have found that African, Asian, Latino, Middle Eastern, and Native American people are misrepresented and underrepresented in commercial marketing campaigns.[25] And on social media, #Oscarssowhite highlights the relative invisibility of people of color in the film industry and their underrecognition when they do appear. But beyond being simply one more example of minority underrepresentation, *The Bachelor* has something specific to teach us about race and *coupledom*.

It's not that people of color don't exist on the show. There have even been Black protagonists. For the most part, though, both *The Bachelor* and *The Bachelorette* feature young, white, middle-class (or higher) conventionally hot people going on dates with young, white, middle-class (or higher) conventionally hot people. The nonwhite contestants, meanwhile, tend to be excluded from serious contention and to take on supporting roles. As the communication scholar Rachel Dubrofsky has observed, *The Bachelor* "is a context in which only white people find romantic partners, a process that women of color work to facilitate."[26]

While we might want to view *The Bachelor* as a relic, jettisoned from an earlier version of our society that was not as diverse or as accepting, in fact it crisply mirrors today's racial dynamics. Even today, most Americans wed people of their same race; one analysis found that in 2015, five out of six (83 percent) newlyweds were married to someone of the same race/ethnicity.[27] In fact, the majority of Americans still marry others who match up with them on a variety of demographic characteristics, including race, but also education level, socioeconomic class, and political affiliation[28]—a concept known as "homophily," or "same love." This continues to happen for a few different reasons. First, we don't have access to just anyone in the world to date. We marry the people we meet, and de facto segregation in housing and schooling, as well as racial disparities in educational attainment, means that we're likely to meet people with our same skin color.[29] And before you jump on the "Tinder is changing all that!" bandwagon, research suggests that extreme homophily persists in online dating as well.[30]

As those internet dating studies suggest, once we have our pools narrowed down, there's also bias in whom we choose. Personal preference and a desire for shared culture play a role, but there's also just plain racism. An analysis by the Pew Research Center, for instance, found that by 2017, still more than one in ten non-Black Americans (14 percent) "said they would be opposed to a close relative marrying a Black person."[31] (And that number includes only people who were willing to *admit* they were not okay with it.) So, while we might bemoan the sparsity of nonwhite representation on *The Bachelor* and chide the network for being behind the times, in some senses it's not behind the times. It reflects the times, as our long-standing racial inequalities continue to filter into our courtship norms, and those in turn bleed into the show.

To be clear, this is not an argument about what the show *should* be doing. Rather, it's evidence that the *Bachelor* world bears the imprint of our own. The coupling on the show is not *just* the result of the contestants' choices (and the producers' maneuvering) but is also a reflection of broader social hierarchies. Tellingly, the ratings for Black protagonist Rachel's season of *The Bachelorette* dipped considerably from the prior season and contained a lower percentage of white viewers.[32] The contestants on these shows highlight how racial boundaries remain in place, not only within the microcosm of the show but also within the outer world that consumes it.

HERE FOR THE RIGHT REASONS

So far, we've seen how our cultural ideas about gender and race impact our assumptions about what a couple should look

like. Same-race heterosexual couples with complementary
gender roles sit atop the apex of cultural legitimacy. Yet for
us to view them as fully real, even these couples must possess
another key ingredient: *love*.

It may seem self-evident that contestants on reality TV
dating and wedding shows—and people on the dating scene in
real life—should be looking for love. However, the association
between romance and long-term relationships isn't biological
and universal; it's something that stems from culture. It wasn't
until the late eighteenth century, as the historian Stephanie
Coontz points out in her book *Marriage, a History: How Love
Conquered Marriage*, that we even began to think of love and
marriage as two things that went together. Before that time,
"most societies around the world saw marriage as far too vital an economic and political institution to be left entirely to
the free choice of the two individuals involved, especially if
they were going to base their decision on something as unrea-
soning and transitory as love."[33] Even by the early twentieth
century, marriage was still largely a mandatory union rooted
in family approval, child-rearing, and economic security.[34]
After that point, couples moved increasingly toward "com-
panionate" arrangements; that is, it became more widely expected that the spouses should like and even (gasp!) love each
other. While we might think of 1950s marriages, for instance,
as hypertraditional, they were actually somewhat progressive
in this respect.[35] This change was likely connected to postwar
prosperity. The generation growing up in this era, overall, was
less consumed with basic survival and had the ability to turn
to loftier goals.[36]

In the fun-house mirror, love and marriage arc together
and become contiguous. Contestants on *The Bachelor*, for

example, constantly face the question of whether they're there for "the right reasons"—the primary "right reason" being romantic sentiment for the suitor, rather than a desire for the flashy trips or the exposure. Participants who are not willing to say the l-word, or who suggest that they may not be ready for an engagement at the end of the season, are viewed skeptically. (Peter, on season thirteen of *The Bachelorette*, for instance, got the boot for this reason.) More directly, the premise of the show *Joe Millionaire* (Fox, 2003) was a group of women competing for a man they've been told is worth millions, only to find out in the end that he's a construction worker. The key tension of the series lay in the question of whether the final remaining woman would still love him despite it all or if she was just in it for the cash. Both programs demonstrate how we tend to proceed as if "the right reasons" are incontrovertible and ahistorical (though they are not). Even a dating show such as Britain's *Love Island* (ITV2, 2015–present), with its strong emphasis on casual hookups, at least nominally pays lip service (pun intended) to the notion of romantic love. It's not *Sex Island*.

Our strong cultural association between coupledom and love becomes particularly apparent on *90 Day Fiancé* (TLC, 2014–present). The show follows Americans who have applied, or are applying, for K-1 visas for their foreign fiancés. The fiancés are able to come to the US to be with them, but only for ninety days, after which they must either wed or leave the country. The constant question of which relationships are "real" hovers thickly over the whole enterprise. Friends and family members on the show, as well as viewers, continually judge the couples for their seemingly transactional relationships. American Jorge and his fiancée, Russian-born Anfisa, for example, face multiple accusations from family; at one point, Jorge's sister snaps at him, "So, when you have money, that's when she spreads her legs?"[37]

Danielle and Mohamed from season two (as well as the spin-offs *90 Day Fiancé: Happily Ever After?* and *90 Day Fiancé: What Now?*) also ignited suspicion, both on and off the screen. "From the beginning, it is clear to everyone but them that things will not work out," an article in *The Cut* summarizes, for instance. "As one of the longest-running story lines . . . this couple provides the highest level of secondhand embarrassment."[38] Throughout this couple's story arc, Danielle's friends and family members refer to Mohamed as a "scam" and a "fraud." Shortly after Mohamed's arrival in the US, we find out that both members of the couple were dishonest about their financial situations. Ultimately, they do tie the knot, but Mohamed refuses to kiss Danielle at the altar. Almost immediately after that, he runs off to Miami, where she sees photos of him cavorting on a boat with another woman. They get divorced. Danielle sues him for fraud.[39]

While Danielle and Mohamed may not have had a love for the ages, to suggest their relationship was a "fraud" presupposes that there is an objectively "real" form of marriage that we can hold them up against. Our collective reaction to this couple illuminates our assumptions about what it takes to make a marriage. Our skepticism about their relationship, for instance, is likely augmented by the physical differences between them. Danielle is a chunky, middle-aged white woman typically outfitted in glasses and sweatpants (no shade: I'm currently wearing sweatpants), and Mohamed is a tall, fit, twenty-six-year-old Tunisian man. Both the viewers and the families on the show seem less eager to cast doubt on its duos when their ages, skin colors, and perceived hotness click into alignment. Case in point, season three's Loren and Alexei—both twenty-seven years old, Jewish, and conventionally attractive, whose drama is focused not on whether their love is real but on other factors, such as Loren's disclosure of her Tourette's syndrome.

These entwined concepts of valid marriages as romance based and homophilous are baked into our social institutions as well. The couples on *90 Day Fiancé* highlight this, as they strive to demonstrate their legitimacy to the government or risk dissolution. It's significant that nearly all of them talk about their relationships in terms of love. In addition to possibly actually loving each other, it's likely they use this kind of language because they're interacting with other social institutions—religion, their families, the government—that view love as a necessary ingredient for marital legitimacy. The whole concept of validating one's relationship for the purpose of citizenship is premised on a notion of authentic marriage that is culturally and historically specific. These couples would gain nothing from explaining to government officials, "He needs a green card and I want a boy toy," or, "She's looking to escape poverty and I have an Asian fetish," even if those explanations are closer to the truth.

So, what makes a relationship "real," under the law? As the sociologist Gina Marie Longo has pointed out, in the United States, couples petitioning for green cards must "demonstrate that their relationships are 'valid and subsisting' (i.e., for love) and not fraudulent (i.e., for immigration papers)."[40] Immigration officers also consider several "red flags" for fraudulent relationships, which include "large age differences, short courtships, or requests for money."[41] A variety of other contingencies have historically surrounded the process of awarding green cards and citizenship as well. Under early US

immigration laws, native-born women weren't able to peti-
tion for citizenship for foreign-born husbands; in fact, they
lost their citizenship if they wed foreign nationals (while no
such laws applied to native-born men).[42] And until very recently, only heterosexual relationships were considered valid
for these purposes.

In showing us how the government reflects and shapes
cultural ideas about valid marriage, *90 Day Fiancé* shows us
how the government also reflects and shapes our expectations
around specific constellations of gender, sexuality, and race.
Analyzing posts on immigration self-help forums, Longo
found that while American men are able to "prove their man-
hood to peers" by pursuing young, attractive women from
foreign countries, "women citizens with the same intentions
are considered desperate fools, incapable of controlling their
emotions or the border. Consequently, their relationships appear more suspect and in need of policing."[43]

Our collective reaction to Danielle and Mohamed plays
into these stereotypes. And I'm not immune; I, too, have
arched my eyebrows and winced at this couple. I have rooted
for Danielle's incomprehensibly sage teenage children as they
tried to convince her of the error of her ways. The skepticism
with which I and others view Danielle and Mohamed is based
on our conception of marriage as a romantic unit; our assumptions about authentic masculinity and femininity and
their relationship to sexuality; and our preconceived notions
of what these pairings should look like. The *90 Day Fiancé*
couples reinforce for us, the viewers, what we consider to be
valid and appropriate for committed relationships. What's
more, they demonstrate the potency of such assumptions, as
they travel through social institutions that have the ability to
bestow benefits on those unions that they deem real.

MARRIED TO MARRIAGE

Our expectations for gender roles in relationships, our expectation that both members of a couple be similar to each other, and our assumptions about the indispensability of love: all of these elements come to a heady boil on *90 Day Fiancé*. Further, in understanding what types of relationships we deem "authentic," the entire premise of the show is key: as a culture, we still cling to the institution of marriage. Marriage remains the government-stamped, church-approved consecration of "legitimate" coupledom.

Anthropologist Gayle Rubin has argued that just as our society distributes its benefits unequally by race and gender, so, too, is it unequal by sexuality—and not just when it comes to sexual orientation. People who participate in certain types of sex are rewarded by society, with "certified mental health, respectability, legality, social and physical mobility, institutional support, and material benefits."[44] Heterosexual, monogamous, *marital* sex, as Rubin points out, is at the top of that hierarchy.

As a society, we remain married to marriage. Though fewer people get married today than in the past, divorce is more widely accepted, and we get married at older ages, the majority of us still tie the knot at some point in our lives.[45] Marriage still holds a high symbolic significance, even for those groups that are doing it less now. Along these lines, the sociologists Kathryn Edin and Maria Kefalas, interviewing low-income women about why they chose to become mothers without getting married first, found that, by and large, it wasn't because these women didn't value marriage. It was because they *did* value marriage that they didn't want to jump into it with someone who might be a poor bet.[46] In fact, some research suggests that the institution may be even more symbolically important to us now than it has been in the past.[47]

We see the cultural resonance of marriage reflected in all of the social benefits we afford to couples who tie the knot. We see it in same-sex couples' fight for their unions to be legally recognized. And we see it on the marriage-themed reality shows that spring up like hothouse flowers. The Wikipedia category "Wedding Television Shows" lists fifty-six currently (or previously) airing programs, the majority of which are reality TV. From *Bridalplasty* (E!, 2010–2011), which featured brides competing to get plastic surgery procedures, to *Marriage Boot Camp* (WE tv, 2013–present), in which couples from other reality shows receive counseling, the proliferation of these programs reflects the prevailing cultural importance of this institution. At the end of the day, reality TV reminds us that our most "legitimate" couples are married couples. At the same time, it illuminates the narrow contours of acceptable marriage. We cast aspersions on those, like Danielle and Mohamed, who have not arrived at the altar for the "right reasons."

This is not to suggest that other types of relationships are absent from the reality genre. Patti Stanger has matched some same-sex couples; Reza Farahan's engagement and marriage to his husband, Adam, were shown on *Shahs of Sunset* (Bravo, 2012–present), and season eight (2019) of MTV's dating show *Are You the One?* (2014–present) featured all bisexual, pansexual, and sexually fluid cast members. The women in *The Girls Next Door* were not in monogamous relationships, nor are the spouses on *Sister Wives* (TLC, 2010–present). Indeed—as we'll see—in some ways, the reality genre gives us more diverse relationships than other forms of media.

Still, the reality TV shows that are focused on dating and,

especially, marriage—for instance, *Bridezillas* (WE tv, 2004–2013, 2018–present), *My Fair Wedding* (WE tv, 2008–present), and *Say Yes to the Dress* (TLC, 2007–present)—generally feature gender-conforming women marrying gender-conforming men of their same race. The reality dating series *Love Is Blind* (Netflix, 2020–present) even acknowledges the homophily that persists in contemporary dating, with its very premise. When the show's potential romantic partners first "meet," they're sitting in pods where they can't see each other. In the first episode, one contestant describes the show as "removing the confounding variables of ethnicity, race, background, and the big one being physical appearance."[48] Ultimately, though, even *Love Is Blind* doesn't *really* remove those barriers, as the contestants are able to see one another long before they walk down the aisle. And even when they're "blinded," they discuss topics such as ethnicity and religion. They also fit the criteria to be selected for this reality show, which means that they're already all similar in some ways. For instance, most have conventionally attractive bodies, they're all within a specific age range, and so forth. And none of the contestants on *Love Is Blind* are looking to be matched with participants of the same gender, just as all of *The Bachelor*'s potential partners have been female. In this way, the genre demonstrates broader society's heteronormativity: the notion that heterosexuality is the presumed and preferred orientation of all people.

When romantic relationships on reality TV do deviate from the model of legitimacy, such differences are often highlighted. The polygamous partners on *Sister Wives*, for instance, regularly discuss their stigmatization. And while the queer season of *Are You the One?* went against the grain, as we'll see, the show was *notable* for its revolutionary premise.[49]

Along the same lines, we can all likely think of examples

of interracial relationships within reality TV and other forms of popular culture—*The Bachelorette*'s Rachel and her ultimate choice, Bryan; John Legend and Chrissy Teigen; the Kardashians and most of their partners; Ernie and Bert; and so on—but these are far more notable than the homophilic ones. Consider, for instance, the intense press scrutiny surrounding Prince Harry and Meghan Markle. While scrutiny is par for the course when you marry into British royalty, attention on this duo was likely amplified by the perceived social asymmetry of a divorced, biracial American actress linking up with an elite British ginger. As one 2016 piece in the UK's *Daily Mail* predicted, if the couple ever had children, "the Windsors will thicken their watery, thin blue blood and Spencer pale skin and ginger hair with some rich and exotic DNA."[50] The prince's own press secretary has remarked upon the "racial undertones" in the "abuse and harassment" that Markle has experienced from journalists.[51] As the couple explained in a 2021 Oprah interview, this was a factor in their decision to retreat from their roles as royals and to flee Britain.

When considering how we've found our mates, we might credit fate, or hormones, or the particular arc of Cupid's arrow. But dating-themed reality TV casts a spotlight on the social mechanisms grinding behind the scenes. These shows are more than just pastiches of wacky premises and zany one-liners ("The penis does the picking!"). They strip American courtship down to its essence, showing us how our society is organized around twosomes and spotlighting our retrograde cultural expectations for those partnerships. While we might consider the stars of *The Bachelor* silly for allowing their pools of potential partners to be selected by producers, our own romantic relationships are heavily shaped by external forces as well. We don't just date whomever we want, in whatever ways we want. Ultimately, reality TV doesn't just show us the importance of twos—it shows us the importance of *specific* twos.

It doesn't *have* to be this way, as Rubin and others have pointed out. It isn't a foregone conclusion that relationships should be monogamous, or be rooted in love, or involve different genders playing specialized parts. Nevertheless, we cast these particular partnerships and their attendant roles as natural and correct. And, of course, we're changing. Women are more sexually empowered now, same-sex marriage is the law of the land, and back in 1990 a whopping 63 percent (not 14 percent) of non-Black Americans said they weren't okay with their relatives marrying Black people.[52] Still, reality TV shows us how sticky our collective assumptions are, about who and what makes a "real" couple, and how these assumptions have infused and settled thickly within our culture.

And perhaps we enjoy watching dating and marriage play out in this way on TV *because* these shows are like pacifiers, soothing our anxieties about cultural change. Despite their often wacky premises, shows about coupledom reinforce many of our long-standing ideas about women, men, race, sex, and love. In doing so, they reflect and bolster our most entrenched and long-lasting social hierarchies—hierarchies that have repercussions far beyond who ends up with that final rose.

3

"Not Here to Make Friends" (Groups)

Seven castaways remain in the Tagi tribe. They move through the dimming daylight, their hands clutching the long stems of tiki torches, their faces taut.

It's time to vote another teammate off the island.

As they pack up their gear and stomp through the jungle in their late-1990s fashion—pocket tees, chinos, sweat socks hiked up over their calves—the action is interspersed with clips of them individually commenting on what's about to unfold.

"I thought it was a done deal that Rudy would be the one voted off, but it could be me," Stacey explains, her eyes narrowing with worry.

Rudy appears, shirtless, sitting in front of a fire, and confirms that he'll be voting for Stacey. "'Cause I don't like her," he explains, laughing a little, "and I never will." His concern is that the younger castaways will work together to get rid of him.

"I gotta think of the team," Sue tells the camera.

Richard, similarly, indicates that he's "prioritized people" based on who is most likely to contribute to the team's success.

When considering strategy, "I don't think anybody's out here to make friends," Kelly tells us, finally. "I'm not out here to make friends."[1]

When Kelly made that comment on the first season of *Sur-*

vivor in 2000, she couldn't have known it would turn into one of the most commonly repeated refrains on competition TV. Just as surely as the tide ebbs and flows on the beaches of Borneo, when you're watching a gamedoc, at some point someone will declare that they're not on the show to make friends. (Or, as the drag queen Lashauwn Beyond once put it, "This is not *RuPaul's Best Friend Race!*") But as we've seen with Heather B. from *The Real World*, who's still hanging out with Julie and Norm more than a quarter of a century later, some reality TV participants do make friends. Even on competition shows, the connections between contestants are not purely adversarial but just as rich and varied as our own.

Writing in the early 1900s, Georg Simmel took note of such connections. We've seen how Simmel theorized the relationship between the individual and society, but he also explored how we do things in groups. In particular, he was one of the developers of "formal sociology." That's not sociology in a tux and tails; rather, it's a way of looking at the world that places an emphasis on the *form* rather than the *content* of basic social structures. Simmel observed commonalities across a wide array of social groupings. For example, while "a religious community," "an art school," and "a band of conspirators" are very different types of groups, similar types of dynamics are happening within each—for example, "superiority and subordination, competition, division of labor," and so on.[2] While he was writing more than a century ago, these commonalities have endured. Examining reality competitions alongside Simmel's writings provides a porthole into our everyday group dynamics, showing us the most basic types of social relationships that have endured for centuries and operate in our own lives today.

Season one of *Survivor*—Mark Burnett's juggernaut that

exiles contestants to a remote location, where they vote one another off until there's a million-dollar winner left standing—is an especially clear mirror of these relationships. Many of the contestants seem to have a naivete about being on camera that's lacking in all subsequent competition TV, and there's more of an emphasis on interacting with one another as they would in the real world. As Sue tells the camera in episode three, "I have personality conflicts every day with people." She adds that she can deal with these conflicts in real life, and "I'm gonna do the same thing here." Season one also reveals social dynamics particularly well because Richard Hatch, the winner, is a corporate communications consultant who is transparent about his strategy for the camera, if not for the other castaways, throughout the show. Richard showed early on that one key to success on *Survivor* was the ability to gain mastery over these small groupings. (Just ask Max Dawson, the former communications professor who taught a course on the microdynamics of the show and then became a competitor himself.) *Survivor* not only highlights these long-standing social forms but also allows us to see how shrewd players can benefit from them—on TV and in life.

THE DYAD: DOUBLE TROUBLE

The most basic small group that Simmel identifies is the *dyad*, or group of two. We've seen how we have built our world around twosomes, in ways that reflect and perpetuate broader power structures. But the *internal* workings of these relationships are also important to understand. As Simmel has observed, groups of two can be some of the strongest and most intimate social forms.

Season one of *Survivor* contains its fair share of dyadic

relationships, though Richard and Rudy perhaps best exemplify the power of two. The ex-military senior citizen and the openly gay corporate guy may seem like an unlikely pair, and while Rudy periodically calls Richard "the homosexual," he also opines that Richard's "one of the nicest guys I ever met." This seemingly unlikely alliance demonstrates the immense power of the dyad, as the two men stick by each other until nearly the end of the season, when Rudy gets voted off—not by Richard. If all goes well, a solid twosome can be extremely advantageous to its participants, as we see when Richard's relationship with Rudy ultimately helps him to secure victory.

The other thing that shows like *Survivor* teach us about dyads is that there's a lot more at stake when there are only two people in a group, because both need to be actively engaged in the relationship to make it work. Simmel explains that "the decisive character of the dyad is that each of the two must actually accomplish something, and that in the case of failure only the other remains."[3] One person slacks off, and the dyad is unstable. One person leaves, and it's kaput. We see this reflected in Sue's vitriol when Kelly turns on her, breaking up the dyad and getting Sue voted off the island.

But perhaps nowhere in reality TV land is this unique characteristic of the dyad more evident than on *Naked and Afraid* (Discovery Channel, 2013–present). In each episode, a male and female survivalist are left together in the wilderness with no food, water, or clothing to see if they can last for twenty-one days. Toward the end of their time together, they need to make their way across the terrain to an "extraction point."

On *Naked and Afraid*, the dyad is the *whole show*. By isolating the dyad, *Naked and Afraid* allows us to examine the pure characteristics of this form. The participants' dependence on each other is established early and reinforced throughout each episode. In the pilot, for example, Shane and Kim are stranded in a Costa Rican jungle.[4] Almost immediately, there is a bit of a clash between the two survivalists, with Shane admitting that he doesn't much care for people in their twenties (which Kim is) and Kim opining that Shane sure talks a lot. He begins referring to her as "kiddo." Regarding the epithet, Kim tells the camera, "At least for now I don't mind it, because I need some moral support and he needs some moral support." *Naked and Afraid* repeatedly emphasizes how Shane and Kim's survival depends largely on the strength of their union.

A central tension between Kim and Shane is the possible breakup of the twosome. If one partner leaves the show, the other can try to make it alone, but it's an uphill battle. When Kim becomes ill and is incapacitated for several days, Shane is nearly unable to keep up all of the work that needs to be done to maintain their fire and shelter. "I'm running down with energy and I can't support two people," Shane tells the camera. "I just can't do it." When Kim begins to feel better, the two are able to join forces and make it to the end. Ultimately, both *Survivor* and *Naked and Afraid* provide neatly packaged examples of how the dyad impacts its members and also how those members can work within the form to achieve success.

THE TRIAD: CHECKMATE IN THE TRIBE

The next basic unit of social life that Simmel pinpoints, and *Survivor* exemplifies, is the *triad*: a group of three. It doesn't matter what the composition of that triad is—friends, family members, coworkers, or castaways—but there are shared aspects across triadic forms. Add just one more person to a dyad, and things get a bit more complicated. Things also get more interesting to watch, which is likely why we see so many iconic trios (from Stooges to anthropomorphized duck nephews) strewn across the pop-cultural landscape. Numerous film and TV plots also revolve around an interloper who changes the dynamic of an established twosome—the 2006 comedy film *You, Me and Dupree* being just one example.

As Simmel points out, triads are somewhat tricky, because it's harder for three people to maintain a "uniform mood"[5] than it is for two. Any two parents who have dragged a cranky toddler on vacation likely know this all too well. And we see this immediately on *Survivor* when Kelly and Stacey, who believe they've developed a friendship with Sue, approach her about axing Rudy. Sue leads them to believe she shares that mood, while in fact she's planning on giving Stacey the chop. "These chicks think I'm voting for one person and I'm not," she tells the camera, grinning. Stacey was right to be worried about that elimination ceremony; she ends up being the third castaway voted off, and Sue makes it nearly to the end. (And, yes, this is the same Sue who later becomes upset when Kelly betrays *her*.)

Another thing that distinguishes a triad from a dyad is that the three people within it can have different relationships with *one another*. This introduces new possibilities for various combinations of antagonisms as well as, to use *Survivor* parlance, "alliances." Indeed, one of Richard's chess moves is to turn interpersonal conflict within triads to his own advantage. When it suits him, he becomes what Simmel calls a *tertius gaudens*: the "rejoicing third" who is able to benefit from a conflict between the other two.[6] For example, in episode four[7] he's able to capitalize on Sue's annoyance with Dirk to bring her into an alliance with him. "Well, I know what the resolution to the conflict that exists right now would be at home," he says in a testimonial, "but I'm actually planning something different from that, that might benefit me, and it's a little sneaky." He strokes his chin. "I think I'm gonna handle this by beginning to develop alliances with some folks to ensure that I move into the next round."

Interestingly, while Richard may be "sneaky," he stops short of becoming what Simmel calls a *divide et impera* ("divide and rule") participant—the third in a triad who actively *creates* conflict in order to profit from it. *Divide et impera* personalities are not lacking on the reality TV landscape, however. Colloquially known as a "shit stirrer," there seems to be at least one on every *Housewives* franchise, and if one doesn't exist or she's not pulling her weight in terms of drama, a fringe character emerges for this purpose. *New Jersey*'s Kim D.—a woman who pops up mainly to host fashion shows for her store POSCHE and to make inflammatory accusations—is one example. One might also argue that the true *divide et impera* role in reality TV is filled by the producers, who plant the seeds for dissent in order to drive conflict and ratings.

When dyads and triads materialize on our screens, it's easy to see how they operate in our own lives. We've invented snazzy modern lingo to characterize some of these relationships: Rudy and Richard's bond might be labeled a "bromance" today, and Sue and Kelly are the consummate "frenemies." But while we develop new words for them, their basic structures and dynamics do not change. Watching these forms on reality TV helps us to see how they're applicable to other contexts— the workplace, our families, school, political life. The *tertius gaudens* exists in the child of divorce who receives gifts from his feuding and guilt-ridden parents, while the *divide et impera* employee can be found stoking conflict between two coworkers in order to keep the boss's eye off her own work.

It would be a challenge to find a reality show where dyads and triads *don't* exist and don't function in the ways Simmel described. And it would be nearly impossible to find a real human biography from which they are absent.

DOING IT IN GROUPS

So, dyads and triads are fundamental to social life—both on and off the screen—but what happens when additional people come onto the scene? We've likely all used the term "small group" at some point, though Simmel defines it in a particular way: as a cluster of people who are engaging face-to-face and who lack formal roles and all have the same status. As opposed to "large groups"—such as military units or classroom setups—small groups, which have no built-in leadership structure, can find it hard to get anything accomplished. From group science projects in middle school to university governance committees, many of us can likely relate to the difficulties posed by these forms!

Small groups are an important facet of reality TV—perhaps because they force interactions between participants and can catalyze drama. Remember how the producers took the TV away and gave the housemates a job after the London season of *The Real World*? The job in the subsequent season (*The Real World: Miami*, 1996) was to create a business using $50,000 in start-up funds. Yet the *Miami* housemates were highly disorganized and never managed to get a project off the ground. Following that season, the cast had jobs or volunteered as part of existing, hierarchical organizations.

Competition shows bring the insufficiencies of such groups into sharp focus. On *Survivor*, this happens almost as soon as Tagi washes ashore. Richard wants the tribe to sit down together and talk through their process; meanwhile, everyone else just begins doing physical labor. Sue, a truck driver from Wisconsin, pushes back against Richard, saying she's "not corporate." Rudy, an ex–U.S. Navy SEAL, complains that "everybody's trying to run the show"; he says things were a lot easier in the military, where they just followed one person's orders.

Ultimately, Richard is able to succeed not only within dyads and triads but within these slightly larger social forms as well. When the Tagi and Pagong tribes merge, for instance, an in-group/out-group structure appears in which ex-Tagi members Richard, Kelly, Rudy, and Sue band together and begin picking off the ex-Pagongs one by one. Now, when we hear the term "in-group" we might be tempted to think it applies only to mean kids in the high school cafeteria. Yet, as Simmel observed, the in-group/out-group distinction is a recurrent form in social life. The in-group holds the social power, and while they're often the majority (e.g., white people in the US), they don't necessarily *have* to be. Going back to the high school cafeteria, the popular kids often wield a great deal of influence despite being low in number relative to the student body as a whole. In the case of *Survivor*, the ex-Tagi alliance is smaller than half the total number of remaining castaways. (Tagi and Pagong merge with equal numbers, but Tagi member Sean is not in the alliance.) However, the ex-Tagi's shrewd organization enables them to become a powerhouse, dictating much of the rest of the game. Again, they're able to do this in part because of Richard's maneuvering.

To be fair, Richard's ability to gain mastery over small social forms is particularly pronounced, even within the extreme world of reality TV. It may have helped that most of the other contestants were not playing a psychological game in quite the same way as he was at the time. It's worth noting that he came back for *Survivor: All Stars* in 2004 and was the fifth castaway eliminated out of eighteen.

"GET HIM!"

If Georg Simmel and Richard Hatch were co-teaching a sociology class, they would undoubtedly emphasize the strength that can be found in our tiniest social groupings. By working together within these forms, we can accomplish many tasks—from surviving in a jungle to defeating a rival team. But there is another side to these groups: they can control *us* as well.

As Simmel has explained, and as the reality genre repeatedly shows us, seemingly normal, well-mannered people can get swept up in collective bad behavior. Discussing the "lowering of practical personality values"[8] that happens in a group, Simmel observes that people commit acts together that they wouldn't if left to their own devices. Groupthink may insulate them from feeling that they're doing anything wrong. Likely, we can all think of examples of this. Childhood bullying. Shopping mall stampedes on Black Friday. Political officials trampling on human rights. "If the individual had to answer for all these acts personally, he would find them impossible—at the very least, they would make him blush," he explains.[9] You've probably heard this described as "mob mentality."

Perhaps nowhere on the reality TV landscape is this aspect of groupthink more prominent than on *Top Chef*, season two. One of the contestants, Marcel, has friction with other cast members throughout the season. His castmate Ilan repeatedly insults him, at one point telling him to "shut the [bleep] up, keep making your foams, and go cry in a corner." This tension comes to a head one night; the crew members have gone home, but they've given the contestants a video camera with which to film themselves.[10] In a testimonial, Cliff tells us that since they were about to go into their last elimination challenge, they "thought it would be a good idea to try to shave Marcel's head." Suddenly, there's footage of Cliff pulling a sleeping Marcel off the couch. Cliff holds Marcel to the ground as he squirms to get away, and then they tussle standing up, with Cliff pinning Marcel's hands up behind his head. From behind the camera, Ilan yells, "Get him! Get him!"

"I was rudely awakened by Cliff," Marcel recalls in a testimonial, "and I'm like, 'Is this for real? What the [bleep]'s going on right now? Why is there this big guy on top of me? Why am I, like, eating the carpet? What are those [bleep]ing clippers doing over there?'"

"It was a very stupid plan or joke," Cliff explains.

"It was weird," Sam says in a testimonial. "It was an uncomfortable situation for all parties involved."

Going back to the incident, Sam sits on a nearby couch, laughing. After Marcel breaks free and angrily storms into the bedroom, Sam smiles and whispers, "Go in there," to Ilan. Ilan does follow Marcel, angering him further. Marcel ends up getting away and sleeping in a locked bathroom. When the footage comes to light, Cliff is ejected from the show for putting his hands on Marcel. The other chefs are allowed to continue in the competition, and Ilan wins the whole shebang.

While *Top Chef* provides an example of groupthink that results in physical violence, we often see the same dynamic in other reality programs, when the cast members gang up verbally on one of their own. Many a *Housewives* reunion show, for instance, has seen a single cast member set upon by the others. Perhaps one thing keeping these encounters verbal and not physical is that there are usually observers waiting in the wings, attuned to the possibility of bad press and legal reprisals. On some shows, such as *Love & Hip Hop* and *Bad Girls Club*, we've seen crew members scramble onto the screen, pulling cast members apart when violence erupts.

How many times have we, like the chefs, been swayed by group emotion? Recently, at a university faculty meeting, I found myself getting caught up in a tide of unfavorable opinion about a minor change to a policy that I hadn't cared a lick about before setting foot in that auditorium. In that moment I felt true anger, which had dissipated by the time I got home. Durkheim describes this phenomenon as a "social current."[11] When people gather together, he argues, "the great waves of enthusiasm, indignation and pity that are produced have their seat in no one individual conscience. They come to each one of us from outside and sweep us along in spite of ourselves."[12] However, "Once the assembly has broken up and these social influences have ceased to act upon us, and we are once more on our own, the emotions we have felt seem an alien phenomenon, one in which we no longer recognize ourselves."[13] Indeed, standing before the judges in the sober light of day, the chefs appear remorseful.

And what about the chefs who simply looked the other way? Such bystanders are there, too, in our daily lives. If we've learned anything from the reality show *What Would You Do?* (ABC, 2008–present), it's that many ordinary people will not intervene when they notice wrongdoing. On the show, actors put on a ruse of morally questionable, and sometimes illegal, behavior in public spaces, to gauge how bystanders will respond. At the end of each scene, host John Quiñones interviews people about their reactions, prompting us to assess what our own would have been. As we've seen, one particular appeal of reality TV is our ability to identify with the participants. In the case of *What Would You Do?*, the show itself explicitly encourages us to slip our feet into the bystanders' shoes. It prompts us to look inside ourselves, to ask ourselves a series of questions, to measure our own ethics by the ruler of the show. Who am I, in this scenario? The bigot? The intervenor? The mute observer? Would I have followed everyone else in remaining distant, unresponsive?

So while we might like to think we would have stood up for Marcel, one thing that's evident from *What Would You Do?* is that many people do not stand up. Ultimately, *Top Chef* is a sobering reminder that violence can erupt anywhere, when the will of the individual gets dissolved within the will of the group. As the show's head judge, Tom Colicchio, wrote on his Bravo blog after the episode aired, "In a flash I understood how frat pranks can morph into ugly acts of hazing, or how a rowdy bachelor party can become the scene of a crime. . . . The whole thing brought to mind that famous quote, 'All that is necessary for evil to succeed is for good men to do nothing.'"[14]

REALLY REAL?

On gamedocs such as *Survivor* and *Top Chef*, the challenges may seem wholly disconnected from everyday experience. In real life, nobody's ever going to ask you to balance on a canoe with a lit tiki torch or whip up a gourmet meal using only Cheez Doodles and a Mallomar. Yet my students often tell me that they find competition shows to be the "realest" of the reality TV subgenres. At least on competition shows the main constraints are obvious, and it may seem that within those constraints the contestants are pretty much allowed to "be real." (The students acknowledge, however, that there is a broad spectrum, with some gamedocs appearing to be more manufactured than others.) Another reason these shows seem "realer" to my students, according to them, is that the group dynamics come across as familiar. While the average viewer may not be able to relate to eating grubs on an island or sliding into a sparkling sheath dress for an elaborate rose ceremony, these shows lay bare the forms of interaction that dominate all of our lives. They're mirrors of our most basic and immediate social groupings.

My students' responses to competition shows may help explain why this is a particularly popular reality subgenre. Audiences will watch people compete for nearly anything on TV. From heirs clamoring over an inheritance (*The Will*, CBS, 2005), to women vying for the affection of a Prince Harry doppelgänger (*I Wanna Marry "Harry,"* Fox, 2014), to a celebrity diving competition plagued by injuries (*Splash*, ABC, 2013), variations on the gamedoc have been myriad. And competition shows can be big business. On a list of the most watched shows of the 2017–2018 season (including sports) among adults eighteen to forty-nine, *The Voice*, *Survivor*, *American Idol*, and *The Bachelor* all cracked the top twenty-five.[15]

When it comes to *Survivor*, there's a reason the droves are still tuning in, decades later. Just as we can see ourselves and people we know in these characters, we can also see our own experiences in theirs. Yet I would go a step further than my students do. Reality competitions aren't simply a showcase for our everyday group dynamics; they can be a *magnifying glass*. Shows like *Survivor* put people in front of a lens, limit their distractions (no TV, phones, internet, music, or even writing implements), and highlight their basic interactions. These shows isolate our small groups like slide specimens, allowing us to peer through the microscope and focus on their dynamics in a way we don't often get a chance to do.

What's more, on reality TV, these conflicts are heightened by fatigue, the constraints of challenges, the demands of filming, and producer intervention. One might argue that because of these factors, reality TV overemphasizes our propensity for group conflict. What makes something like the head-shaving incident all the more impactful, though, is that *Top Chef* is a cooking competition. It arguably has more in common with the HGTV fix-it shows than it does with more conflict-driven reality TV. The biggest drama in a given season might be that a chef is accused of serving too many dishes with the same protein. (Cue season five's Fabio: "This is *Top Chef*. It's not *Top Scallops*!") And despite the head-shaving incident, these contestants are never presented to us as monsters. Sam goes on to win "Fan Favorite" for the season.

On other competition shows, such as MTV's *The Challenge*, the conflicts are more overt and expected. These are not your grandma's small-group interactions, to be sure. Still, by turning up the dial, these shows amplify the latent dynamics that exist in all of our lives. Out here in the real world, an important figure in a triad might be an online troll who tries to drive a wedge between two factions of her rival political party. It might be your normal-seeming colleague who eats your lunch from the fridge and blames it on somebody else. But such figures are particularly *noticeable* on reality TV, when they're in the form of cartoonish villains like Kim D. When they're Housewives stirring metaphoric shit with exaggerated swirls. When they're Richard Hatch stroking his chin and flashing a Grinchy smile.

Ultimately, for all of their convoluted premises, *Survivor* and other competition programs expose Simmel's forms and show us how they might apply to our own lives, as we struggle with two friends who are feuding or attempt to maintain order in a meeting. Watching these groups—versions of our own, taffy-pulled into entertaining caricatures—doesn't just show us what happens when explosive personalities are pushed to the brink. The little groups that populate these programs show us who we are, and who we have historically been, as social beings. Indeed, perhaps one of the reasons gamedocs continue to resonate with us is that these social forms and their internal dynamics have never become outdated. They were relevant around the turn of the twentieth century when Simmel was writing, they were relevant around the turn of the twenty-first when *Survivor* first aired, and they remain relevant today. The pocket tees and chinos may have been retired, but the *tertius gaudens* remains.

4

"Kim Is Always Late" (Families)

"Kim is always late."

The chaos of daily life in a family with six kids is set to self-consciously hokey theme music.

Kris is the mother hen, arranging her children for the camera and ordering her husband to make an outfit change ("Awful!"). Each of the siblings then gets a moment in front of the lens:

Khloé asks whether the wind effects are necessary.

"No, that is not cute," Kourtney tells the camera, touching her hair.

Rob says he needs someone to make him laugh.

Preteens Kylie and Kendall pose back-to-back, *Charlie's Angels* style, angling their fingers into guns.

Finally, Kim—recognizable from her ubiquitous sex tape—sweeps in, "late," in a red bandage dress, positioning herself dramatically in front of the others. The clan jostles one another for a bit before they finally come to rest, settling into a group pose in front of their suburban home.[1]

When reality TV first introduces us to the Kardashian/Jenners, in the 2007 title sequence to their show, it is as a family. Indeed, the cover of *Cosmopolitan* dubbed them "America's First Family" in 2015, sparking outrage that this seemingly vapid gaggle could serve as ambassadors of our culture.[2] But while critics might scoff that nothing is sacred to this clan, as the religion scholar Kathryn Lofton has pointed out, the Kardashian/Jenners suggest that what's sacred for them is the clan itself.[3] They use the word "family" over and over on their show and in their social media posts. Their devotion to one another is a useful narrative that no doubt helps to sustain their popularity. But it's not *just* a narrative. Functionally, they were a family before the E! network came into their lives, and they will still be one now that it has departed.

More broadly, stemming back to 1973's *An American Family*, families have always been a central focus of the reality genre. And this makes sense. The genre supposedly showcases unscripted human experience, and families are fundamental to that experience. As the sociologist William J. Goode has observed, the family is the one institution besides religion that has been "formally developed in all societies."[4] Though reality TV relatives may not always look or act like ours, they show us what our families do for us and the reasons that these groups remain such an integral part of our lives. And they demonstrate that while families and our roles within them may have changed, we continue to conceptualize "the family" in a fairly homogenized way.

KEEPING UP WITH FAMILY

Why do the Kardashian/Jenners need one another? As Goode has explained, families shoulder a tremendous weight for all of us, doing things that it would be infeasible to pawn off on other social groups. While we might rely on the public school system to teach our kids calculus, for instance, family members are most likely to be the ones teaching their children how to talk, hold a spoon, and brush their hair. Families provide "physical maintenance" of their members—for example, feeding, bathing, grooming—as well as emotional support.[5] And especially in the United States, where we don't have universal health care or childcare, families do a lot of the caring for the ill, elderly, disabled, and very young. During the COVID-19 pandemic, for instance, many of us hunkered down in our family units, drawing emotional, physical, and financial support from our kin. Others were devastated to be severed from their family support systems. Similarly, while the government sometimes steps in to punish those who violate our social rules, families do much of the labor of keeping their members on an even keel. You're probably not going to initiate legal action when your teen sasses you or your toddler pilfers candy from the cupboard.

Not only do families fill in the crevices where other social institutions can't extend, but there are also clear advantages to our participation in these groups. Goode points out that we can divide up our labor among our kin, ultimately easing the load for everyone. Families also enjoy economies of scale; for instance, it's cheaper per person to buy food in bulk for a family than it is to feed a single individual. Families receive support from outsiders; this includes not just emotional support but structural support as well. As *The Bachelor* and *90 Day Fiancé* have taught us, marriage (in general) bears the stamp of cultural approval as well as legal, governmental backing. (This explains why I've attended lots of joyous weddings but only one divorce party.) And we often have long, shared histories with our families and can communicate and plan with them based on our prior knowledge of their personalities. Not all of these benefits apply to everyone—some families do more emotional harm than good, for instance—but overall, families provide these advantages in ways that other social institutions do not and cannot, given the way our society is currently organized.

All of the social functions and benefits that Goode describes are present on *Keeping Up with the Kardashians* (E!, 2007–2021). Throughout the series, Mama Kris swoops in as "momager"; in episode one,[6] she uses Kim's sex tape scandal to fuel her daughter's career. "Physical maintenance" of family members? We see the Kardashian/Jenners continually feeding, grooming, and clothing one another. Economic functions? The Kardashian/Jenners are actually more of an economic unit than most families, as they work together on the show; spreading beyond it, their careers are entwined in one another's. Education, social control, and socialization of the kids? When the show begins, youngest daughters Kendall and Kylie are eleven and nine, respectively. Kris and the gang teach the two girls the morals and norms associated with being a part of the Kardashian/Jenner clan. And at least in the early episodes, the family makes efforts to rein in the girls' behavior, with Caitlyn often taking the role of disciplinarian. "I have little sisters," Kim tells us in the pilot episode, "I need to teach them what not to do." Support from outsiders? The series begins with the family preparing for the parents' anniversary party, which is attended by friends and relatives. Emotional support? Episodes regularly slake our hunger for resolution by concluding with the fast food of expressive conversations, tears, and hugs. And shared knowledge about one another's idiosyncrasies? "Kim is always late."

While the Kardashian/Jenners may or may not be a functional family in a psychological sense—an assessment that is beyond my expertise—in a sociological sense they function as a family and derive advantages from that grouping, even if the content of those benefits may be different from ours.

It's not likely that your mom has ever counseled you about how to address your sex tape on *The Tyra Banks Show*, but she may have given you advice of some sort. And Kris and her brood are similar to other reality TV families in that way. *Sister Wives*, for instance, shows us what families do—making money and allocating it, laying down a set of values, feeding their kids and propelling them through school and out into the world. While "functional" may not be the term that comes to mind when we think of reality TV kin, they show us the essential characteristics of families that have caused these social groupings to endure.

SISTER WIVES GO BANANAS

But just because this institution has persisted doesn't mean that our roles within families have remained the same. Much has been written, for instance, about how the family has become more "individualized."[7] Researchers have found that, over time, our own wants and needs have become more important to us,[8] and we've become more likely to value our personal autonomy within families.[9] One group of researchers, for example, found that between 1980 and 2000, people increasingly emphasized personal choice within their marriages and that the percentage of couples who said they generally shared decision-making equally rose from 49 percent to 64 percent.[10] On wedding-themed reality shows, we often hear brides declare, "This is *my* day!" In uttering this line, they're conceptualizing their weddings, and by extension their marriage and family roles, in an individualistic way that's specific to the contemporary Western world.

There are a few different reasons we started thinking about our families in this way. As the male breadwinner/female homemaker model began to decline and women entered the workforce in larger numbers—gaining greater financial security and greater decision-making power in their marriages—our attitudes about family life got swept along with those currents.[11] (Other catalysts for this shift included rising life spans and increased standards of living.)[12]

And *Sister Wives* offers us a microcosm of this shift. As a reminder, the show focuses on the Browns: a contemporary, polygamous fundamentalist Mormon family. In season one, the family is housed together with a clearly defined collection of roles. The first three wives and their husband, Kody, live in one home in Lehi, Utah, with their various children. At this time, Kody is courting Robyn, who will become the family's fourth wife. In an approximation of the breadwinner/homemaker model, Kody and wife Janelle both work outside of the home, wife Meri is in school studying psychology, and wife Christine provides childcare for the youngest kids. Meri describes how they are functionally reliant on one another: "If you're looking at this lifestyle as 'What can I do to help you?' or 'What can you do to help me?' it works out totally well." There is a communal pantry from which they all draw food. As Janelle explains, "The family functions as a whole, but we all have our own autonomy."[13]

Over the course of multiple seasons, the wives' autonomy skyrockets. At the end of season two, the family moves to Las Vegas, ostensibly to avoid prosecution for their lifestyle by the state of Utah. There, they live on a cul-de-sac, each wife with her biological children in her own home, and the wives increasingly spin off into their own orbits. (In 2019, the family moved again—this time to Flagstaff, Arizona, where as of this writing they continue to live in separate houses.) Some drama occurs because Meri wants a large house, even though she has only one child while the others have multiple. Janelle joins a gym and gets a personal trainer. Robyn takes the helm of a new business, My Sisterwife's Closet, which offers polygamy-themed jewelry; she tries to get the others on board with the project but finds lackluster support. Meri sells leggings.

And in perhaps their most extreme manifestation of individualism, at the end of season nine it's revealed that Meri has been catfished by a woman posing as a man. Meri's been chatting with "Sam" online and sending suggestive voice mails and photos—including a notable close-up of her mouth eating a banana. When talking about this incident, Meri tearfully tells her husband, "I feel like I'm just doing my life by myself."[14]

Likely, some of the women's increased autonomy is due to their income from the show, just as sociologists have attributed the growth of individualization partly to women's rising financial independence and the democratization of household roles. As polygamists steeped in a fundamentalist religion, the Browns may not seem like the quintessential American family. Indeed, three out of four of their marriages are not even legally recognized—further evidence of our societal emphasis on monogamy. Yet even in this seemingly unusual brood—in fact, *especially* within it—we see how it's become increasingly acceptable to wonder what it is *we* want, both within our families and outside of them.

"HOW COULD I HAVE KNOWN?!"

While the reality genre highlights our culturally specific expectations for various family members, it *particularly* highlights our rigid expectations for our mothers.

Partly this is because reality TV land is just teeming with moms.

Sure, a few shows have focused on dads—*Snoop Dogg's Father Hood* (E!, 2007–2009), for example, and the short-lived *Project Dad* (Discovery Life/TLC, 2016–2017) and *Modern Dads* (A&E, 2013). However, these shows rest on the apparent paradox of manly men performing fatherly tasks. As we've seen, part of the appeal of reality TV, and part of what makes it an apt sociological subject, is how it pulls together disparate social elements. Just as *The Real World* transposed Alabaman Julie onto the frenetic backdrop of New York City, contemporary reality shows give men in the home fish-out-of-water narratives. Even shows that focus on families with famous dads, such as *Gene Simmons Family Jewels* (A&E, 2006–2012) and *Run's House* (MTV, 2005–2009), while depicting the dads' relationships with their kids also portray these men as multifaceted, highlighting their business endeavors and how they navigate celebrity. On the contrary, from *Teen Mom* and *Dance Moms*, to *Pretty Wicked Moms* and *The Mother/ Daughter Experiment*, motherhood is a central theme across reality TV subgenres.

For those of us who are mothers, and perhaps even for those of us who aren't, these shows can resonate with us deeply, cutting to the heart of our own insecurities about our ability to adequately fill this role. For example, I used to belong to a book club of about one dozen women. They were mainly suburban professionals—doctors, executives, professors, university coaches, foundation directors. These women intimidated me with their knowledge of politics and theater, history and wine. They could lay down random facts about the Tudors coolly like silverware. And they had all seen the reality show *I Didn't Know I Was Pregnant* (TLC, 2009–2011).

The show, as the title suggests, is about women who did not know they were pregnant until they found themselves giving birth. We get to hear from the mothers themselves in testimonials, and we watch dramatic reenactments of their stories. Sometimes these women have medical conditions that obfuscate their pregnancy symptoms; in other cases, the signs are clearly there. The women in the latter group are easy targets for our ridicule. Comedian Kathy Griffin, for instance, does a bit in which she mocks the women on the show; in an exaggerated southern drawl, she describes all of the classic markers of pregnancy (e.g., weight gain, morning sickness) and adds, "How could I have known?!"

I can't look away from *I Didn't Know I Was Pregnant*, and judging from that book club I'm not the only one. Perhaps our gratification here is the voyeuristic glee we get from watching circumstances different from our own and our smugness in feeling that *we* could never be so foolish. Or, conversely, perhaps we watch for the same it-could-happen-to-me jolt we enjoy from a scary movie. One reason the show may have reverberated with the women in my club is that all of us are mothers, and this show shakes us to the core.

The very premise of the show violates a notion that the sociologist Sharon Hays[15] refers to as "intensive mothering": the idea that women should singularly devote their time, resources, and emotions to their children. The women on *I Didn't Know I Was Pregnant*, who aren't even aware that they're about to be moms and haven't prepared, fail at this before they've even begun.

"Intensive mothering" is a fairly narrowly defined, yet widespread, cultural model for parenthood. And it may seem biologically self-evident. Obviously, mothers should closely attend to their children! Isn't that what all animals do? Yet it's important to note that our notion of intensive mothering, like our ideas about individualism, is particular to our

time and place. As Hays points out, the idea that mothers—
and *primarily* mothers (hence: few dad shows)—should be
constantly emotionally available to their children, monitor
them fully, and occupy them with organized activities is a
historically specific, Western ideal. In fact, individual moms
are the primary caretakers of their kids only in a minority
of cultures.[16] Even in the United States, child-rearing hasn't
been strictly a mother's domain; in late-seventeenth- to early-
eighteenth-century New England, for instance, fathers were
the ones charged with instilling discipline and "moral for-
titude" in their children.[17] And the model of baby being at
home with mom while dad brings home the bacon is far from
a universal one. As Stephanie Coontz has pointed out, "Exclusive child care by mothers and sole breadwinning by fathers
have been exceedingly rare in history."[18] Along similar lines,
we haven't always considered it healthy for moms to lavish
love and affection on their kids, as it might make the children
soft. On the contrary, in prior eras, it was considered good
mothering to feed your baby opium if it got fussy, to toss your
infant in the air to entertain it, and to whip your kids when
they misbehaved.[19]

CRACKS IN THE MODEL

So, we are taught to think about motherhood in a fairly specific
way. And for all of its *unusual* moms—celebrity moms, survivalist moms, polygamous moms, drag moms, Kris Jenner—
reality TV illuminates this way. The genre shines a light on the
model of intensive mothering and illuminates its fault lines.
It shows us how we subscribe to this cultural ideal, while also
offering us an array of women who fail to meet its bar.

From the girls on *16 and Pregnant* who leave their babies

with their parents while they go out partying to *Here Comes Honey Boo Boo*'s Mama June allegedly dating the same convicted pedophile who had molested her elder daughter,[20] many reality TV women fail to grab the brass ring of intensive motherhood. We collectively acknowledge this, and we are harsh in our rebukes. On social media, viewers dissect and debate these mothers' choices, from what their children eat to how they dress and their very presence in the spotlight. Articles, listicles, and tabloid items sizzle with titles such as "The Worst Parenting Moments from Reality TV Moms"[21] and "The 10 Worst Moms on TV Who Had No Business Having Kids"—a list including fictional moms such as Cersei Lannister from *Game of Thrones* as well as reality TV's Kris Jenner and Mama June.[22] The strength of our cultural association between moms and child-rearing is evident in the minimal or absent references to the children's fathers in these pieces. For instance, on a 2012 list titled "The Worst Parents on Reality TV," all were mothers, except for two cases in which fathers— Stephen Fowler of *Wife Swap* and Jon Gosselin of *Jon & Kate Plus 8*—were listed alongside their female co-parents.[23]

Jon and Kate, particularly, show us our collective assumption that the responsibility for children's well-being lies primarily with their mother. Their show, originally titled *Jon & Kate Plus 8* and later *Kate Plus 8*, initially focused on the couple's everyday lives with their toddler sextuplets and older twin daughters. Eventually their marriage unraveled and Jon moved out of the home, leaving Kate as the primary parent of the children. During the heyday of the show, and even in the years following it, Kate's purported misdeeds were regular tabloid fodder. *Is she getting plastic surgery? Is she dating her bodyguard? Should she have really gone on* Dancing with the Stars? Often implicit, and sometimes explicit, in these questions is purported concern for the welfare of her children. *Who was watching the kids while she trained for* Dancing with the Stars? One website, for instance, included an array of fifteen photos "proving" Kate's lack of fitness as a mother. "Is Kate Gosselin a good mom?" it asked. "Does she have the temperament to raise eight kids with love, calmness and kindness? Evidence to date says the answer to both questions is 'no.'"[24] The article briefly mentioned Jon but did not dwell on his participation in the children's lives. Pieces like these often focus on Kate's career ambitions, and they display paparazzi photos to cast doubt on her parenting choices (*Why is there a spoon in her pocket? Is she hitting her children with the spoon?*). But Jon, who is purportedly now estranged from six of his eight children,[25] is largely left out of these investigations.

It's not that the mothers on reality TV are all "good moms," but they're not "bad moms" either, from a sociological perspective, because either designation presumes there is some universal, ahistorical standard by which motherhood might be assessed. When it comes to the specific model of intensive motherhood, however, many reality TV moms do fall spectacularly short. From the *Toddlers & Tiaras* moms who wax their preschoolers' eyebrows to Jenelle from *Teen Mom 2* who flouts the basic rules of car seat safety, these women do things we might find unsettling. When they fail the litmus test of modern motherhood, they reveal the parameters of the test itself. Our reactions to these women highlight the artificial, historically specific conditions that we place on valid, acceptable mothering. After all, we're not expecting any of these women to pump their babies full of opium and fling them in the air to entertain them. Not even Jenelle.

By failing to rise to the standards of intensive motherhood, the moms of reality TV both shed light on this model and hint at its lack of universal viability. There are contradictions and tensions inherent in this model, as Hays notes. One such tension is that mothers are expected to be intensive, but not *so* intensive that they border on helicoptering and smother their children.

Unscripted TV often tells the cautionary tales of these two extremes. Kris Jenner, for instance, is portrayed as somebody who is simultaneously too inattentive and too attentive to her children. On the one hand, in early episodes of *Keeping Up with the Kardashians*, when Kylie and Kendall are pre-teens and young teens, they appear to have copious amounts of unstructured, unmonitored free time; in the first episode alone, they're found swinging on a stripper pole and mixing cocktails. On the other hand, as a "momager," Kris has her hands in every aspect of her children's professional lives. The ubiquity of her presence is something they often complain about on the show. Her ability to somehow straddle both negative extremes of motherhood is likely part of what lands her on so many "Worst Mom" lists.

This premise that moms need to be intensely attentive, but not *too* intensely attentive, is a central narrative thread on *Celebrity Wife Swap* (ABC, 2012–2015). On the show, just as on its noncelebrity forbearer, two spouses (usually wives) switch families for a period of time. Both shows follow the reality TV recipe of artificially throwing together people from different social contexts and, in doing so, exposing their differences. At the end of each episode, the two sets of parents come together, talk about what they've learned from the experience, and offer suggestions to each other. A regular theme on *Celebrity Wife Swap* is that one mom is overly monitoring of her children while the other is overly lax. Often, they reach a kind of Goldilocks's porridge resolution, collectively ushering us toward a mode of mothering that's *juuuust right.*

In the inaugural episode, for instance, former *Growing Pains* actress Tracey Gold trades places with singer Carnie Wilson of Wilson Phillips fame.[26] The two mothering polarities are clear from the beginning. Carnie begins by telling us that their family motto is "Love before rules" and that she has a set of people who help with the children and the house, as she has been traveling extensively for performances. Tracey, on the other hand, describes her family as "extremely organized" and lists the set of chores she performs personally every day. Throughout the episode, the show hints at the notion that perhaps Tracey does too much for her children (e.g., picking out her teen's clothing for him) while perhaps Carnie does too little. As the narrator explains, Carnie "isn't used to running a house without an army of help." When Tracey tries out Carnie's life, we mainly see her sitting around the house, looking in the fridge, and flipping through a magazine, while two employees attend to the kids. In similar ways across its episodes, *Celebrity Wife Swap* is often a show that cautions women about straying too far from the sweet spot of the intensive ideal.

A second wrinkle in the model of intensive mothering is its paradoxical expectation that women have a natural aptitude for mothering but also must solicit the input of other, better-informed people. The intensive model, as Hays describes it, tells us that child-rearing "should be carried out primarily by individual mothers and that it should be centered on children's needs, with methods that are informed by experts, labor-intensive, and costly."[27] As we'll see, reality TV seizes on the notion of expertise in multiple domains, showcasing loosely credentialed professionals who show us how to repair ourselves. When it comes to mothering specifically, the demand for expertise creates a tension with the notion that women are natural nurturers who are biologically programmed to know what's best for their own kids.

This tension comes into play on *Supernanny* (ABC, 2005– 2011; Lifetime, 2020), where British nanny Jo Frost goes into American homes, observes family life, and teaches parents how to deal with their unruly children. From the beginning, the show frames Jo as an expert; she has "fifteen years of childcare experience," the narrator states. While seeking Jo's professional know-how, the women on the show often express guilt at not knowing how to handle their own children themselves, as they ostensibly should be genetically predisposed to do.

But *Supernanny* does more than show us how certain individuals are unable to accomplish intensive motherhood; it shows us how, at the societal level, the model falls apart. In one episode, for instance, we meet the Wischmeyer family.[28] The mother, described as a "stay-at-home working mom," has difficulty attending to her four-year-old twins and their older brother while sitting in front of the computer for her job all day (a scenario that likely seemed far more unusual to us prior to the COVID-19 pandemic). One of the solutions that Jo ultimately provides is for her to cut back on her hours so that she can be more present for the children. While this was seemingly an easy fix, viewers may be left to wonder why she had not previously tried this or if it's economically feasible. More broadly, this moment on *Supernanny* begs the question of what happens to those who are unable to provide the "labor-intensive and costly" mechanisms of intensive mothering.

Economically strapped people on reality TV aren't the only ones portrayed as "bad moms." The affluent parents on shows such as *My Super Sweet 16* (MTV, 2005–present) are depicted as spoiling their kids, for instance. But the idea of continuously monitoring your kids is class-specific. Indeed, the sociologist Annette Lareau has found that working-class parents are more likely to use a strategy she terms "accomplishment of natural growth" (i.e., "providing the conditions under which children can grow but leaving leisure activities to children themselves"), while middle-class parents are more likely to "engage in concerted cultivation" (i.e., "attempting to foster children's talents through organized leisure activities and extensive reasoning").[29] Within the framework of intensive mothering, we tend to think about these as "bad" and "good" strategies, respectively. In real life, we see this play out in the arrests of mothers who, unable to afford childcare, leave their children unattended while they run to the store, go to work, or participate in job interviews.[30] Ultimately, legitimate mothering gets tied to class privilege because it's generally the privileged who have the bandwidth to be intensive.

BAD MOMS

One might observe that there are moms, on reality TV and elsewhere, who stray from the intensive model and don't get flak for it. We may even celebrate them! Perhaps the most prominent example is the 2016 film *Bad Moms* and its objectively awful sequel, *A Bad Moms Christmas* (2017), in which actresses Mila Kunis, Kristen Bell, and Kathryn Hahn play mothers who band together and reject the intensive model. Ultimately, Kunis's character requires her children to be more independent, and Bell's husband pitches in more.

Yet there are limits on who is able to push back and how we respond to those pushes. On *Snooki & Jwoww: Moms with*

Attitude (go90, 2015–2018; MTV YouTube, 2018–present),
for instance, the two *Jersey Shore* cast members drink, curse,
and laugh together about their deficiencies as parents. But, as
the media scholar Racquel Gates has pointed out, one reason
we're able to find their narratives compelling and smile along
with their misadventures is that they, like the women in *Bad
Moms*, are white—or "in Snooki's case [she has] a certain degree of racial ambiguity."[31] (We'll return to this point.) It's not
that women of color on reality TV don't do things that are incongruous with idealized notions of mothering, Gates points
out. On *Love & Hip Hop*, for example, "they fight, they drink,
they enter into sexual relationships with same- and opposite-
sex partners."[32] Yet white women—particularly straight white
women who are middle-class or higher—can be insulated
by privilege in a way that women of color cannot. "It should
come as no surprise," Gates explains, "that white women like
Snooki and Jwoww . . . get to be 'bad' with no consequences
by adopting the same markers of rebellion that would characterize black mothers as unfit."[33]

We see this double standard not only on reality TV and in
movies like *Bad Moms* but also in real life. It rears its head, for
example, in our response to "mommy wine culture." The popular blog *Scary Mommy* defines this term as "a classification of
moms who enjoy drinking wine and do so as a practice to un-
wind, in a non-judgmental setting."[34] There are hashtags and
paraphernalia dedicated to the theme—for example, a T-shirt
that says "Will Trade Husband for Wine," a children's book called
If You Give Mommy a Glass of Wine, and a wineglass emblazoned
with the words "mommy's juice." And it is likely no coincidence
that a Google search of the term returns mainly images of white,
seemingly middle-class moms clinking glasses. If, say, poor
Black mothers or immigrant Latinas were participating in this

pastime, it's likely that we as a culture would fail to treat it with such good humor. Such behavior would play into our collective stereotypes of women of color being unfit—of Black mothers, for instance, as welfare queens, as "lazy, dishonest, and irresponsible."[35] In the end, reality TV reveals not only how our notions of acceptable mothering are socially constructed but also how they're *specifically constructed in ways that validate mothers within certain demographics*. Not only are the relatively privileged more *able* to adhere to the ideal, but we're more forgiving of them when they do stray from it.

OUR FAMILIES, OURSELVES

Reality TV illustrates our lingering homogenized notions of what mothers, and what American families in general, are and should be. That's not to suggest that the genre never shows us alternative realities. Indeed, on the face of them, these shows beam out a dizzying kaleidoscope of family experiences: spouses who are fixed up by experts, by their parents, and by matchmakers; single moms, breadwinning moms, pageant moms, teen moms, soccer moms; transnational families, little-people families, "Gypsy" families, families with more than a dozen kids; transgender parents, same-sex marriages, gay kids who come out on TV; sextuplets, conjoined twins, incarcerated parents, and families struggling with addiction.

It also provides some representations of types of families, and of family members, that have historically been hidden from public view. For example, some queer participants on reality TV—such as Meri's daughter Mariah on *Sister Wives*— are shown within family contexts. In fact, going back to the embryonic stage of reality TV, in 1971 elder son Lance's homosexuality was a theme on *An American Family*. PBS, which aired the program, has called Lance "the first openly gay person to appear on television as an integral member of American family life."[36] Many of us likely also remember Pedro Zamora from *The Real World: San Francisco* (1994) as the first openly gay man we got to "know." But as the queer theorist José Esteban Muñoz has pointed out, the revolutionary thing about Pedro wasn't just that he was openly gay, or that he was openly HIV positive, but that he was an openly gay, openly HIV-positive Cuban immigrant in a committed relationship with another man of color.[37] Their commitment ceremony was broadcast on TV. At a time when it was widely believed that same-sex attraction was incompatible with being loved by one's parents, having a long-term partnership, or raising children,[38] reality TV was quietly showing us some new possibilities for family life.

Still, the genre *centers* particular families, showing us how we do the same. The clans that populate these shows are predominantly middle-class or wealthier. Racially and ethnically, reality TV families don't represent the demographics of the populace either. For instance, while Hispanics are the second-largest racial/ethnic group in the US,[39] as of this writing there have been only two US reality shows—Universo's *The Riveras* (2016–2019)[40] and Bravo's *Mexican Dynasties* (2019–present)—that focus on Hispanic families. Similarly, there are few Asian American families on the reality TV landscape. (As we'll see, this reflects the dearth of Asian Americans within the genre in general.) And while there are LGBT+ people—for instance, Mariah and Lance and Caitlyn Jenner—no program has centered on the nuclear family of a same-sex couple. Most of these families also seem to be some flavor of Christian,[41] leaving aside the approximately 30 percent of Americans[42] who don't follow these faiths. Yet even these gaps in visibility provide us with valuable cultural information, showing us how certain narratives and perspectives remain dominant, even within such a sprawling genre that ostensibly offers images of our diverse world.

The expectations that we hold for our family members are culturally specific and cannot possibly apply to everyone, yet we cling to them as though they are universal truths. Which families are legitimate? What roles within them are valid? In taking a thick highlighter to the inconsistencies and tensions in our expectations, unscripted television demonstrates how ways of looking at the world that may seem obvious to us are in fact built on the shifting sands of culture. *Every family member needs to be personally fulfilled. Weddings are about the bride. It's natural for women to remain in the home and care for children.* The reality genre takes our collective assumptions about family and exposes how our society shapes our senses of what's normal, what's natural, and what's real.

Paradoxically, one reason we may crave clear-cut meanings and sharply defined marital and familial roles is that families are increasingly diverse in meaning and structure. Premarital cohabitation, out-of-wedlock childbearing, divorce, and remarriage are becoming both more common and more culturally acceptable.[43] As the sociologist Andrew Cherlin points out, these days "social norms about family and personal life count for less" than they once did.[44] Indeed, scholars have argued that the reality genre captivates us precisely because it seizes upon our collective anxieties about changing families.[45] These anxieties, in turn, play into long-standing concerns about families being "in decline,"[46] becoming less important, fading away.

And that may be a reason we watch. But, taken as a whole, reality TV isn't showing the American family in free fall. In many ways, it's not even acknowledging the variety that exists within families. Nothing's dissolving here. The genre gives us sensationalized families, to be sure, but it also demonstrates that family is still a cultural touchstone on which we can all rest. Though one could probably write a dissertation on why the Kardashian/Jenners became a phenomenon, a key chapter would be about their emphasis on family. The dramatic changes in their lives—Caitlyn coming out as transgender, their feuds, their various marriages, divorces, and births— may have kept us riveted, but they were in this together from the beginning. Though we may not have been able to relate to their struggles with the paparazzi, their atypical use of the word "Bible," or the evolving configurations of their faces, we could locate other points of connection. Many of us have received unwelcome advice from our parents, sparred with our siblings, or attempted to arrange rowdy kids for group photos. Most of us are in families, they are central to many of our lives, and they perform crucial work within our broader society. This is perhaps why it's so difficult to imagine what society would look like if it weren't divided into these units. Perhaps our minds drift to some dystopian future where we all wear burlap tunics and have shaved heads. Any notion of a family-free society exists outside the boundaries of our current reality.

Ultimately, reality TV teaches us that, contrary to our cultural anxieties about the decline of family values, in no way are families in jeopardy. When Kim first careened across the screen and let us into her world, she gave us a glimpse into an institution that is still central to who we are, and that isn't going anywhere anytime soon.

5

"Sparkle, Baby!" (Childhood)

Eden Wood is "having a diva moment," her mother explains.

For the "Outfit of Choice" category at the Universal Royalty Beauty Pageant, Eden's mother, Mickie, has told us, "We're going to do our 'Vegas Showgirl' [costume]—which is a real Vegas showgirl outfit that was cut down" to fit her daughter.

"I don't want lipstick!" the four-year-old protests now, flapping her winged arms. Her hot-pink bodice drips with beads and feathers. A rhinestone-encrusted beret is pinned to the side of her head. Mickie is able to distract her daughter with a hand puppet, and in the next scene, Eden is all happiness, bopping and spinning on the pageant stage. Out in the audience, Mickie can be seen miming the routine to her daughter, making fish faces, and looking coyly over her shoulder.

Eden smiles radiantly, ending her routine with an arm raise and a head nod.

"The judges and the audience ate it up," Eden's pageant coach tells us afterward. "It was precious."[1]

Maybe you've never, like the moms on *Toddlers & Tiaras* (TLC, 2009–2016), entered your young child in a beauty pageant. You've never spray-tanned her legs or glued a hairpiece to her scalp. You haven't stood in the audience, exaggeratedly cuing her routine with kissy faces and sweeps of the arm, hollering, "Get it, girl!" and "Sparkle, baby!"

But maybe you've done other things. Let her sit too long in front of the TV, perhaps, her face slackened and her mind empty. Allowed yourself to get flustered by her obstinacy, throwing up your hands, yelling. Bribed her with chocolate to wear an itchy dress for an Easter photo. Become overly invested in the outcome of an elementary school spelling bee.

We've seen how, as the moms of reality TV march toward us in lockstep, they brandish at us our own flaws. But just as what it means to be a "good mom" has varied historically, the meaning of "real" childhood has always been in flux as well. Nowadays, as the historian Steven Mintz[2] has pointed out, we "sentimentalize" childhood, drawing a thick line around those years as a separate and special time of life. But the enthralling and revolting carnival of reality TV shows us that this distinction between childhood and adulthood is to some extent artificial—and not quite as clear-cut as we'd like to believe.

PIROUETTES AND SILLY STRING

While we might conceptualize childhood in a narrow way, in reality—like marriage, families, and motherhood—it has never has been any one thing. As Mintz explains, in some ways today American children are more protected than they've been before. For instance, we have free public schools, child labor is outlawed, and there's more awareness about child abuse.[3] In other ways, though, contemporary children experience their own harsh realities. Large numbers of American children still grow up in poverty and without access to health care.[4] And some subsets of parents, particularly within the middle class, push their kids to succeed more than they have before. These latter parents are well represented on kiddie competition shows—for instance, *Dance Moms* (Lifetime, 2011–2017, 2019), which featured a group of young competitive dancers, their mothers, and their harsh dance instructor, Abby Lee Miller.

But despite these historical changes, we tend to *think about* childhood as though it's a universal constant. Specifically, we hold fast to the idea that it's a whimsical and innocent period of life, completely separate from adulthood. The flip side of the expectation that mothers must intensively monitor their children is the assumption that children need intensive monitoring. And central to *this* notion is the idea that children are fundamentally different kinds of creatures from adults.

Our sentimentalizing of kids as separate beings with their own spheres, abilities, and pursuits is a relatively recent cultural construct. As Mintz has pointed out, before the eighteenth century, children were largely treated as "miniature adults."[5] It wasn't until around then, for instance, that furniture makers started designing pieces specifically for kids, their pastel colors and nursery rhyme themes reflecting "a growing popular notion of childhood as a period of innocence and playfulness."[6] Around that point, childhood "came to be seen not simply as a prelude to adulthood but as a separate stage of life that required care and institutions to protect it."[7] Further, as Hays points out, in the past (and in some contexts still), children have been viewed as economic assets rather than the needy creatures suggested by the intensive model.[8] During the European Middle Ages, for instance, it wasn't unusual for children to work as servants or be sent into apprenticeships at six or seven years of age.[9] Indeed, in many different eras, children worked outside of the home rather than being gently clasped in its confines. Even our assessments of our children's biological abilities are in some ways specific to our place and time. For example, while in the United States today we typically potty train kids when they're toddlers, this is not the case in every country and has not always been the case for us. In the 1920s, for example, the U.S. Children's Bureau advised parents that "toilet training may be begun as early as the first month."[10]

The reality genre provides a snapshot of how we think about children today: as distinct beings with unique needs and capacities. On the episode of *Celebrity Wife Swap* described in the prior chapter, for instance, Carnie tells Tracey that her oldest son has too much responsibility for taking care of his siblings. She forces him to play with Silly String and hair dye, advising his parents that he "needs to be a kid." Many competition shows have specific "junior" versions; much like the pastel furniture of yore, these tend to have a more upbeat, lighter tone than their adult counterparts. For example, on the cooking show *MasterChef Junior*, judge Gordon Ramsay tones down his typical cantankerousness for the young contestants, which suggests they need to be shielded from the level of critique he applies to the adults. In these ways, presentations of childhood on reality TV tap into our specific, contemporary notions about the capabilities of our youth and their role in society.

"A DOLLA MAKE ME HOLLA"

Yet it's in part *because* we think of children as different and in need of protection that reality TV also has the potential to make us wince, to make us laugh, or perhaps to make us sick to our stomachs. This is often how shows about kids reel us in. As we've seen, the genre thrives on juxtaposition of differences. That includes propelling tiny humans into contexts that we assume to be the domains of grown folks. On *Toddlers & Tiaras*, the kids have false lashes, faces full of makeup, and other accoutrements we'd typically associate with adult women. They veer into the domain of adult sexuality as well—for instance, when their parents tell them to "flirt" with the judges with their eyes during their routines. On one episode, three-year-old Paisley dresses up like Julia Roberts's prostitute character for a *Pretty Woman* routine,[11] while on another, two-year-old Mia re-creates Madonna's cone-bra look from the 1980s.[12] And then there's the breakout star of the show, six-year-old Alana Thompson, who tells the camera she wants to win big money at the pageants because "a dolla make me holla, honey boo boo!" She gets her own spin-off show, *Here Comes Honey Boo Boo* (TLC, 2012–2014).

The kids of reality TV also blur the boundary between childhood and adulthood by displaying skills and capacities that we would typically expect from people much older. Every week, the girls on *Dance Moms* must learn a new routine, complete with flips, spins, and death drops—a feat that's all the more impressive when we consider that they were not professional dancers prior to appearing on the show. *Chopped Junior* (Food Network, 2015–2017), a cooking competition featuring chefs between the ages of nine and fifteen, also showcases children's physical abilities. We watch as the contestants deftly employ knives, blenders, skillets, and deep fryers. On one episode,[13] for instance, four eleven- and twelve-year-olds have thirty minutes to cook a meal including ingredients like alligator, daikon radish, and a century egg (a type of "funky" fermented egg). Eleven-year-old Kennedy says she's been cooking since she was "about four." At one point, Cassidy says that if she's victorious, she'll donate some of her winnings to a local food bank. One of the judges then reminds us that "one in six kids in America don't have enough food"—revealing a crack in our fiction of a universal, protected childhood.

At the same time, the show never fails to remind us that these are kids, after all, when the chopping knives flash cartoonishly large in their little hands, when Logan opines that the century egg "smells like my brother's room," or when Kennedy's face crumples upon her elimination. By showing that they can simultaneously act like regular kids and perform adult functions, *Chopped Junior* muddies our notion that the kids *we* know are helpless, innocent beings who need to be catered to (literally).

This is not to suggest that adults and kids are indeed physiologically identical. Before you're tempted to mention secondary sex characteristics or neural connections in the brain,[14] yes: kids and adults *are* biologically different in some key ways. Still, the ways we think about those biological differences have varied over time, and this has translated to different social understandings of childhood. If we didn't have such steadfast ideas today about the bright line between childhood and adulthood, the mini chefs on *Chopped Junior* would likely not be as entertaining. At the same time, such shows demonstrate that the firm line we draw between children and adults isn't a universal certainty at all. As they chop daikon, land pirouettes, hit the high notes, and make football tackles, reality TV's young people—simultaneously talented and commonplace—call into question our certainty about what our kids' bodies can do.

"NIKE!"

It is perhaps *because* the demarcation between childhood and adulthood is not actually set in stone that we are so invested in maintaining it. It requires our constant curation. This is particularly true when it comes to sexuality. While we conceptualize childhood as a time of innocence separated from the erotic realm with a thick line, we remain ever vigilant about the blurring of that line—as we can see on *19 Kids and Counting* (TLC, 2008–2015).

This reality show (previously called *17 Kids and Counting* and *18 Kids and Counting*) peers into the family life of parents Jim Bob and Michelle Duggar and their nineteen offspring. Jim Bob and Michelle, part of the evangelical "Quiverfull" movement, do not believe in birth control.

On the surface, this is far from a racy program. Common Sense Media, which reviews the appropriateness of various content for children, indicates that the show is suitable for ages eight and up, classifying it as a "mild behind-the-scenes look at an unusually large family."[15] If we look a bit more deeply, though, we see that this family is highly concerned with childhood sexuality. Rather than engaging in conventional dating, for instance, their teens have chaperoned "courtships" and save their first kiss for the altar. Even the youngest children are not allowed to dance, as wiggling one's body in that way is deemed inappropriate. Their parents teach them the concept of "defrauding," which means that females cause males to have lustful thoughts through their choice of dress. The older Duggar girls call out the code word "Nike!" whenever a passing woman is wearing something that might cause her brothers to have such thoughts. "That's a signal to the boys, and even to Dad, that they should nonchalantly drop their eyes and look down at their shoes as we walk past her," four of the girls explain in their 2014 book, *Growing Up Duggar: It's All about Relationships*.[16] The children even give their siblings sideways hugs, avoiding full frontal contact. In these ways, the show exhibits a broader cultural tension: sexuality is not the realm of children, yet children are constantly at risk of being sexual. This tension is especially jarring in light of the fact that, in 2015, eldest brother Josh publicly admitted that when he was a young teen he had molested five girls, including some of his sisters—a revelation that led to the cancellation of the show.[17] (A spin-off of the show, *Counting On*, which focuses on the older girls and their spouses and children, began airing in 2015.)

While the Duggars are particularly invested in regulating adolescent sexuality because of their extreme conservatism, they're far from the only ones on the reality TV landscape who do this. On *To Catch a Predator* (MSNBC, 2004–2007), for example, operatives posing as teens are contacted by adults over the internet for sexual encounters. The "teens" then invite these adults to a filming location, where they are confronted by host Chris Hansen and ultimately detained by law enforcement. And by showing teens who have voluntarily engaged in sexual behavior, *16 and Pregnant* (MTV, 2009–2014) drives home the point that our adolescents aren't asexual at all. (Indeed, research indicates that the "majority of adolescents will become sexually active between the ages of 15 and 19.")[18] In these two instances, again, reality TV entertains by capitalizing on our desire to crisply separate out child and adult domains and our inability to do so. A reality show titled *26 and Pregnant* would have been much less compelling.

Both *16 and Pregnant* and *To Catch a Predator* show us that one way we attempt to shore up the blurry boundary between childhood and adulthood is by problematizing and prohibiting teenage sexuality. This is not to suggest that sexual predators shouldn't be stopped or that teen pregnancy isn't problematic in some ways. (Studies have shown that teen moms are more likely than other young women to drop out of school, become single parents, and live in poverty,[19] and their offspring are at a higher risk of leaving school early, being unemployed, becoming teen parents themselves, and becoming violent offenders.[20]) But both programs show us how, in the United States, we respond to these potential threats in a specific way: by insisting that sex is not, and cannot be, the providence of minors.

In her interviews with both Dutch and American parents of teens, the sociologist Amy Schalet has found that in the Netherlands, teen sex is "normalized"—seen as a part of life. Dutch parents, according to Schalet, "describe teenage sexuality as something that does not and should not present many problems."[21] In the US, conversely, it tends to be "dramatized"—seen as a social ill.[22] And *16 and Pregnant* is a dramatization. It selects one potential outcome of underage sex and unreels the physical toll it takes: the broken relationships, the fights with parents, the sleeplessness, the loss of freedom.

Our dramatization of teen sexuality extends far beyond the collection of rounded bellies on *16 and Pregnant*. Pregnant girls have long been popular fodder for movies and scripted TV; *For Keeps?* (1988), *Juno* (2007), and *The Secret Life of the American Teenager* (2008–2013) are simply a few examples. And our understanding of teen sex as a social ill is fundamental to how we address these topics with our kids. Some American teens are asked to sign "virginity pledges," indicating that they will remain abstinent until marriage. Some conservative Christian groups even host elaborate "purity balls"—dances that teen girls attend with their fathers, at which they publicly make that same pledge.

But perhaps nowhere is the aforementioned difference between the United States and countries such as the Netherlands more obvious than in the ways we teach kids about sex in our schools. As of 2019, for example, thirty-seven US states required their youth sex education programs to provide information on abstaining from sexual activity (with twenty-seven requiring that it be emphasized), and eighteen required their programs to teach that sexual activity should occur only within marriage.[23] Many school districts take this idea even further, teaching abstinence-*only* (or abstinence-until-marriage-only) sexual education—sidestepping topics such as contraception, consent, and sexually transmitted infections. By one estimate, between 1996 and 2018, Congress allotted more than $2.1 billion in taxpayer dollars to such programs.[24] Though studies have shown that they are ineffective and may even increase pregnancy rates,[25] these programs reflect our broader cultural anxieties about teen sex and our continual gatekeeping between childhood and the adult realm. Along these lines, it is telling that few of the girls on *16 and Pregnant* say that they were using birth control properly at the time they got pregnant.

More broadly, this sexual gatekeeping extends beyond the walls of high school health class, becoming a routine part of the way we treat our children. As the social theorist Michel Foucault has pointed out, beginning in the eighteenth century, educational institutions became preoccupied with childhood sexuality in a new way. While "one can have the impression that sex was hardly spoken of at all in these institutions," in fact, "one only has to glance over the architectural layout, the rules of discipline, and their whole internal organization: the question of sex was a constant preoccupation."[26] While that may seem like an extreme or outdated example, today, too, we have separate boys' and girls' bathrooms, even for elementary school students—a practice that arguably stems from an anxiety about (heterosexual) sexuality. In the United States, we cover up little girls' torsos at the beach, even though they don't have breasts. While many of these tactics to protect children from sex presume heterosexuality—further evidence of our heteronormativity—parents try to shield their children from homosexuality as well. Consider, for instance, the father who will not let his son play with a kitchen set or take ballet class, for fear of "turning him gay." As one father of a preschooler told the sociologist Emily Kane, "There are things that are meant for girls, but why would it be bad for him to have one of them? I don't know, maybe I have some deep, deep, deep buried fear that he would turn out, well, that his sexual orientation may get screwed up."[27] Paradoxically, kids get treated as potential sexual beings through this everyday vigilance—not just by reality TV's pageant moms who outfit them in Madonna cone bras.

"EVERY MINUTE OF MY LIFE I HAVE SOMETHING SCHEDULED"

So, *16 and Pregnant* teaches us a number of things about contemporary American notions of childhood. It reveals a central paradox in how we think about childhood: that children's sexuality is both unthinkable and a constant risk. The show also teaches us how teen sexuality plays out in reality. And the episodes, taken as a whole, reveal broad patterns in the experiences of US kids.

While MTV clearly makes some attempts at diversifying its cast—featuring teens of different races, from different geographic locations, and with different family configurations— the patterns on the show tend to align with the contours of teen pregnancy in reality. Although there are exceptions, these girls generally do not have socioeconomic privilege. They regularly mention that money is an issue, and at least one teen father wasn't at his child's birth because he was unable to afford the trip.[28] Research has found that adolescents who live with both biological parents, whose mothers have more education than high school, whose mothers didn't give birth as teens, and who live in wealthier neighborhoods are less likely to give birth or father a baby as teens.[29] Childbirth rates are also higher among Hispanic and Black teens than among their white peers.[30] While there are teen moms across all demographic strata and family situations, overall those teens who wind up pregnant tend to have less social advantage—that is, less to lose. When we see this play out on *16 and Pregnant*, it not only demonstrates the risk factors for teen pregnancy but also reveals the various types of childhoods that various slices of privilege have to offer.

Indeed, as Steven Mintz has emphasized, both in the past and today, there's been a large degree of diversity in children's experiences. Leading up to the early twentieth century, the children of working-class white parents, the children of enslaved and free Black parents, and the children of the white urban middle class or more prosperous farmers tended to have very different childhoods.[31] These divergences persist today, and we can spy flashes of them within the reality genre. On *Cops*—which followed police officers on their patrols and aired on various networks from 1989 until 2020—young faces blurred for privacy hovered in the background. Meanwhile, the grown-ups in their lives—often poor or working class and living in ramshackle conditions—interacted with the law. As Mintz argues and the reality genre suggests, privileged white kids, overall, are still more likely to have the types of sentimentalized childhoods that we falsely view as universal and worthy of protection.[32]

While it may seem obvious that parents are able to pass on their social advantages to their kids, many of us may not understand the full extent of this process. It certainly runs afoul of the "pull yourself up by your bootstraps" and "land of opportunity" types of meritocratic narratives we like to tell about the United States. While there are exceptions, more privileged parents are generally able to transmit that privilege to their kids, not only in the form of money and the things that money can buy but also in the ways they teach their children to engage with the world. The sociologist Pierre Bourdieu used the term "habitus" to describe these ways of thinking that parents of various class strata impart to their offspring.[33] Just as wealthier families provide their children with economic capital, Bourdieu noted, so, too, do they provide "cultural capital," which he defines as nonfinancial assets (knowledge, tastes, etc.) that benefit these children socially.[34] Parents' level of education, for example, is an extremely strong predictor of their children's subsequent level of education.[35] This is not only because more highly educated parents also tend to have higher incomes, enabling them to provide better educational opportunities for their kids. It is also because these parents can give their children the cultural capital to facilitate this journey: the expectation that they will attend college, knowledge of what it takes to get in, information about how to navigate once they've arrived, and the habits of mind that allow them to blend in with their peers.

Throughout *Child Genius* (Lifetime, 2015–2016), we can see how class-privileged parents are able to use their own forms of capital to spur their children to excel. On this game-doc, children between the ages of eight and twelve are asked questions relating to a variety of areas of knowledge (e.g., geography, math, literature, current events). The final contestant left standing wins a $100,000 college fund and the title "Child Genius." The narrator states in the first episode, "Behind every child genius there's often a driven parent determined to maximize their child's potential."[36] As Ryan's dad puts it, "I always tell [my kids], 'People will remember number one. They don't remember number two.'"

Remember how Annette Lareau drew a distinction between middle-class parents, who often strove to "cultivate" their children through "organized activities and extensive reasoning," and working-class parents, who were more likely to give their children unstructured time to flourish independently?[37] Ryan's parents, and others on *Child Genius*, are the poster parents for the former. "My days are pretty busy and, like, every minute of my life I have something scheduled," says Ryan. Indeed, in one scene he's working on geometry and in the next he's taking a violin lesson.

And Ryan's parents are far from the only "concerted cultivators" on the show. In addition to sending her to school, for instance, Vanya's family has set up a classroom in their house for additional training. "We're not just parents but we also coach her and we're also mentors," her father tells us in a testimonial.[38] Like *Wife Swap*, the show also touches upon the Goldilocks's porridge of intensive mothering. As Lisa Van Gemert, the "Gifted Youth Ambassador" for American Mensa, tells us in the first episode, "Sometimes parents will cross that line from being really great facilitators for gifted kids to being almost hovercraft. They leave helicopter parents in the dust."

It's no coincidence that most of the families on *Child Genius* live in an array of similar-looking middle-class or upper-middle-class suburban homes. Nor is it a coincidence that most of the kids have highly involved parents who have the time and capacity to drill them on the various subjects required for competition. These parents brim with cultural capital, their hands flying across whiteboards and their mouths spewing information: mnemonic devices, relevant facts, the Latin and Greek roots of words. It's also not a coincidence that these kids seem to share a constellation of advantages—the language and instrument lessons, the chess tutors and martial arts classes. Watching these advantages in action, we can see some of the mechanisms behind why kids of higher social classes tend to score higher on IQ tests and why schoolteachers are less likely to nominate poor children for gifted programs.[39]

Junior competition shows such as *Child Genius*, with their caricatures of stage moms and football dads, also show us that the *ability to compete* is itself a form of cultural capital. As Lareau has argued, putting their children in organized activities is one way in which parents transmit class advantage to their children.[40] Along these lines, it's significant that *Child Genius* season one's victor is Vanya, who's had previous experience competing at both the Scripps National Spelling Bee and in the Science Olympiad.

And research has shown that parents themselves are aware of the social advantages these extracurriculars provide. Interviewing middle-class moms and dads about why they place their offspring into competitive activities, for instance, the sociologist Hilary Levey Friedman found that these parents tended to emphasize the constellation of broad abilities that would be applicable to life—rather than necessarily the specific, technical skills the children learned (e.g., how to dribble a ball). In a riff on Bourdieu, Levey Friedman introduces the notion of "Competitive Kid Capital," or "the various elements of capital that parents hope to instill in their young children through participation in competitive after-school activities."[41] These elements include "internalizing the importance of winning," "learning how to recover from a loss to win in the future," "managing time pressure," "performing in stressful environments," and "feeling comfortable being judged by others in public,"[42] and they all apply not just to childhood pursuits but to life more generally. They're also represented on almost any reality show involving child competitors.

On *Dance Moms*, for instance, dance instructor Abby Lee Miller teaches the girls to internalize the importance of winning. "Does it feel better when you win or does it feel better when you lose?" she asks young Mackenzie, quickly answering the question herself: "When you win."[43] Each week the girls must memorize at least one new dance routine in a short amount of time, perform that routine in front of an auditorium of strangers, and receive a score from a set of judges. Abby then stands in front of them the following week, conducting a postmortem on all of their errors. Again, it is no coincidence that the girls on *Dance Moms* all live in seemingly middle-class homes similar to the ones seen on *Child Genius*. Their parents are able to afford the lessons, the outfits and shoes, and the competition fees. Their mothers are readily available, as needed, to strap them into minivans and shuttle them where they need to go.

Now, Abby Lee's teaching methods may or may not be *psychologically* advantageous for the girls; she calls them names, overtly plays favorites, and punishes them for the sins of their mothers. But her pupils are nonetheless paying Abby, in part, to teach them how to compete. Writ large, these competitive-kid programs demonstrate how class status gives children an edge when it comes to competition—and, subsequently, to life.

THE REAL KIDS OF TV

To point out that the majority of kids on shows such as *Child Genius* and *Dance Moms* appear to be middle-class is not to suggest that their abilities are wholly the result of social influence. But while some kids have inborn brilliance, natural athletic talent, or an inherently stronger work ethic, their advantages are not wholly sealed in their genes. The hyper-involved parents and talented offspring on these shows demonstrate, in augmented form, how our raw biological tools work collaboratively with our social inheritance. Just as, historically, the kids of prosperous farmers had different outcomes from those of less fortunate parents, today our children's life experiences tend to differ markedly by their social positions.

The real kids on our screens teach us how we falsely naturalize and idealize youth in ways that don't take into account these broader social divisions. When Carnie Wilson tells Tracey Gold that her son needs to experience "being a kid," we know what that means, and it's not that he needs to learn to make an off-the-cuff alligator sous vide or watch his father get shackled outside of a mobile home. Reality shows illuminate how we think about childhood in a specific way that we believe to be universal and fixed, even though different kids have different life experiences based upon their positions in the social structure.

But these kids don't simply *reflect* their class positions. When relatively privileged kids learn to embody the cultural capital of their parents and get primed for success in a way that's consistent with their class position, they then become active agents in *reproducing* the class structure. And that's why sociologists such as Bourdieu are so interested in cultural capital—not because it inherently matters, say, whether one knows which fork to use for shrimp at a fancy dinner. These forms of knowledge and habits of mind are important because they all add up—and, taken together, they help to transmit social status across the generations, systematically disadvantaging some groups and advantaging others.

Reality TV illuminates how we all use kids as extensions of ourselves. They become vectors not only for our personal goals and dreams (see: the starry-eyed parents on *Toddlers & Tiaras*) but, more broadly, for the reproduction of the social status quo. These tiny humans become agents through which we transmit our most deeply held cultural values and uphold the systems of power that govern all of our lives. Kids become ambassadors for the broader social norms and practices that buzz through our culture, lodging in our social institutions and leeching from their walls.

The real kids of TV are precocious, talented, spoiled, and heartbreaking. Their parents often appear on our screens as screeching caricatures. But these parent/child duos and our reactions to them paradoxically expose the tidy boxes we use to contain "legitimate" childhood. They expose the limited way we conceptualize our kids: as sentimentalized, asexual, incompetent creatures with assumed class and racial privilege. At the same time, reality TV's kids also reveal the flawed nature of such assumptions, as they lift their feathered arms and emerge, bedazzled, from those neat boxes.

Part II

6

"I Question Your Taste Level" (Class)

The first time we meet Alana's family, they're throwing paper towel rolls at one another.

Six-year-old Alana is a competitor in the Precious Moments Pageant and a featured child on *Toddlers & Tiaras*.[1] Her family has amassed a large quantity of paper towels because her mother buys things in bulk. Introducing herself as "the coupon queen," Mama June explains that, all told, pageants have cost them about $8,000 to $9,000. "But that's okay, because I've saved it all with my coupons!"

On the inaugural episode of their spin-off show, *Here Comes Honey Boo Boo*—which focuses on Alana, Mama June, and the rest of their nuclear family—they attend an event called the Redneck Games. Mama June describes the games as "similar to the Olympics, but with a lot of missing teeth and a lot of butt cracks showing." There, they bob for pig feet and compete in the "mud pit belly flop." ("I like to get in the mud because I like to get dirty like a pig," Alana tells us.) Elsewhere in the episode, they're farting audibly, washing their hair in the kitchen sink, and eating cheese balls for breakfast out of a communal jar. Alana lifts up her shirt and shows us her stomach chub, folding it into a mouth and making it "talk" to the camera.

On the one hand, reality TV may not seem like great

fodder for a rumination on class inequality in America. The tone of these shows is often light, and they tend to focus on individual behavior without overtly contextualizing it within broader structural processes. Generally, as the media scholar June Deery has observed, if reality programs touch on issues of social inequality at all, it is "only briefly, in order for individualized and apolitical solutions to proceed."[2] And the genre does not show us the full spectrum of class in America. We rarely see the very poor, for instance. When *The Real World*'s Julie spends time with the homeless or the Kardashians volunteer at a soup kitchen, the poor are ancillary to, and serve mainly to shed light on the thoughts and feelings of, the central characters.

On the other hand, reality TV reveals a *wider* spectrum of class positions than some other forms of media. Some have argued, for instance, that working-class people are more visible within the reality genre than on scripted TV.[3] From southern rednecks to Manhattan millionaires, reality TV casts a searchlight across large swaths of our socioeconomic terrain. In doing so, it reveals the tenacity of class: a monetary category that isn't *just* that. It shows us what class is, what it means to us, and how we buffer our class system using a set of relatively rigid, ingrained assumptions about what's right, normal, and good.

CLASS: IT'S ABOUT THE MONEY, HONEY!

Few would disagree that social class is related to how much money one has. Writing in the mid-1800s, for instance, Karl Marx defined class as a group of people who share the same material circumstances. While acknowledging various gradations within these central categories, he pointed to two

primary social classes that exist under capitalism: the bourgeoisie (who control the means of production) and the proletariat (the worker bees). The proletariat perform the manual
labor that's essential for a capitalist, industrial society, while
the bourgeoisie disproportionately profit from that labor.
Marx and his coauthor, Friedrich Engels, conceptualized history, writ large, as the story of conflict between groups fighting
over limited economic resources.[4] Indeed, Marx suggested
that any kind of struggle (political, religious, etc.) essentially
could be distilled to a class conflict.[5]

Marx's two class categories career into view on *Undercover Boss* (CBS, 2010–present). On the show, high-level executives go incognito to find out what's really happening during
the everyday operations of their companies. In one episode,
Rick Silva, president and CEO of Checkers and Rally's, poses
as a trainee at the restaurants.[6] The show emphasizes the
class divide nearly as soon as it begins. Scenes of a suit-clad
Rick, sitting at a desk and shuffling papers, are interspersed
with shots of his employers frying up burgers and passing
them through the drive-up window into outstretched hands.
While both Rick and his employees work, it's clear that they
perform the manual labor and that his share of the profits is
much larger. The show crystallizes this distinction, on this and
many episodes, by revealing the boss's ineptitude at the physical tasks required by the low-level jobs in his operation. Here,
Rick nearly burns some burgers and struggles to work a cash
register and an intercom. The fundamental distinction, both
within Marx's theory and on *Undercover Boss*, is monetary.
The main chasm here is between the CEO and his workers on
the line, who are of varied genders and races but who are *all*
subordinate to him within the class hierarchy.

In having the boss pose as a worker bee, the show reveals

forms of labor that are often obscured. It's this obfuscation, Marx argues, that allows for the oppression of workers to go unchecked. He discusses "commodity fetishism," which doesn't mean just that we love to buy stuff (although we do: see below) but is the idea that we don't tend to think about the things we buy in terms of the social relationships that have created them.[7] Since we as consumers are separated from the labor process, the relationship that is central to our minds is between each item and our money. And then we take for granted that apples just *are*, inherently, $1.32 apiece, without thinking about the human dynamics that make that so. Yet *Undercover Boss* exposes these dynamics. While the show doesn't reveal exploitation per se—which would be terrible PR for these companies—it does show us hierarchies of labor and the power relations enmeshed within them.

At one point, for instance, a manager at one of the restaurants speaks harshly to his workers. Rick takes aside one of the employees, Todd, and asks him why he puts up with this treatment. "I couldn't work there for ten minutes," Rick says. "I would never let someone talk to me like that."

"It's my job," Todd replies. "I do it because I need to help my mom."

Rick suggests that they talk to the manager.

"I don't think so," Todd repeats several times, shaking his head. "I need my job, by any means necessary."

Ultimately, Rick does speak to the manager, because he is really the boss and he is empowered to do so. This scene highlights the different experiences Rick and Todd have of the world, not just because Rick makes more money but because of the privileges that accompany that money—including social respect and the ability to make choices. Notably, when

Rick discloses that he's the CEO, the manager immediately begins speaking to him more respectfully.

"BUT WE'RE STILL ENTERTAINING PEOPLE"

People in the higher classes, like Rick, have more money. But, as both Marx and *Undercover Boss* demonstrate, this is not necessarily because the work that these people do has inherently higher value. Yes, Rick and Todd are in very different types of jobs that necessitate different levels of education and skill. Still, that doesn't mean that labor requiring a college degree is more important to the actual functioning of society—though we may try to tell ourselves that.

For Marx and Engels, ideology is not something that stems organically from each of our individual brains; rather, it's born from our social relationships and functions as an instrument of power.[8] We sustain the current arrangement of power when we interpret work that involves manual labor as less important. The classical sociologist Max Weber makes the related point that engagement in physical labor tends to disqualify one from status. He gives the example of artistic work that's more labor-like (such as masonry) being lower-status work than artistic practice that's less labor-like (such as oil painting).[9] While we can likely all think of exceptions to this rule—for example, professional athletes—it's still generally true that our most esteemed work is more intellectual than physical, and vice versa.

Indeed, some of our most highly compensated work is not the work that's crucial to the functioning of society. For instance, if we look at the list of professions that people view as the most prestigious, food preparer doesn't make the cut.[10]

Yet food preparers literally hold our lives in their hands daily, as we discover anew each time there's an *E. coli* scare. During the height of COVID-19, the people deemed "essential" to our infrastructure included relatively low-paid grocery store stockers, delivery people, and sanitation workers—*not* those in jobs like Rick's. Within our capitalist system, the objective importance of one's work is not necessarily aligned with compensation, as Rick and Todd show us.

In a different way, the Kardashians teach us this as well. The fact that this brood has been compensated so handily despite their ostensible lack of talent has clearly ruffled some feathers. In 2011, Barbara Walters interviewed Kris, Kourtney, Kim, and Khloé, as the family was on her "10 Most Fascinating People" list for that year—a list that included Steve Jobs, Pippa Middleton, and reality host turned future president Donald Trump. "You are all often described as 'famous for being famous,'" Barbara Walters stated bluntly, addressing the four women. "You don't really act, you don't sing, you don't dance, you don't have any—forgive me—any talent."

Several of the women nodded in response to the comment. "But we're still entertaining people," Khloé replied.[11]

As this interview suggests, a common critique of reality stars is that they don't do anything to warrant their stardom. Of course, there are exceptions, such as the contestants on skill-based competition shows or programs featuring stars who are already famous for having recognizable talents, such as singing, acting, or comedy. But for the most part, reality TV participants seem to rise in stature by simply . . . *being*.

But in this sense, reality stars aren't showing us anything new. They're showing us something old. In 1867, Marx drew a distinction between "use value" and "exchange value"—a distinction that may be used, for instance, to demonstrate why gold is more expensive than water. Water has higher use value than gold, because we need it to survive. Yet gold has higher exchange value than water because even though it's a hunk of metal that serves virtually no inherent function, it's a universal currency. Weber, writing in the early 1900s, made a related argument, observing that most highly esteemed occupations were not necessarily the ones that garnered the highest wages, and vice versa. If we aligned prestige and compensation, Weber argued, society would look very different.[12] Indeed, research suggests that even today, the job categories that people view as most prestigious—for instance, firefighters and clergy—are not necessarily the highest paying, and the other way around as well.[13] So while it may chafe us that Kylie Jenner earns a million dollars per Instagram post,[14] there's precedent for this. (Even the concepts of "skill" and "talent," though, are social constructions, presuming excellence at tasks that are socially valued. I can wiggle each ear independently, which I think is pretty special, but I've never earned a cent for it.)

Of course, this all presumes that the Kardashian/Jenners *don't* have any type of marketable skill or talent—which, to be clear, is not a foregone conclusion. These women (and maybe Rob) have managed to parlay a sex tape into international stardom. At some point, in some form—perhaps in Kris's expert momaging or Kylie's keen sense of consumer trends—it is reasonable to believe they did something to hasten their ascent. But whether these particular reality stars just fell upward or made shrewd decisions or some combination of the two, it's not unique or contemporary that they get paid handsomely for something that many people think is worthless.

They simply reveal how our conceptions of talent, money, and social worth were never connected to one another in straightforward ways.

FROM RAT PITS TO "RATCHET"?

In part *because* objective value, status, and compensation are misaligned, we have to tell ourselves stories justifying our class system. Job hierarchies become prestige hierarchies as we interpret certain types of work—and, consequently, certain *types of people*—as legitimate, valuable, and morally correct.

Reality TV, with its emphasis on archetypes and difference, amplifies these typologies. The sociologist Patricia Hill Collins uses the term "controlling images" to refer to media's stereotypical portrayals of marginalized groups—which, she argues, serve to normalize the power structure and allow us to view facets of culture such as racism and sexism as natural and inevitable.[15]

This brings us back to Honey Boo Boo.

In Alana's family, we see controlling images that legitimate the class system. Though there is some debate within the family about whether they actually qualify as "rednecks" ("We all have our own teeth, don't we?" the dad says),[16] the show repeatedly emphasizes their stereotypical southern-hick qualities. Their grammar is creative, they intersperse their sentences with words not found in *Merriam-Webster*, and they offer medical advice like "If you fart twelve to fifteen times a day, you could lose a lotta weight." Notably, the show also includes their bodily emanations, rather than editing them out.

But, again, this isn't anything new. We've been wringing

enjoyment from lower-class stereotypes for hundreds of years. In the next chapter, we'll see how minstrel shows historically caricatured Black people, but here it's important to note that they satirized poor white "rubes" as well.[17] As the sociologist Jennifer Lena has explained, "The idea of respectable people being entertained by demonstrations of working-class or poor lifestyles is as old as the bourgeoisie is as a class."[18] For instance, she describes how, beginning in the 1800s, "slumming parties" in London and New York brought upper-class white people into poor and immigrant urban areas. These trips allowed elites to participate in activities such as "rat pit" gambling—that is, betting on how long it would take a terrier to kill a rat in a hole in the ground. "When elites slum," Lena argues, both then and today, "lower-class culture is enjoyed as a commodity, and the experience of consumption is designed to satisfy and thrill without too much discomfort."[19]

It's hardly a stretch to draw a line from the rat pits of yore to the weave-pulling and mud-pit-belly-flopping "ratchet" fare of today. While critics panned *Here Comes Honey Boo Boo*, it was one of the most popular programs on TLC during the time it aired.[20] In 2013, *Deadline* reported that the show had ended its season in the number one spot for its time slot "among ad supported cable networks in virtually all key demos."[21]

Were *all* of those viewers "slumming" when they watched *Honey Boo Boo*? Maybe not. It's plausible that some people watched because they personally identified with the characters and/or because they found them likable or even aspirational as everyday, working-class people turned TV stars. Still, these types of programs arguably *also* attract viewers because they enable us to slum. For instance, perhaps there was a reason that the reality-adjacent *Tiger King* (Netflix, 2020) became so popular during the early days of the coronavirus pandemic. Part of that reason, likely, had to do with the show's many riveting plot twists. (Did Carole Baskin really feed her husband's corpse to her tigers? I still don't know what to believe!) But perhaps seeing the working-class criminality and buffoonery on the show also allowed us to think less about, or explain away, the fact that many low-wage "essential" workers were being placed at daily risk for COVID-19. Meanwhile, the more privileged among us were able to work safely from home with the luxury, in our downtime, to get sucked into the world of Joe Exotic.

Indeed, research has shown that middle-class viewers who watch and enjoy reality TV are able to hold it "at a distance," emphasizing the us/them distinction.[22] One study of teens in England, for instance, found that some of these young people reaffirmed their own middle-class statuses by "positioning themselves as TV critics" and expressing "disgust at working-class participants" on reality programs.[23] This dovetails with the idea that we receive voyeuristic pleasure from reality TV.[24] *Here Comes Honey Boo Boo* teaches us that we may want to visit the rat pit to remind ourselves that we are not *of* the rat pit. Just as slumming parties ultimately bolstered elites' senses of their own superiority and reinforced class boundaries, middle-class viewers today are able to use these programs to symbolically distance themselves from working-class culture—and working-class people.[25]

"ALL THAT VAJIGGLE-JAGGLE IS NOT BEAUTIMOUS"

In order for us to accept the class system, we have to naturalize the class system. We have to believe that people are where they are for reasons that are inherent and objective. *Here*

Comes Honey Boo Boo demonstrates how we do this by showing us how we think about bodies and how we think about class and how those two things are intertwined in the American imagination.

The family's fatness is not lost on viewers; critics and fans alike have made it a central part of their commentary. Virtually every initial review of the show mentioned it in some way. For example, a review of the show in the *A.V. Club* referred to Alana's "overweight, heavy-lidded coupon-queen mother June,"[26] and *Time* magazine observed that the show "is less like *Toddlers and Tiaras* than it is a reality-show version of *The Fatties: Fart Two....*"[27] Indeed, in the first episode, Mama June vaguely breaks the fourth wall by referring to the viewers' nickname for her, from her *Toddlers & Tiaras* stint: "Jabba the Hutt."

The program implicitly strings together the family's round bodies, their class status, and their outrageous behavior. The first time weight is mentioned in episode one, it's at the Redneck Games. Here, the focus is not on the central clan but on their reaction to the other participants. We see shots of various attendees, their flesh drooping over their minimal clothing, and Mama June and her daughters are critical of the physiques on display. "Her body is eatin' the bikini," Mama June says of one large woman. In a testimonial, she advises "women that are of voluptuous size" to cover themselves up. "All that vajiggle-jaggle is not beautimous," she opines. Later in the episode, the focus shifts to the family members themselves. They discuss the prospect of losing weight as they sit on couches munching on cheese balls from the ubiquitous shared jar. Mama June agrees to participate in a "family weight-loss challenge," though she is ambivalent about the goal. At one point in the episode, she says she's happy with her body—at another, that she'd ideally lose one hundred pounds.

By presenting fat bodies initially at the Redneck Games, *Here Comes Honey Boo Boo* almost immediately contextualizes fatness within a particular class category. Indeed, female thinness has become something of a privilege marker. Small and taut bodies translate into "embodied capital"—Bourdieu's term for "external wealth converted into an integral part of the person."[28] This becomes evident in fashion markets; high-end boutiques, for instance, seldom carry plus sizes, while cheaper mass retailers such as Walmart do. It's also quite telling that as the income from *Here Comes Honey Boo Boo* began rolling in, Mama June underwent weight-loss surgery and sloughed off those one hundred pounds—emerging from her chrysalis on her spin-off show, *Mama June: From Not to Hot* (WE tv, 2017–2020). (In 2020, as the main characters went through a variety of personal and legal struggles, the show was rebooted as *Mama June: Family Crisis*.)

As the title *Not to Hot* bluntly states, in the contemporary United States fatness is socially undesirable. No, it's not *always* undesirable. We might point to putative counterexamples, such as Kim Kardashian's round derriere, or racial/ethnic differences in the acceptability of thick bodies,[29] or the existence of arguably fat-positive media, including TLC's own reality show *My Big Fat Fabulous Life* (2015–present). Which bodies we consider to be "fat," and how we interpret that fatness, has also changed over time.[30] But in general today, within dominant American culture, fat bodies are generally presented as socially problematic.

They're also often presented as signs of *individual failings*. The sociologist Amanda Czerniawski has observed that we stereotype fatness "as a defect, a symbol of gluttonous obsessions, unmanaged desires, and moral and physical decay; the fat body is one that is out of control and takes up too much space, a failed body project. These controlling images of fat are rife with moralistic innuendos that place blame on the individual and ignore culture's impact."[31] Indeed, the controlling images on *Here Comes Honey Boo Boo* suggest that this family's bodies, like its behavior, cannot be contained. Guts tumbling over pants, belches escaping from mouths, bodies exploding with impulses—this family is just spilling out, in every sense.

Mama June and her offspring show us how lower-class status and fatness are culturally aligned, how we convert both into moral categories, and how we lay them at the feet of individuals. Of course, the individual members of the *Boo Boo* clan (the adults, at least) *do* have some ability to control what they put into their mouths. Mama June feeds her daughter sugary foods, including "go-go juice" (a mixture of Red Bull and Mountain Dew), to keep her alert for pageants. And there's the cheese ball jar. But by presenting these individual decisions as *just* individual decisions made by out-of-control people, without interrogating the broader mechanics of food production, marketing, and distribution, or underlying inequalities in the educational system, *Here Comes Honey Boo Boo* obscures the large-scale social dynamics that have helped move the go-go juice to Alana's lips.

When we look at *Here Comes Honey Boo Boo* as a slumming adventure, we can see the types of cultural mechanisms that we use to normalize class hierarchies. Portraying this clan as lazy, impulsive, and not that bright, the show contributes to a narrative that naturalizes the class structure as correct and appropriate.

And it's far from the only reality show to do this. The entire subgenre of makeover TV reminds us which bodies we perceive as acceptable and good. On these shows, as in our lives, our bodies are understood not simply as collections of cells that exist neutrally in the world; they can be evaluated and altered accordingly.[32] On *Dr. Pimple Popper* (TLC, 2018–present), for instance, the dermatologist and YouTube sensation Dr. Sandra Lee remedies extreme skin conditions, while over on *Botched* (E!, 2014–present), Drs. Terry Dubrow and Paul Nassif (both formerly of *Housewives* shows) remedy the mistakes of prior plastic surgeons via additional plastic surgery.

These shows "fix" their participants in ways that sustain existing class hierarchies. Transformational television is like other types of reality TV in that it promotes middle-class norms of fitness, thinness, and goodness.[33] As we've seen on *Supernanny* with the mother who tamed her disobedient children by scaling back on her work hours, sometimes these remedies also presume access to middle-class (or higher) resources. Competition programs regularly frame failure as a product of laziness, lack of grit, lack of seriousness, or lack of talent, rather than a lack of resources. On *RuPaul's Drag Race* (Logo, 2009–2016; VH1, 2017–present), for example, success on the runway hinges on having fabulous garments; the judges often attribute contestants' deficiencies to their lack of polish or failures of imagination, rather than the thinness of their wallets. And makeover shows such as *What Not to Wear* (TLC, 2003–2013; 2020–present)—on which hosts Stacy London and Clinton Kelly fix the wardrobes of supposed fashion victims—sometimes offer cost-prohibitive advice, such as urging viewers to have their clothes tailored. The culture scholar Brenda R. Weber has argued that these types of programs endeavor to produce the "perfect citizen"—that is, "one whose insides and outsides are in perfect alignment, . . . one whose female or male body evokes 'appropriate' gender and sex information, one who is not glaringly marked as raced or working class. . . ."[34] These shows thus link together unruly bodies, lower-class status, and moral failure. Similarly, when *Honey Boo Boo* displays its clan speaking unintelligently and behaving impulsively, it suggests that they're responsible for both their corpulence and their own social position—and that rather than consider too deeply the structural realities of that position, our appropriate response is to sit back smugly and watch.

"I QUESTION YOUR TASTE LEVEL"

Shows like *Honey Boo Boo* teach us how monetary distinctions ultimately become moral distinctions, as we put bodies and behaviors into class categories and interpret them as good or bad. We further reinforce the class hierarchy by maintaining hierarchies of *taste*.

Recall that, for Marx, a class is a group of people who share the same material conditions. Building on that theory, Bourdieu argued that a class is actually a collection of things. It includes people who have similar amounts of money but also who share the same habits, practices, and internalized understandings of the world. Bourdieu observed that when it comes to our cultural preferences, we have "the illusion of spontaneous generation."[35] That is, while we tend to think taste is random and highly individualized, it has a socialized component. Indeed, he found that our preferences in things such as music and cuisine are highly aligned with socioeconomic class; in particular, there is lowbrow culture and there is highbrow culture, and elites are socialized to enjoy the latter. For example, it's telling, but also probably not surprising to viewers, that the *Boo Boo* clan attends the Redneck Games and not the opera.

These distinctions matter, Bourdieu argues, because taste then becomes a signifier of social status and a form of shared culture that helps to coalesce those within the same class. Elite tastes become a form of capital that facilitates the transmission of social status from one generation to another, thus maintaining the class structure. Consequently, certain tastes are connected with certain class positions, and a hierarchy is created. It's not just that the opera and the Redneck Games, say, are different pastimes. It's that one becomes codified as more "high class" and, subsequently, *more socially valued* than the other.

These types of hierarchies, and their social importance, come to life on *Project Runway* (Bravo, 2004–2008, 2019–present; Lifetime, 2009–2017). On the show, aspiring fashion designers compete in a series of challenges. In each episode, they construct garments that models wear during a runway show and then receive commentary about their work from a panel of judges. Nina Garcia, the fashion journalist and editor who has been one of the judges on the show since its inception, invokes the designers' "taste level" so often that "I question your taste level" has become her catchphrase and a meme. On one episode, for example, the contestants must create clothing with video game heroines in mind.[36] Judge Brandon Maxwell tells one of the designers, Venny, regarding his female "savior" outfit with feathered cuffs: "It is not that you do not know how to make clothes. What you do not know how to do is to restrain yourself in that process."

Nina agrees: "One challenge, you can produce something beautiful and tasteful, and the next challenge you present us with this. From head to toe, it's a disaster."

Later, when the judges examine Venny's garment up close,

Nina reiterates, "He really missed out on the fantasy here. And then, on the reality, there's a taste level issue that is concerning." Here, as in the case of *Honey Boo Boo*, lacking class and taste is associated with lacking control over oneself. This is a common theme on *Project Runway*, as overuse of feathers and excessive bedazzling are interpreted as an inability to rein in one's designs. Instead, designers are expected to hit the sweet spot of being restrained without being dull.

The very concept of a "taste level," and indeed the whole premise of the show, also suggests that our fashion preferences aren't just personal and arbitrary—rather, there is some objective, tiered index by which they can be evaluated. And the judges often confirm that this taste hierarchy is aligned with economics. On a different episode from that same season, for instance, Nina heaps praise on one of the designs.[37] In evaluating Tessa's garment, she comments, "This look does not look like a $250 look." There is a pause, dramatic music swells, and she adds, "This looks expensive. This is luxe."

"Good. Good," the designer says, looking relieved.

Later, when Tessa is announced as the winner of the challenge, Nina proclaims, "It felt like any of us [judges] could be wearing that."

"This looks expensive" is a common compliment on the show, across judges and across seasons. Here, Nina specifically links that compliment to people in her own class category, for whom $250 might be seen as relatively cheap. She thus illuminates spectra of taste, economics, and social value and the interrelation among the three. These interconnected hierarchies don't appear just on reality TV but pervade our lives; for instance, they're baked into the English language, in evaluative terms such as "cheap" and "classy." *Project Runway* teaches us how we all conceptualize certain types of material culture as tasteful or trashy, expensive or cheap, good or bad, worthwhile or not, right or wrong, and in doing so, we implicitly reinforce class boundaries.

CAVIAR DREAMS

Nina Garcia shows us the flip side of what we see on *Honey Boo Boo*. If we view the lower classes as morally compromised and responsible for their predicament, then for the rich it must be the opposite. By demonstrating how we equate class privilege with legitimacy and happiness, some reality shows about wealthy people also illustrate how we normalize the class hierarchy.

Why do we perceive wealth as good? One might argue that it's only natural to crave nice things, to want to live in the greatest comfort possible, and to feel the urge to telegraph our success to our neighbors like a peacock fanning its tail. Yet to some extent, these impulses are a particular product of Western capitalism. Tracing the origins of our capitalist system, Max Weber has argued that we can locate its roots in late-1800s Protestantism. At that time, financial success in the present life became seen as a marker that one was destined for greatness in the afterlife as well. Thus germinated the "Protestant ethic," in which people are inspired to work hard and accumulate money, to demonstrate that they are among the Chosen. This ethic wasn't the sole catalyst for capitalism, but it did contribute to the "spirit" of capitalism.[38] In some Christian megachurches we still see this ideology of wealth both as a goal and as a sign of God's blessing. And even though most of us today are not working hard to demonstrate our fitness for the afterlife, we're still fanning out those peacock plumes of money to demonstrate our legitimacy.

Under capitalism, to *have things* becomes a goal in and of itself. The concept of modern-day consumerism, as the sociologist Dalton Conley explains, "refers to more than just buying merchandise; it refers to the belief that happiness and fulfillment can be achieved through the acquisition of material possessions."[39] Consumerist ideologies take effect on television programs such as the reality-adjacent *Lifestyles of the Rich and Famous*. On the show, which ran on CBS for more than a decade (1984–1995), host Robin Leach (with cohost Shari Belafonte toward the end of the show's run) swept viewers along on journeys through the homes of the wealthy, ending each episode with his signature tagline, "Champagne wishes and caviar dreams." More recently, VH1's *The Fabulous Life of . . .* (2003–2013) similarly gave us a glimpse into celebrity lives, specifically focusing on their various forms of luxury consumption.

Even a show such as *The Girls Next Door* was aspirational in its portrayal of money and privilege. Hef's three central girlfriends during the majority of the series—Holly, Bridget, and Kendra—are all platinum blond, conventionally attractive, and decades younger than the elderly Hef. Their bodies are offered to us not as objects of ridicule, as in *Here Comes Honey Boo Boo*, but as sites of sensuality. Further, though the show has received critiques related to sexuality, gender roles, and its participants' values,[40] its tone is not derisive. The women live in a mansion, receive lavish gifts, and go on exciting adventures. They are presented as sexually desirable and happy, ensconced within a thrilling world of celebrity and privilege. Glamorous music plays when Hef enters the room. These types of series reveal our zeal for consumption, our desire to gawk at the slick lives of the rich, and our tendency to conceptualize wealth, material possessions, and contentment all as part of the same package.

MONEY CAN'T BUY YOU CLASS

Yet we don't simply rebuke the poor and love the rich. We aspire to be the rich, and we interpret their types of bodies and their types of things as morally correct, but we love them in a complicated way. While some reality programs about rich people are aspirational in tone, the genre's relationship with the elite—and *our* relationship with the elite—is more complex than just that.

Successful people are not exempt from our mockery. In fact, we may particularly enjoy watching them stumble. Reality TV, specifically, reveals how we delight in the shortcomings of well-to-do people, because the genre thrives on these kinds of seemingly incongruous intersections. *The Simple Life* (Fox, 2003–2005; E!, 2006–2007), for instance, places the socialites Paris Hilton and Nicole Richie in everyday contexts for comedic effect. In season one, for instance, the women live with a family on an Arkansas farm for a month. Like Rick on *Undercover Boss*, they are often portrayed as inept at manual tasks, both on the farm itself and within their various low-wage jobs. The show suggests that wealth hobbles one's ability to function in the real world. This is perhaps an attractive prospect for those of us who are not millionaires.

More specifically, the reality genre shows us how, just as we like to cast aspersions on poor people, we also like to cast aspersions on rich people *who don't know how to be rich*. The *Housewives* programs, for example, are not simple paeans to the rich in the manner of *Lifestyles of the Rich and Famous*. There's champagne and there's caviar, but there's also drunken fighting, occasional mug shots, and an endless parade of shiny, unflattering dresses. The mismatch becomes a shared joke between Bravo and the viewer.

It is significant that many Housewives were not born into upper-class families, and this information trickles out on the show. In a scene from season twelve, for instance, Countess LuAnn revealed to her autobiography's ghostwriter that she'd had a hardscrabble childhood. Bourdieu's concept of habitus suggests that your position in the class hierarchy is key to your general orientation toward the world. But specifically, for Bourdieu, it's where you were *born and raised* in the hierarchy that most strongly impacts this "internalized form of class condition."[41] Yet we live in a society where there is some social mobility: some people move up or down. While Bourdieu acknowledges that an individual's habitus can change in response to social circumstances, when people jettison out of one class and into another, they can also experience friction. This scenario has played out in various forms of entertainment, from the Frank Capra film *Mr. Deeds Goes to Town* (1936) to *The Fresh Prince of Bel-Air* (NBC, 1990–1996), focusing on characters who suddenly become rich and lack the corresponding habitus. Because it focuses on social asymmetry, and because many of its wealthier participants are nouveau riche (perhaps *because*—Paris Hilton aside—an elite habitus might deter reality-show participation), the reality genre is particularly primed to reveal this potential gap between a privileged economic position and its accompanying habits of mind.

The Housewives are an imperfect example of this mismatch between socioeconomic status and upper-class habitus because, frankly, some of them are not all that rich. Some of them do appear to have legitimate wealth and/or fame—for example, *Beverly Hills*' restaurateur Lisa Vanderpump, *New York City*'s heiress Tinsley Mortimer, *Miami*'s cosmetics queen Lea Black, and *Atlanta*'s Grammy winner Kandi

Burruss. But *Orange County*'s Gina Kirschenheiter's small, sparsely furnished house littered with inspirational signage ("GATHER") is a far cry from Lisa Vanderpump's sprawling mansion with miniature horses and a swan moat. Other Houseswives are shown living in rented houses, filing for bankruptcy, and tucking the tags into their designer dresses so that they can return them later (I'm looking at you, Sonja!). These women have a lot in common with Karl Marx's category of "petite bourgeoisie," the middle managers who are not *of* the bourgeoisie but affect their airs.

But even among the Housewives who have amassed considerable fortunes, their constant emphasis on that wealth is not always consistent with an upper-class habitus. The juxtaposition between these women's current (purported) economic level and their internalized class condition is mined for entertainment. Indeed, these shows present the women's ignorance of their own crass materialism as a kind of dramatic irony.

On the *Beverly Hills* franchise, for instance, Dana brags that her sunglasses cost $25,000.[42] Some of the other women perceive this to be a bit gauche—not, specifically, paying that much for the sunglasses but the mentioning of it. On that season's cast reunion,[43] Camille notes that people who genuinely have a lot of money don't boast about it, and Lisa agrees, "It was a bit weird when you were saying the prices."

"Your dog wears attire for every event," Dana retorts, pointing out Lisa's own excesses. But the women—and the show itself—ultimately suggest that there are limits to our valorizing of consumption, as flaunting our wealth in some ways can be a social disqualifier. Here again we see that while class is an economic category, it's typically accompanied by a particular set of cultural practices. The *Beverly Hills* women draw a distinction between authentic and inauthentic class status, with authenticity linked to a particular habitus and the whispering of wealth. Money alone, as the Countess points out, can't buy you class.

TRUMP DYNASTY

It's crucial to note that not *all* mismatches between class status and habitus are treated the same way on reality TV. *Duck Dynasty* (A&E, 2012–2017), for example, is a very different show from *The Real Housewives*. The former show, which juxtaposes the common and the regal in its very title, lets us into the lives of the Robertsons, who run a business selling duck-hunting supplies. While the family was not always wealthy, its patriarch, Phil, invented a tool for calling ducks that has been quite lucrative. The disconnect between the family's income and their class conditioning is evident from the beginning of the pilot episode.[44] As the show opens, Phil's adult son Willie explains, "The backwoods of Louisiana is now home to a new breed of millionaire: my family." We see boots sloshing through a swamp, followed by a shot of a gated mansion. In the title sequence, the family emerges from an expensive-looking car with a gleaming duck ornament on its hood—the men sporting long beards and scraggly hair, Willie clad in a camouflage blazer. "Money didn't change some things . . . ," Willie narrates, and during the episode we see the clan hunting, cutting off the heads of bullfrogs, and frying up squirrel brains. By presenting sweaty millionaires in bandannas capturing frogs from a fishing boat, and demarcating this as atypical, the show reveals how socioeconomic status is normally associated with certain cultural practices.

But despite this family's unusual combination of culture

and class, and probably even *because of it*, the Robertson clan became folk heroes for a certain segment of working-class America. While *Duck Dynasty* was a mainstream hit (the season four premiere, for instance, was watched by 11.8 million viewers—a cable record for a nonscripted series),[45] it's significant that the show was *particularly* popular in rural markets similar to the Robertsons' milieu.[46] And within the first year of its airing, it had generated $400 million in product revenue—about half of which was from the low-end retailer Walmart.[47] As we've seen, our ability to identify with its broad character types has long drawn us toward reality TV. Part of *Duck Dynasty*'s appeal, perhaps, lay in its suggestion that the wealthy aren't a separate species; they're everyday Joes like us who happen to have cash. It portrayed a manageable distance between the rich and the poor, fitting neatly into the tantalizing American narrative of ingenuity, meritocracy, and individual achievement.

Donald Trump's reality show, and his subsequent presidency, capitalized on a similar narrative. In the introductory sequence to *The Apprentice*, set to the song "For the Love of Money" by the O'Jays, the trappings of wealth are front and center: a stock market ticker, hundred-dollar bills, a luxury car, a private jet, and Trump's silhouette on a golden money clip. Nothing about either Trump's show or his public persona has ever "whispered" wealth. *The Apprentice* was all about the things that money could buy: helicopters, skyscrapers, connections to influential friends. In addition to his overt materialism, Trump long publicly embraced low culture—for example, when he served McDonald's and Burger King to White House guests. (In one particularly striking photo, he stood behind the fast-food buffet, his arms outspread, as a painting of a pensive-looking Abraham Lincoln loomed in the background.)[48] There's a reason that Trump was able to package himself as a new kind of candidate to voters, as a renegade who went his own way. His messaging promised, and perhaps his atypical behaviors suggested, that although he was rich he would be different from the queue of other rich white men who had preceded him. He was the billionaire who "kept it real"—the one you could get a beer with.

With his braggadocio and his penchant for gold decor, Donald Trump might have made an excellent Real Housewife. Yet these women are still throwing wineglasses at one another on Bravo, and he's been president. Both Trump and the Robertsons, though arguably "low class" in their actions at times, have been lionized among white, working-class audiences in a way that the Housewives have not. (Tellingly, if anyone is given a hard time on *Duck Dynasty*, it is Willie for supposedly becoming overly educated and failing at "redneck" tasks like frog hunting.) Why the difference? Gender certainly plays a role in how these reality stars are received. As we'll see, men—particularly rich, white men—are given more space to play at being crude and offensive.

Still, what the Housewives, the Robertsons, and Trump do have in common is that their class/habitus mismatch is *notable*—whether because it renders them particularly appalling, kitschy, or refreshing. They all confirm that low culture and high income is an unusual pairing. And in doing so, they all solidify our standard ideas about class.

REALITY TV: THE GREAT EQUALIZER?

Although Bourdieu's initial scholarship on taste is now decades old, more recent research and reality TV shows both continue to suggest that there's still a relationship between class and cultural preferences.[49] Still, as Donald Trump and other reality stars show us, one can be a socioeconomic elite without exhibiting an upper-class habitus all the time.

Elites don't listen *only* to opera. Indeed, as the sociologist Paul DiMaggio has observed, they actually have a wider range of tastes than just the highbrow. One of the reasons for this, DiMaggio proposes, is that upper-class people have larger and more diverse social networks, necessitating "broad repertoires of taste."[50] They are exposed to more things and need to connect with all different kinds of people. Other researchers have found similarly, observing not only that high-status people are "omnivorous" when it comes to cultural consumption[51] but also that this group has become *more* omnivorous over time.[52] (True story: I worked as a research assistant to Paul DiMaggio when I was in college, and upon my graduation he gave me a notepad with Snoopy on the cover, saying, "Shit." He really *got* my lowbrow tastes.)

One might argue that reality TV itself is a key site for the democratization of taste. As we've seen, one of the reasons people watch the genre is for the social aspect: so that they can connect with others about its content.[53] While reality TV retains a stigma,[54] it is also potentially versatile as a mechanism for promoting interaction and solidarity across class lines. The ubiquity of this genre's fans, even among the elite, is evident in everything from a piece about the show *Vanderpump Rules* by Emily Nussbaum in *The New Yorker*[55] to the revelation that Hillary Clinton is partial to Dorinda on *The Real Housewives of New York City*.[56] One 2014 analysis of Nielsen data found that six of the twenty most popular nonsports shows in households earning $150,000 or more per year were reality series.[57] Another analysis found that *The Bachelorette* was the

2018 summer show whose viewers had the highest median income.[58]

Participating in this form of low culture, furthermore, does not exempt reality stars from elite status. In some cases, their involvement with reality TV even seems to enhance their status. Kim Kardashian has amassed (greater) wealth and secured a front-row seat at Paris Fashion Week. Kylie Jenner graced the cover of *Forbes* magazine on her ascent to becoming the youngest-ever self-made billionaire in our country's history.[59] Bethenny Frankel, who first hawked the Skinnygirl Margarita on *The Real Housewives of New York City*, ultimately sold her low-calorie cocktail for a reported $100 million.[60] And then there's Donald Trump: wealthy businessman, *Apprentice* judge, US president. Whether or not his work on *The Apprentice* hastened Trump's ascent to the White House, it did not disqualify him. High-status people may look down on reality TV, but they're not wholly snubbing it. To some extent, they are allowing it to permeate their spaces, and vice versa.

Reality TV occupies a curious place in contemporary life, in that while it's not always socially acceptable to discuss our viewing of these programs, it can sometimes be socially useful. Over the past several hundred years, and arguably even since Pierre Bourdieu wrote about taste in the 1980s, high-status people have been commingling with the masses more than ever—both physically and now within the virtual world.[61] While we may not consider last week's *Bachelor* elimination to be socially weighty, when we know which contestant rode home weeping in the limo, it potentially enables us to forge points of connection beyond our immediate social circle, extending to the wide swaths of the populace that tune in to the show.

Still, we should be wary about considering reality TV a
great equalizer. Just because some groups of people have become more omnivorous does not mean that taste hierarchies
have fallen by the wayside. As the *Project Runway* judges
make clear, and as Jennifer Lena emphasizes, "Elites are still
elite—they still have and display sophisticated tastes."[62] Elites
who consume reality TV likely *also* participate in elite culture. There's also some evidence that while rich and poor alike
may be tuning in to reality TV, they're watching slightly different programs. The aforementioned analysis of 2018 summer
shows also suggested that the viewers of shows such as *So You
Think You Can Dance*, *American Ninja Warrior*, and *America's
Got Talent* had relatively high median incomes; *Showtime at
the Apollo*, *Little Big Shots*, and *Undercover Boss*, on the other
hand, relatively low.[63] This is not definitive evidence that people
in different income brackets watch different types of reality TV,
as it relies on averages and does not control for age or race. But
it *suggests* that reality TV viewership, like most forms of cultural consumption, might be patterned by class.

Additionally, while reality TV is in some ways a democ-
ratizing force, the fact that some relatively high earners may
watch *The Bachelor* doesn't mean that low-income people are
more likely to listen to classical music or amble through muse-
ums. When scholars originally wrote about omnivorousness,
the concept referred to elites elevating previously lowbrow
forms of art to highbrow status, though not really vice versa.[64]
And anyway, reality TV has not been elevated. Whether or
not some elites watch reality TV, few would characterize it as
an elite form of culture. In fact, as we've seen, this type of
elite crossover into mass media can actually help to preserve
the class hierarchy, as the upper classes symbolically distance
themselves from the lower-class groups they are viewing. They

can peer into the rat pit and emerge with their own status affirmed.

Along the same lines, the reality stars who have managed to parlay their exposure to other venues tend to be the ones who were already class privileged. Kylie Jenner may be a "self-made" billionaire, but she was born into a comfortable life with a Wheaties-box Olympian parent. Growing up, Bethenny Frankel attended an elite boarding school. Donald Trump was born to a real estate developer and graduated from Wharton. The *Boo Boo* clan, in contrast, may have made enough money to pay for weight-loss surgery and they may keep getting spin-off shows, but they're not sitting in the front row at Paris Fashion Week, inking multimillion-dollar business deals, or helming a nation. When *Duck Dynasty* was canceled in 2017 (in the wake of flagging ratings and some controversial comments from patriarch Phil about homosexuality and civil rights), the cultural frenzy surrounding the Robertson family subsided. As Bourdieu reminds us, "Individuals do not move about in social space in a random way . . . All positions of arrival are not equal from all starting points."[65] Those who begin on third base are the ones most likely to end up on third base or to make it home.

BOO BOO AND BEYOND

Nearly all unscripted programming has class lurking in the background in some way, revealing how our material circumstances impact our movement through life—from where we live and how we're educated to what we like and buy. Indeed, class has always been a part of reality TV, going back to *Queen for a Day*—a show that exposed the limitations of existing on a particular socioeconomic tier. Reality programs take us on a tour through our class system, from the cheese ball jar to the $25,000 sunglasses. In doing so, they illuminate this system and the types of narratives and cultural practices that we use to keep it buoyed. They show us how class designations ultimately translate into evaluations of taste, morality, and legitimacy that impact the types of people we giggle at and the types of practices we admire. The genre itself occupies an interesting place in that hierarchy, as "guilty pleasure" fare that has some appeal across class lines. But ultimately, while some high-class people may watch it, and while it might give visibility to people like the *Boo Boo* clan, it doesn't change anything about the reality of social class in America.

It does, however, broadcast that reality in sparkling detail.

We are a country starkly divided by social class. Further, this divide is increasing, not diminishing. The gap between middle-income and higher-income households, for instance, has been widening for decades.[66] And class is sticky. By one estimate, it can take ten to fifteen generations for a family to either lose its wealth or move out of poverty.[67] Another study found that class is vastly more important than intelligence in determining a child's future; in fact, a low-income child with high test scores in kindergarten is significantly less likely to attend college and get a good entry-level job than a high-income child with low test scores.[68] The fact that a reality star could ascend to the presidency, and that we could tweet at him directly, has not rattled the fundamental structure of the class system. While there are some nuances to this structure (laughable heiresses! redneck TV stars!), and while it may sway slightly, it remains heartily intact.

Myths about meritocracy are central to our national discourse. We tell ourselves that Americans, with the right amount of skill and effort, should be able to improve upon the circumstances of their births, and indeed some people do. Yet we don't have completely meritocratic systems in place. With controlling images as our lodestars, we navigate the gap between our meritocratic national narrative and the reality of life in the United States. We watch these shows, perhaps, because they reinforce the long-standing narratives about class we want to hear: that there's an objective hierarchy of morality and goodness that aligns with the socioeconomic spectrum; that people are in the "right" places; and that if they're not, they'll be exposed as buffoons. Because ultimately, while the class system is sturdy, the narratives we use to buffer it are underlaid by precarious, socially manufactured assumptions—about what's natural and right and who's real.

7

"Who Gon' Check Me, Boo?" (Race)

Shereé is having a party.

She's been chatting with Anthony, her planner, from her cell phone in her gargantuan car. The call did not go well. She explained to him, and reiterated to us in a testimonial, that he was not being responsive to her concerns about the event. Then she got out of her car, glancing at her phone.

"This fool hung up," she said in a measured tone.

Now she's arrived at his office to continue the conversation.

"Hey, Anthony," she says, shaking his hand. There's tension in their voices but a coolness as well. They're cordial.

Anthony leads Shereé into a conference room, where he begins to take her through the event, as he's planned it. When Shereé arrives at the party, he explains, "the women are dropping the rose petals at your feet. They're gonna carry you in, sit you on a throne . . ." Then there's more back-and-forth, with Shereé telling Anthony she's concerned because she hasn't yet met the person who is supposed to compose a poem about her for the event.

Their discussion begins to crescendo. Shereé says she needs to be included more in the planning, while Anthony contends that she doesn't respect his time. Their voices are now slightly raised.

"Anthony promised a helicopter," Shereé explains in her

testimonial, "and it's not happening now." She tells us that Anthony can't just admit he screwed up.

Back in the conference room, Anthony's now drumming his fingers on the table, telling Shereé she needs "a reality check." They're both still seated.

"You need to get your face out of my face," she tells him.

"You need to watch yourself before you get checked," he fires back.

"Who gon' check me, boo?" she asks, peering at him over her sunglasses.

There's a quick cut to her testimonial, where she recalls that all of a sudden, "things went haywire."

Now they're yelling at each other. Anthony's emphatically listing his professional credentials, and Shereé's waving a water bottle around. Words are bleeped. His staff members have arrived and hover in the doorway, looking confused.

In her testimonial, Shereé reminds us that she's from Cleveland: "The Cleveland girl was ready to get on the phone and call Pookie and them to come over there and whip yo' ass."

Back in the conference room now they're standing, hands flying, moving into each other's spaces. Anthony's arm flaps in Shereé's face and she goads him repeatedly: "Put your hands on me! Put your hands on me!"

"Get out of my office, you trashy bitch!" he's screaming, now being physically restrained by his staff members, who pull him out of the room.

The scene concludes with a shot of Shereé in her testimonial, calmly asking, "Whatever happened to customer service?"

This moment from *The Real Housewives of Atlanta* (Bravo, 2008–present)[1] leaves a lot of open questions. For instance, how did things escalate so quickly? And who is this Pookie?

The stereotypes that it splashes across our screens, however, are unambiguous. As the action in the conference room progresses, Shereé slides right into the category of the bitchy, difficult Black woman, while Anthony fills the roles of both the incompetent Black man and the angry one with the latent propensity for violence.

In Anthony's conference room and beyond, reality programming plumbs the depths of our deepest social rifts, shows us how they intersect, and highlights the cultural narratives we use to sustain them. As in the case of social class, controlling images of Black people have filtered down through the years and we use those to help us stomach the current racial order. But in the end, the genre's caricatures expose how race is a story we tell ourselves in order to organize our worlds—a tale with tremendous power, but a tale nonetheless.

THERE GOES THE NEIGHBORHOOD

From an aerial view, the landscape of reality TV reflects the topography of race in America. These shows—like our neighborhoods, our schools, our marriages, and even the tables in our high school cafeterias[2]—are not segregated under the law but are profoundly impacted by our long history of racial divisions. The sociologist Henri Lefebvre has observed that there is "social space" (the space in which social relations lie), which is distinct from "mental (or 'cognitive') space" and from "physical space."[3] While it's not something that one can reach out and touch, social space is still "real" in the same way that other social constructions like money are real. Reality TV reveals how racial stratification exists physically but also mentally and socially, as we classify and interact with others based on deeply inscribed hierarchies.

Yes, some people of color are sprinkled into predominantly white casts, just as there are people of color in other primarily white spaces. We might point to these examples as evidence that we're moving toward a postracial model, where skin color has less salience. Similarly, we might observe that some reality shows are extremely racially diverse—for example, *America's Next Top Model* (UPN, 2003–2006; The CW, 2006–2015; VH1, 2016–present) and *RuPaul's Drag Race*, though it's worth noting that both of these programs are helmed by Black celebrities who are in unique positions to move the needle on nonwhite representation.

But while there is some movement across categories, both in life and on our screens, the spatiality of race endures. For instance, our job categories are patterned by skin color. In 2018, Black people represented 37.7 percent of all baggage porters, bellhops, and concierges but only 7.6 percent of all physicians and surgeons.[4] African Americans are overrepresented in prisons—constituting 40 percent of the US incarcerated population but only 13 percent of the total US population.[5] De jure racial segregation in schooling may be an artifact of the past, but de facto school segregation is a current reality.[6] Meanwhile, the legacies of slavery, legal segregation, and discriminatory real estate practices have seared themselves onto housing grids, creating and sustaining "Black" and "white" neighborhoods that aren't *only* the products of socioeconomic differences between the groups.[7] When Black families begin moving into a neighborhood, the white residents start to trickle out, and seldom are white people choosing to move to all-Black areas.[8] As the journalist Isabel Wilkerson has observed, America has a racial "caste system," which "is as central to its operation as are the studs and joists that we cannot see in the physical buildings that we call home."[9]

In parallel, there are places that reality TV specifically reserves for Black bodies. *The Real Housewives*, for example, is a segregated domain, with the mostly Black casts of *Potomac* and *Atlanta* existing in marked contrast to the other, primarily white franchises (or primarily Latinx, as in the case of *Miami*). While *Cops* and shows about prison, such as *Lockup* (MSNBC, 2005–2017), weren't explicitly about people of color, they were places where we saw an aggregation of Black and brown bodies, both being featured and hovering in the background. There are also the aforementioned "ratchet" shows, including the ones, such as the *Love & Hip Hop* franchises, that predominantly feature women of color. Many of these shows cluster on particular networks, such as Bravo and VH1.[10]

Then there are the white spaces. As we've seen, although there are people of color on *The Bachelor* and *The Bachelorette*, these remain essentially "white shows." As Amy Kaufman has pointed out, it took fifteen years for the producers to cast an African American lead. Between 2009 and 2012 there were no Black women on the show, and there were no Black male contestants on *The Bachelorette* between 2009 and 2011. In other years, there were only a few Black contestants. "We always had to cast a black girl or two," a former producer of the show told Kaufman. "It was very obvious to me that it was token."[11] This reflects racial homophily in dating practices, as I've argued, but it also reflects how both our population and the reality TV world remain broadly stratified. During the first Black Bachelorette's season, former *Bachelor* contestant Leah Block tweeted, "I'm sitting here watching @BacheloretteABC and my roommate just sat down on the couch and said, 'What is this? @LoveAndHipHop?' DEAD."[12] Leah's post reflects the reality that Black people are often confined to these "ratchet" arenas. Further, the tweet captures more broadly the dissonance created when Black bodies move into predominantly white spaces—physical, mental, and social. Historically, we've seen this in the furor over school desegregation and "white flight" from racially mixed urban areas into the suburbs. The implicit question: What is this person doing here, in this space generally reserved for white people?

And the genre shows us how, just as we do with class, we sustain and naturalize these racial divisions by propagating certain narratives about race. Many scholars and journalists, for instance, have drawn a thick line connecting the reality programming of today with minstrel shows of yore.[13] These traveling variety programs, which sprang up in the early 1800s and had tremendous followings well into the 1880s, featured white men in blackface (and sometimes Black men in blackface) presenting racist and stereotypical versions of Black people and Black culture. These portrayals fundamentally shaped Americans' views about race, particularly since many of the white actors and viewers alike had never had any actual contact with African Americans.[14]

Every now and then, blackface boomerangs back into public consciousness, as when the morning show anchor Megyn Kelly (a former Fox News fixture who also interviewed the Duggars about Josh's sexual predation) defended blackface Halloween costumes or when it was revealed that Virginia governor Ralph Northam had included a blackface photo in his medical school yearbook. Kelly was fired for the comments,[15] and Northam was urged to resign (though he did not).[16] Blackface has emerged in the reality TV sphere as well. The competition series *America's Next Top Model* has come under fire more than once for photo shoot challenges in which the contestants were asked to wear paint and emulate other races.[17] In 2018, Countess LuAnn showed up at a costume party dressed as Diana Ross in an Afro wig and what appeared to be dark facial makeup. ("I was wearing bronzer," she has insisted. "I always wear bronzer.")[18] And on a 2012 episode of *The Challenge*,[19] cast member Emily attempted a humorous impersonation of Ty, a Black contestant on the show, by wearing his clothes and smearing chocolate on her face. When she emerged in the getup, the mood in the house became somber. "I am shocked," Paula, another white cast member, recalled in a testimonial. "It is so offensive on my level that I am thinking they have to be out of their minds." While Emily claims to have been raised in a cult separated from mainstream society—a fact that some cast members later used to explain her ignorance—it's telling that the other *Challenge* contestants, generally known more for their physical prowess and sloshed hookups than their intellect,[20] immediately pegged Emily's actions as unacceptable. These instances illuminate both our cultural prohibitions against blackface and the fact that these portrayals have not completely fallen by the wayside.

While most of its stars aren't literally doing blackface, there are still strong notes of minstrelsy in the reality TV brew. Broad, stereotypical characterizations of Blackness have percolated through mass media for hundreds of years[21] and have pooled in the well of this genre. Because archetypes are integral to these programs, reality TV has become a prime locale for the reactivation of these tropes. Minstrel shows, which exaggerated supposedly "inherent" differences between racial groups,[22] reaffirmed racial separateness. Similar portrayals on unscripted TV demonstrate how we're still using popular culture to re-entrench and naturalize these deep rifts. As the filmmaker and author Justin Simien has explained in his book, *Dear White People*, "Though the catchphrases have gone from 'Who dat?' to 'Who gon' check me, boo?,' reality

TV has kept the stereotypes tap-dancing along and made them more popular than ever!"[23]

"WITH WOMEN, IT'S DIFFERENT . . ."

We've seen how reality TV's one-dimensional archetypes allow us, the viewers, to mentally classify characters in order to select the ones with whom we most identify. In a similar fashion, we're able to slip these characters neatly into stereotypical categories that exist at specific junctures of race and gender. The critical race theorist Kimberlé Crenshaw initially coined the term "intersectionality" to refer to the interlocking categories of difference (both race and gender) shaping Black women's lives.[24] More broadly, the concept describes how the combination of social categories—race, gender, class, sexuality, and so on—that we inhabit fundamentally shapes how others perceive us and our own experiences in the world.[25] A wealthy white woman in America will likely have different life experiences, and be perceived differently, than a poor white woman, or a wealthy white man, or a wealthy Black woman.

We've seen how this concept comes into play on that first episode of *The Real World*, when Kevin and Heather discuss how their shared history with racism has manifested in slightly different ways because of their genders. Along these same lines, American mass media has typically portrayed Black women in specific ways that are qualitatively different from the way both Black men and white women are portrayed,[26] and reality TV is no exception. Looking at the genre through an intersectional lens allows us to identify how specific portrayals have deep historical roots that are entwined with, and uphold, structural racism in different ways.

Two of the most salient images of Black masculinity in

popular culture, for instance, have been the Lazy Black Man and the Angry Black Man. Characterizations of both laziness and angriness were initially used to buttress and justify slavery and the notions that African American men needed to be simultaneously motivated and tamed. As the historian J. Stanley Lemons has pointed out, it's no accident that minstrel shows rose in popularity around the 1840s, "just when the slavery issue was becoming a serious political question."[27] In minstrelsy, notions about Black laziness crystallized in the character of the "slow-thinking, slow-moving" Jim Crow.[28] This stereotype has trickled down to the representations on reality TV—for instance, *Survivor* season one's Gervase, who doesn't like to do physical labor.

While African American men on minstrel shows were often portrayed as lazy and/or as buffoons, they also appeared to have an underlying anger that needed to be corralled. This was embodied, for instance, in the character of the Brutal Buck: the sexual predator with a propensity for violence.[29] We've seen flashes of this putative Black male anger, simmering under the surface and occasionally erupting, on prison shows and on law-and-order-themed programs such as *Cops*. Two key facets of the reality genre—broad stereotyping and heightened conflict—combine to create a habitat for this particular representation.

Indeed, the Angry Black Man emerged on reality TV almost right out of the gate, with the inaugural *Real World*'s Kevin. "I think you're very bitter," Julie tells him in the first episode, accusing him of being "prejudiced against white people." We then see Kevin reflecting on that moment in a testimonial:

"I was like 'I'm not bitter,' but when I think about it now, I think I have a right to be very angry and I'm not apologetic about that." Kevin's quiet and thoughtful anger in this moment may appear subdued to us, particularly since the genre has become exponentially more physical and dramatized since those early days. But when Kevin explains how he was kicked out of school for his radical politics; when he is repeatedly shown talking about racial inequality; and when he alludes to the possibility of a criminal past, his character begins to take shape as the brooding Black man with the latent potential for violent behavior. We then got a whiff of the sexual predator stereotype with season two's David, who was ejected from the show after pulling a blanket off his roommate, Tami, who was wearing only underwear at the time.[30] As the communication scholar Mark Orbe has pointed out, Kevin and other African American males on *The Real World* "function to signify Black men as inherently angry, potentially violent, and sexually aggressive."[31]

While minstrel shows mainly portrayed men, other stereotypes have been used to justify Black women's separateness from white society in different ways. For example, the concept of the "Jezebel"—the sexually licentious Black woman—wends back to the days of slavery. As Patricia Hill Collins has observed, this stereotype was initially used to justify the rape of Black female slaves by defining "Black women's bodies as sites of wild, unrestrained sexuality that could be tamed but never completely subdued."[32] This archetype has traveled over to reality TV land, where it takes root in the "hoe" character. We see her, for instance, in the form of Tiffany Pollard[33]—aka "New York"—who initially competed for rapper Flavor Flav's affections on *Flavor of Love* (VH1, 2006–2008), then received her own spin-off show, *I Love New York* (VH1, 2007–2008), and subsequently appeared on multiple other reality shows. Within the first five minutes of *I Love New York*, before we even glimpse her face, she's rubbing Vaseline on her legs and breasts.[34] "I was willing to stop at nothing to get my man," she tells us, recapping her time on *Flavor of Love* amid flashbacks of her wearing lingerie, entwining her body with Flav's, and aggressively grabbing another contestant by the hair. Flash forward to *I Love New York* and she's preparing to meet her suitors—not, as the Bachelorette does, in an elegant gown but with a furry robe left open to reveal ample cleavage and a cigarette positioned between her lips.

As exemplified by Shereé from *The Real Housewives of Atlanta*, another common image of Black femininity in popular culture has been the "Sapphire"—a term originating with the show *Amos 'n' Andy* (1928–1960) and its emasculating character of Sapphire Stevens, who constantly berated her man.[35] On reality TV, we know her as the "Angry Black Woman" or the "Black Bitch." Not the same potentially dangerous criminal as the Angry Black Man, she is portrayed as seldom satisfied, explosive, and poised to offer an opinion with a finger wag and a swerve of the head. Like the Angry Black Man, though, she's been part of the genre nearly from the beginning. As the communication scholar Donnetrice C. Allison has observed, nearly every season of *The Real World* has featured a Black female, "and nearly all of those black females have been described by their roommates using terms like: 'controlling,' 'harsh,' 'overbearing,' 'bossy,' 'quick-tempered,' 'independent,' 'diva,' 'outspoken,' and 'gold-digger.'"[36] Omarosa Manigault Newman, whom we know from *The Apprentice* (2004), *Celebrity Apprentice* (2008), *All-Star Celebrity Apprentice* (2013), and *Celebrity Big Brother* (2018), and who also served as director of African American outreach for President Trump, is the quintessential Sapphire. Allison points out that during her original nine-week stint on *The Apprentice*, Omarosa was called a "bitch" by other contestants, either to her face or behind her back, seven times.[37]

One might point out that there are non-Black reality TV stars who fit these stereotypes as well. And there are "ratchet" programs that primarily involve white people. We've watched these white folks vying for the heart of Poison singer Bret Michaels in *Rock of Love* (VH1, 2007–2009), for example, and brawling on *My Big Fat American Gypsy Wedding* (TLC, 2012–2016, 2018). Conversely, not all Black people on reality TV fit into minstrelsy archetypes. Yet these stereotypes are applied *particularly* to Black people, in spaces and on networks specifically set aside for "ratchet" portrayals. Further, there are few alternative images of Blackness on unscripted TV, in comparison with the broader spectrum of portrayals of white people.[38]

When applied to Black people specifically, these controlling images[39] do a particular type of societal work—and show us how we *all* do that work. We use the stereotype of the Lazy Black Man, for example, to facilitate racial discrimination in the labor market. Indeed, studies repeatedly demonstrate that employers apply strongly negative characteristics to minority workers—in particular, African American men.[40] One might argue that perhaps there *are* differences between Black and white applicants, and that's what employers are responding to, but studies show that this discrimination occurs even when employers are given résumés for hypothetical candidates with objective qualifications.[41] Similarly, the Angry Black Man doesn't dominate just our screens but our broader imaginations as well; research has shown that people tend to perceive Black men as bigger, more menacing, and in need of more aggressive physical control than white men, even when they are objectively the same size.[42] And if we can see Black women as finger-wagging shrews always on the precipice of anger, it's easier to delegitimize their concerns. This allows us to think less deeply about the fact that they make 65 percent of white men's earnings,[43] that more than one-fifth of them live in poverty,[44] and that they die younger than white women.[45] Stereotyping isn't the sole cause of these disparities, but it stems from, and fortifies, the structures that support these disparities. By looking at reality TV, we can see not only how the cross section of social life we inhabit impacts our experiences of the world but also how we normalize and reinforce that segmentation through the narratives we tell ourselves. When we draw upon these controlling images, consciously or not, we keep them real.

LEAVING THE GHETTO

In the previous chapter, I argued that the class system fundamentally impacts our life experiences, and here we've seen how racial stereotypes differ by gender category. But race, gender, and social class are not completely separate systems of power—in reality, they cannot be disentangled. Crenshaw's notion of intersectionality allows for multiple, entwined dimensions of difference. For instance, we've seen how we enjoy laughing at reality TV's wealthy buffoons. However, this is *particularly* true when they are wealthy or wealth-aspiring Black women. And this tells us something crucial about ourselves as well.

Our cultural practice of portraying African Americans who have ascended the social ladder as silly and unnatural is nothing new. Going back to minstrelsy, for example, the character of Zip Coon was a Black man whose dandified clothing and overinflated, malaprop-riddled speech rendered him absurd.[46] Today, reality TV presents the Black nouveau riche along similar lines. The genre, as the historian Sheena Harris maintains, "has provided an avenue for this new class of elites to showcase the grandeur, possessions, and an affluent quality of life, while the viewing public makes a mockery of them and their lack of a more refined behavior generally associated with the upper class."[47]

This brings us back to Shereé.

She may be wearing Chanel earrings, and Anthony may have a crisp pocket square protruding from his business suit, but they soon engage in shouting, finger wagging, and "boo" language.

Unscripted programming illuminates and perpetuates the controlling image of the wealthy Black *woman*, specifically, as someone whose "ghetto" core lurks just under a veneer of civility. Shows such as *The Real Housewives of Atlanta*, *Married to Medicine*, and many others featuring relatively well-off Black women have a "ratchet" undercurrent despite their opulent scenery. *Married to Medicine* (Bravo, 2013–present), for instance, follows a group of mainly African American women— some wives of doctors, some doctors themselves—in Atlanta. At first glance, the show is about Black people who have made it; it references their education and showcases their luxury goods. "One of the great things about the medical community in Atlanta is that it's a huge population of young, Black Americans, and they're doin' it. You know, they're makin' six figures," one of the doctor's wives, Toya, tells us in the first episode.[48]

But the ghetto is never too far out of frame. The women repeatedly mention that Toya does not come from privilege. At one point she tells us that she grew up in "somewhat of a ghetto—you know, hood," but that "being a doctor's wife, you

have to leave that ghetto mentality, that behavior, at home."
Quad, in contrast, is presented as someone who is unable to
discard that mentality. "I wasn't born with a silver spoon in
my mouth, so I can see ghetto from a mile away," Toya tells
us, describing Quad. "She probably dated a drug dealer at
some point, and she lucked up on a doctor dude at the grocery store." At one point, Quad herself exclaims, "I'm trying
not to be what I once was!" her face crumpling.

Throughout the episode, the women emphasize that Quad's
behavior is not befitting a doctor's wife. "You can't be grabbing people's hair, pointing your finger at them," Kari, the one
white cast member, explains. "That kind of behavior is no PR
for your husband." Kari's comment about hair pulling and
finger wagging suggests an awareness of the standard reality
TV stereotyping of Black women. Later, during a conversation between two of the other women, this awareness comes
into even sharper focus.

"When women lose their manners and act out in a social
setting, especially women of color, I'm deeply saddened," Dr.
Jackie explains. "We don't fight and pull hair," she adds.

"Point fingers. Smack hands," Mariah responds.

"Yes," says Dr. Jackie.

Here, Mariah and Dr. Jackie use respectability politics to
distance themselves from Quad (i.e., "I'm *different* from *that*
Black person, over there"). But, more broadly, they also symbolically distance themselves from a specific historical archetype of Black femininity. It's a spin on the image of the
out-of-control Black woman: the one who has ascended the social ladder but still cannot outclimb her "ghetto" self.

Why are these types of programs so popular? Beyond our
general delight in mismatched habitus and incompetent rich

people, the proliferation of these shows about *Black women specifically* is difficult to ignore. Beyond *Married to Medicine*, this archetype infiltrates *The Real Housewives of Atlanta*, *The Real Housewives of Potomac*, *Basketball Wives*, and the *Love & Hip Hop* franchises—to name just a few programs. When considering controlling images, Collins suggests, we need to think about the social function they serve. The caricature of the out-of-control Black lady packs the one-two punch of naturalizing standard hierarchies of both gender and race. And the notion that a Black woman, like Quad, born in "the hood" cannot reasonably assimilate within elite society packs the threefold punch of naturalizing standard hierarchies of race, gender, and class.

Again, this is nothing new for us.

Author bell hooks has described how, during Reconstruction, African Americans who attempted to improve their social standing were met with derision. Specifically, "A black woman dressed tidy and clean, carrying herself in a dignified manner, was usually the object of mud-slinging by white men who ridiculed and mocked her self-improvement efforts. They reminded her that in the eyes of the white public she would never be seen as worthy of consideration and respect."[49] Today, while white women on shows like the *Housewives* are not immune from this type of mockery, the reality genre gets particular traction out of taking putatively elegant Black ladies and cutting them down to size.

The image of a well-to-do Black woman behaving in a "low-class" way is not a random one. It has a history and a function, and there's a reason that Americans gravitate toward it. While, just as in the case of *Honey Boo Boo*, some of us may identify with these characters or strive to emulate them, our zeal for these programs also suggests that we have a more compli-cated and intersectional relationship with the wealthy than one of Robin Leach–style adoration.

Additionally, we've seen how reality TV recommends per-sonal redress to problems that in reality are deeply connected to social structure. In doing so, it helps us to naturalize our underlying systems of power. Similarly, the reality TV nar-rative that Black women, like Quad, cannot truly escape the ghetto because of their personal failings is a story that makes our social hierarchy easier to swallow.

This narrative is perhaps most memorable and poignant during Tiffany Richardson's stint on *America's Next Top Model*. We first meet twenty-one-year-old Tiffany during the first episode of season three, in which thirty-four semifinalists are whittled down to the final fourteen aspiring models who will compete on the show.[50] The first time Tiffany speaks, she tells the judges that she "may seem a little ghetto." The as-piring models go out drinking in Los Angeles, and a bar pa-tron pours beer on Tiffany's head. In retaliation, Tiffany lobs a glass at the woman, and a fight breaks out. Outside of the bar, Tiffany heatedly sputters, "That skank poured beer on my weave!" On the bus ride back to the hotel, she leans against the seat in front of her, tears streaming down her face: "I'm not go-ing back to no hood. I can't." Booted from the show at the end of the episode, she gazes down sadly: "It would've been a big change to go from hustling to being Glamour Girl anyway."

However, after undergoing anger management training, Tiffany returns for season four. "In a lot of ways, I'm a better person," she assures us in the first episode.[51]

"Tiffany grabbed her problems by the reins," photo shoot director Jay Manuel observes approvingly.

In this season, she makes it until episode seven,[52] when

she is ejected along with fellow contestant Rebecca in a double elimination. While Rebecca is visibly upset about the decision, Tiffany smiles and cracks jokes as she's hugging the remaining contestants goodbye.

"Tiffany, I'm extremely disappointed in you," host Tyra Banks tells her. "This is a joke to you. . . . This is serious to these girls, and this should be serious to you."

"Looks can be deceiving," Tiffany says. "I can't change it, Tyra . . . I'm sick of crying about stuff that I cannot change. I'm sick of being disappointed."

"You ain't sick of being disappointed, Tiffany," Tyra replies. "No you're not. If you were sick of being disappointed, you would stand up, and you would take control of your destiny. Do you know that you had a possibility to win? Do you know that all of America is rooting for you? Do you know that? And then you come in here and you treat this like a joke."

As the two women proceed to talk over each other, Tyra becomes visibly angry.

"I have never in my life yelled at a girl like this!" she screams at Tiffany. "When my mother yells like this, it's because she loves me. I was rooting for you! We were all rooting for you! How dare you?!"

Both of these seasons highlight Tiffany's personal failures: her "bad habits," her unchecked anger requiring professional intervention, her decision to throw a glass at a stranger. The show suggests that she, like Quad, was just not strong enough to climb out of the ghetto and leave it behind.

THE INVISIBLES

When Kimberlé Crenshaw initially wrote about intersectionality, she wanted to address the fact that in politics and under the law, Black women were "theoretically erased."[53] When we discuss the concerns of women, she argued, we often tacitly mean white women, and when we talk about politics relating to Black people, we're often discussing Black men. In this way, Black women and their specific needs and experiences become invisible. Though Crenshaw was writing in the late 1980s, we still struggle with these assumptions—as seen, for instance, in critiques that the 2017 Women's March reflected a narrow, white feminism and failed to address intersectional concerns.[54] Yet while Black women continue to be "erased" in this particular way, they're relatively *visible* on unscripted television. In fact, by some accounts, the reality genre provides a larger platform for Black representation than other forms of media.[55] The premiere of *I Love New York* in 2007 was the most watched debut in VH1 history at the time, with 4.43 million viewers,[56] and in 2017 *Love & Hip Hop: Atlanta* was the highest-rated reality series on cable (followed by the original *Love & Hip Hop*).[57] In some ways, reality TV is a vehicle for the diversity that we don't always see elsewhere. And, as we've seen, we can plumb those representational depths in order to understand how we organize society into racialized and gendered categories and build narratives to sustain that organization.

But *invisibility* tells us something, too. Despite the elasticity and breadth of the genre, there are racial and ethnic groups we *don't* see much on reality TV, and their erasure provides additional lessons about ourselves. For example, Latinx characters have historically been less visible on television than Black characters,[58] and this extends to the reality genre.[59] It is significant that while a small body of scholarship looks at constructions of Blackness on reality TV, there's almost *no* research that focuses on Latinx populations in a reality TV context.[60] The scarcity of this demographic on our screens is striking when more than one out of every six people in the US is Hispanic.[61]

When we do see Hispanic characters on unscripted TV, they're often women (some of whom are biracial) mixed in with Black women in "ratchet" spaces. In these spaces, many of the same stereotypes applied to Black bodies get applied to brown ones as well. For example, there's the controlling image of the bitchy, trash-talking, finger-wagging woman of color—who may, in this case, be described as "spicy" or "fiery."[62] Elsewhere on reality TV, Latinx and Black people share the violent criminal archetype. One study looking across TV genres between 1955 and 1986, for instance, found that Hispanic characters were regularly portrayed as criminals: "The worst offenders were 'reality' shows, whose version of reality often consisted of white cops chasing black and Hispanic robbers."[63] And Latinas also appear on reality TV as domestic workers—a role that has historically been played by Black women on scripted TV.[64] While many representations of Latinx people on reality TV dovetail with those of Black people, the former are also the subjects of unique controlling images. For example, there is the Latino character who is problematic or humorous because his English is not very polished—a stereotype we see, for instance, on *RuPaul's Drag Race*.[65]

In these ways, the reality genre highlights the particular narratives that we tell about brown bodies, how they dovetail with those about Black bodies, and how they stand on their own. We can then see how these controlling images of Latinx people—as refusing to play nicely or to assimilate and as purveyors of violence and crime—help to enforce the physical separation of particular categories of people. For example, these very narratives converge in political rhetoric about immigration. In its paucity of Latinx characters, and its representations of the ones that do appear, reality TV illuminates whose perspectives we see as central and whose we see as marginal—and the narratives we construct to sustain that marginality.

Another group whose stories seldom get told on reality TV are Asian Americans. Asian American *women* occasionally appear, sometimes as submissive or unmemorable background players (*The Bachelor*), sometimes as hypersexualized personas (Tila Tequila), sometimes as exoticized creatures (the Asian American contestants on *America's Next Top Model*), and occasionally in the role of abrasive and demanding "Dragon Lady" (Ryan's mom on *Child Genius*). Other than in a few notable cases (e.g., *Dr. Pimple Popper*'s dermatologist Sandra Lee), they're generally marginal to the main action of the show. Asian American men, though, are even less visible. For example, while some Asian American females have appeared on *The Real World*, during its entire run there has never been an Asian male on the show. Similarly, between 2013 and 2018 *The Bachelorette* included only five Asian men, four of whom did not make it past the first round.[66] As in the case of Latinx representation, the near absence of Asian men on reality TV is particularly jarring when Asian Americans are not an insignificant portion of the US population. By one projection, they're expected to become the largest immigrant group in the country, surpassing Hispanics in 2055.[67]

Where are all of the Asian men? What does their absence from our screens tell us about this particular intersection of gender and race? Our cultural stereotype of the Asian man—intelligent, hardworking, asexual[68]—exists in direct opposition to the quintessential reality TV participant—the raucous ne'er-do-well, primed to fight. Further, the same cultural stereotypes about Asian men that likely assist in keeping them off reality programs are evident when they do appear. The cultural theorist Grace Wang, analyzing the shows *Top Chef* and *Project Runway*, observes how Asian American competitors often take the role of the "technical robot."[69]

Because one might argue that technical adeptness is a "positive" attribute, and because Asian Americans in the aggregate have objectively achieved success in America in some ways,[70] we might not think of "technical robot" as a controlling image that contributes to racial marginalization. But Asians *have*, objectively, been marginalized—for example, historically placed on the bottom rung of a racially stratified labor market,[71] shuttled into US internment camps during World War II, and scapegoated during the COVID-19 pandemic. When, today, we frame Asian men as not very passionate or very compelling, that stereotype does a particular kind of societal labor for us. As Wang points out, we continue to use the "technical robot" stereotype to characterize these men as lacking necessary personality attributes in white-dominated fields where they threaten to be successful. This stereotype gets activated in the college admissions process, too. We saw this in 2018, when an audit revealed that even though Asian American applicants to Harvard University scored higher than other racial/ethnic groups in areas such as test scores, grades, and extracurriculars, their scores on various "personality" ratings significantly reduced their chances of being admitted.[72] When we turn on *The Bachelorette* and see only a few (if any) Asian men, who never stay long, we're confronted with an intersectional reality: that the experiences of Asian American men and white men have not historically been identical, and they're not now. From fleeting domestic workers to "technical robots," unscripted television demonstrates

how we still think of both Hispanic Americans and Asian
Americans—in different ways—as "Other" to white Americans and how we tell ourselves particular stories to maintain
that separateness.

(THIS IS NOT AN ARGUMENT ABOUT) THE POLITICS
OF REPRESENTATION

When people of color do appear on reality TV, are these portrayals ultimately more harmful or valuable? Where are we,
the viewers, in all of this? When we tune in, are we morally
culpable of perpetuating controlling images?

While these are not the questions on which I am focused,
they are nonetheless important questions, and they have
nuanced answers. Other authors have written extensively
about the politics of representation on these shows. Some
have critiqued these programs for bringing marginalized
populations to the fore only to perpetuate their marginalization.[73] Others have observed that the fact that reality TV is
presented as "reality" may give these stereotypes particular
life.[74] But rather than, say, boycotting the negative portrayals of Black women on *Love & Hip Hop*, some have suggested
that we can still consume these programs, albeit critically, applying an "oppositional gaze."[75]

Others still, while acknowledging the problematic stereotyping on these shows, point out the potentially liberating
qualities of some of these portrayals.[76] They point out how
Black women on reality TV, for instance, have been able to
work within these stereotypical categories to earn money
and to render themselves culturally visible.[77] We've seen how
Cardi B has used the category of "ratchet" to facilitate her
superstardom. Shereé, to a lesser extent, has capitalized on

"Who gon' check me, boo?"; for example, she incorporated the catchphrase alongside an image of her own face on a T-shirt for her clothing line, SHE by Sheree. One of the few Asian American males on reality TV, William Hung from season three of *American Idol*, was able to capitalize on his public persona of the dorky Asian male who is clueless about his terrible singing. He parlayed the exposure into a successful, albeit brief, music career; his first album, *Inspiration*, sold about two hundred thousand copies.[78]

As reality stars become savvier about the ways these shows are produced and packaged, some become adept at working in and around intersectional stereotypes. One key example from *Dance Moms* is Holly Hatcher-Frazier, an African American former school principal. On the series, Abby Lee variously asked Holly's daughter Nia (the only Black girl in that cast) to wear a dog collar, to twerk, and to don a leopard-print outfit and Afro wig for a solo dance about a pimp character named "LaQueefa." Holly registered nearly *no* emotion, even though she was arguably goaded into acting in accordance with the Angry Black Woman stereotype. Not only did Holly express her objections coolly, but she was a marked contrast to the white moms on the show who repeatedly got into heated confrontations with Abby Lee.

Holly appeared acutely aware of the burden of representation. This was true throughout her time on the series but particularly during season two, when the show briefly introduced another mother, whose name was Kaya but who went by "Black Patsy" and who aligned more closely with the Black Bitch archetype (and, indeed, appeared to be consciously working within this categorization). On the reunion special at the end of that season, Black Patsy said that she wished Holly and Nia, as the other people of color in the cast, would have

been more welcoming to her. While Holly conceded that Nia
was excited to have another Black girl in the studio, she also
told Black Patsy that she doesn't "get a pass" because they're
the same race. She went on to critique Black Patsy's behavior
on the show, describing a "huge eruption" that "was something out of some '70s B movie, to me. It was almost—it was
very stereotypical."[79] In this moment, Holly, like Dr. Jackie
and Mariah from *Married to Medicine*, invoked a prior history
of racist portrayals in order to symbolically separate herself
from both Black Patsy and these stereotypes writ large.

While both the white Dance Moms and Holly need to
grapple with audience responses to their behaviors, Holly
must shoulder the added burden of navigating through racist
stereotypes. She exemplifies the sociologist W. E. B. Du Bois's
notion of "double consciousness." While we all look into the
social mirror and change our behaviors accordingly, Du Bois
observed that this was specifically true for African Americans, who must take into account both their own frames of
reference and those of a potentially racist onlooker. For Du
Bois, double consciousness means "always looking at one's
self through the eyes of others, of measuring one's soul by
the tape of a world that looks on in amused contempt and
pity."[80] Although he was writing in 1903, the concept remains
relevant today. We see it in the way Holly actively distances
herself from Black Patsy and her "very stereotypical" actions.
And people of color experience it in real life: monitoring their
behaviors and responses when they get stopped for speeding
violations, when they're walking around high-end clothing
stores, or when they're locked out of their homes and need to
find a way back in.

Perhaps the answer to the question "Are these programs
doing social good or doing social harm?" is that it's always

and inextricably *both*. Along similar lines, writing about TV talk shows, the sociologist Joshua Gamson has argued that they give voice to historically oppressed people, albeit in exploitative ways: "There is in fact no choice here between manipulative spectacle and democratic forum, only the puzzle of a situation in which one cannot exist without the other. . . ."[81]

But here, my central question isn't whether this genre is exploitative. Rather: What do these programs about people of color shouting, pulling each other's hair, and getting chased by the police *say about us*? And what does it say about us that they are massively popular? The answers to these questions are complicated by the fact that Black people are large audiences for these shows, just as women are large audiences for gender-stereotypical shows like *The Bachelor*. A 2013 Nielsen report, for instance, found that *Love & Hip Hop: Atlanta* was the top-rated reality program for Black Americans aged eighteen to forty-nine, with more than twice as many tuning in to that program than to *American Idol*.[82] Indeed, that same year, six of the top ten prime-time shows for African American audiences were in the reality TV genre.[83] But this does not mean that Black people—or women, or Asian Americans, or Latinos, or queer people, for that matter—uncritically accept their stereotyped portrayals. As Donnetrice Allison suggests, one answer to the question "Why are we contributing to our own subjugation and misinterpretation?" is simple: "We want to see ourselves on television, even if the depictions are distorted and inaccurate."[84]

But part of the broader appeal of these programs likely lies in the fact that these representations are familiar to us; they confirm our dominant narratives. Indeed, research suggests that such shows help to *reinforce* these narratives as well. One study in a mock employment setting, for example, found that when participants were shown images of Jezebels, it negatively influenced their perceptions of African American interviewees.[85] Whether or not reality programs are, on balance, "positive" or "negative," whether they're ethical or not, and whether or not we should be ashamed of ourselves for watching—all of which are beyond the scope of this book—reality TV teaches us about the stark inequalities that still exist, the stereotypes we still mobilize, and how those two elements work together in a circular way.

"I COULD BE BIRTHED FROM, LIKE, DRAGONS AND SQUIRRELS"

Finally, in shining a light on our racial divides and the stories we tell to maintain them, the genre exposes the fallacy of race itself. People aren't "born Black" in the same way that they aren't "born gay," as much as being born into a society that interprets their natural skin color or inborn sexual desires (as we'll see) within a particular framework. Race *matters* deeply, in all the ways I've discussed, but while there are some biological features that go along with racial categories (e.g., skin color, hair texture, eye shape), race itself is a social construction. It's something humans made up.

Reality TV's Nicole LaValle (née Polizzi), whom we know as "Snooki," exposes this construction by eluding easy racial classification. We initially met Snooki in 2009 on *Jersey Shore* (MTV), a show focusing on a group of men and women placed together in a vacation home at Seaside Heights, New Jersey. The cast members were presented as a subcategory of Italian Americans, with gelled hair and a penchant for tanning, who self-identify as "Guidos" and "Guidettes." The show was controversial from the beginning, drawing negative feedback from Italian American groups opposed to its stereotypical portrayals; indeed, it was so widely rebuked that "Controversy and Criticism of *Jersey Shore*" has an independent entry on Wikipedia.[86]

What are race and ethnicity, and what is Snooki? Is she actually Italian American? This is where things get sticky. Sociologists define race as a group of people who share various traits (typically, physical ones) and who theoretically have a common bloodline; it's distinct from ethnicity in that it's hierarchical and is often imposed upon us by others, while ethnic categories (such as Italian American) can be voluntary, non-hierarchical affiliations.[87] Yet race and ethnicity can blur together; for instance, Hispanic, which some would consider to be a racial category, is treated as an ethnicity on the US Census.[88] As discussed, both Snooki and her costar, Jennifer "Jwoww" Farley, are arguably presented as white on their shows.[89] Yet Latina.com has placed both Snooki and Jwoww on a list titled "55 Latinas Who Keep It Real on TV!"[90] Jwoww has some Spanish ancestry, and Snooki was adopted from Chile by an Italian American family, though when she took a DNA test on *Snooki & Jwoww: Moms with Attitude*, it suggested that she is not actually of Chilean descent.[91] The test also revealed no Italian American heritage, though culturally Snooki has been raised with Italian American traditions and self-identifies as a "Guidette." Over the years, Snooki herself has suggested she does not have one clear-cut, stable, racial or ethnic identity. She has made jokes about being "orange" (a nod to her penchant for tanning), and prior to taking the DNA test, she pointed out that since she was adopted, "I could be birthed from, like, dragons and squirrels."[92]

Genetically, Snooki is the result of her DNA test, but DNA does not equal race. We saw this reflected in the public

controversy when the Massachusetts senator Elizabeth Warren produced a genetic report to justify claiming the identity
of Native American.[93] While, again, race has some biological
correlates, our creation and interpretation of racial categories
are social processes. Historically, even full siblings could be
classified as different races given variation in their skin tones,
and this disparately impacted their life experiences. One analysis of the 1910 and 1940 censuses found that mixed-raced
children who were able to pass as white had substantially
better economic outcomes than their siblings.[94] And if race
were purely about our DNA, then racial categories would remain static. Yet some groups that were previously considered
to be racial, such as the Irish, are now thought of as ethnic
groups;[95] conversely, other groups, such as Arab Americans,
have become more racialized over time.[96] Snooki, a pastiche
of genes and culture, destabilizes race as a classificatory system, exposing the blurriness of the taken-for-granted categories that are the basis for our deep social inequalities. Our
difficulty in neatly placing her in a racial category exposes the
fact that race itself is a set of stories we tell ourselves to make
sense of the world, rather than a fixed, natural reality.

But race, though not inherently "real," is "real in [its] consequences."[97] The images that appear on reality TV are part of a
broader collection of narratives, of stereotypes, and of assumptions about moral failure and individual effort. They show us,
through exaggerated imagery, our deeply ingrained racism and
its intersection with the other-isms that govern our lives.

REALITY TV AND RACE IN A POST-FLOYD WORLD

Reality TV sweeps us along on a tour of American inequality. These shows participate in our broader national narrative

about pulling oneself up by one's bootstraps—a narrative that helps to keep us comfortable with our unequal allocation of money and resources and power. But despite its controlling images, the genre shows us glimmers of something broader happening behind the curtain—clues that our social positioning is not just about our personal choices or morality. America's interwoven classism and our racism, which the genre splays out for us in gargantuan caricature, are part of our culture, but they're also *structural*—baked into our institutions, in the way we house, educate, police, and care for our citizens.

This is not to say that our national ideas about race, and their expression via reality TV, are completely static. In a relatively recent development, shows such as *Married to Medicine*, *Dance Moms*, and *The Real Housewives of Potomac* now explicitly break the fourth wall, with the participants discussing their own portrayals in the context of historical stereotyping. It's not shocking that people of color on reality TV are savvy to the ways in which they're portrayed and that they sometimes refuse to play along. This has likely always been the case. (In season three of *America's Next Top Model* back in 2004, for instance, Tyra famously told the potential contestant Eva Pigford that she didn't want to select "another Black bitch" for the show.) But it is telling that the *programs themselves* seem more willing to air these discussions now. If *I Love New York* had included such reflexivity, it would have been a very different show.

Other developments at the intersection of reality TV and race have been less subtle. *Cops* was canceled in 2020, in the wake of George Floyd's death in Minneapolis at the hands of a white police officer and widespread protests over police brutality. *Live PD* (A&E, 2016–2020), which also followed officers on their patrols, was similarly given the chop around the same time. As protesters put on masks and marched with Black Lives Matter during a pandemic, the events surrounding Floyd's death (and Breonna Taylor's death, and Ahmaud Arbery's death, and many others) felt to many like a pivot point for our national dialogue on race. For some of us, the images on shows like *Cops* were always more nauseating than fun, and it seems that, for the moment, mainstream sentiment has also tipped in that direction. The fact that these shows "don't hold up" in a post-Floyd era is perhaps indicative of our country's large-scale reckoning with history.

It remains to be seen whether these events will change the way we think about, and operate around, race for the long haul. Dashcam and cell phone footage now create mini reality shows that make racial inequalities visible to vast swaths of the population. Still, the issues that these new technologies illuminate are not new, and reality TV has shown us this all along. The things Kevin was "angry" about on the first season of *The Real World*—discrimination, lack of access, the structure of the criminal justice system—are the same things that antiracism activists are protesting now. (Indeed, Kevin and his original housemates were still discussing racial injustice when they convened for a reunion series in 2021.) Unscripted programming has long given us a porthole into a culture where a handcuffed and pleading Black man dying from an officer's knee on his neck is horrific but not unbelievable.

And, *Cops* aside, racial stereotypes continue to pervade reality TV. Perhaps one reason for this, besides the fact that *everything* is more amped up on reality TV, is that the genre can get away with being more overtly racist because it purports to represent "reality." One might raise the point that Shereé, Quad, and Tiffany are actual people and that these shows simply present their behavior. But these programs have specifically selected casts who are framed, through editing and curation, by particular narratives. It is not an accident that virtually every dominant stereotype from minstrelsy can still be found on VH1 today. And, like minstrelsy, the genre is a gaudy reflection of how America has historically profited off Black bodies, as labor and as entertainment, in sites specifically designated for that work.

Ultimately, whether or not these representations are appalling or entertaining, and whether or not some performers are working shrewdly within these archetypes or even overtly challenging them, they still cast a bright light on the fundamental distinctions we draw between different swaths of society, the conversations we use to bolster them, and the dire consequences of these distinctions.

8

"We're All Born Naked . . ." (Gender)

A glittering marquee. A maniacal laugh. A figure standing alone in a spotlight, one hand propped on her hip and the other dramatically raised.

Music begins to play, and she struts down the catwalk.

"Covergirl, put the bass in your walk."

Her multicolored dress cascades downward from her cinched waist.

"Head to toe, let your whole body talk."

A coral hoop earring peeks out from beneath her wavy blond wig.

The music stops and she poses again. And then she, drag queen RuPaul, introduces the judges who will be evaluating the contestants this week.

This week, she reminds us, each drag queen competitor has been tasked with transforming one "straight male athlete" into a drag queen. We watch each queen/athlete pair perform a cheerleading routine, followed by a runway walk as "drag sisters" in glamorous attire. Then all of the competitors and their "jocks" assemble on the stage for judging.

"You really embraced your feminine side," guest judge Sharon Osbourne tells one of the jocks, adding that his drag queen "did a great job on the makeup and the hair."

"You're giving me Kardashian!" comedian Margaret Cho tells the same duo. "I'm 'keeping up' with you."

Raja and her partner get less praise, with Sharon likening the jock's walk to a sailor's.

"You did such a good job giving that Madonna face," Margaret tells another of the duos, "which I think is fierce."

"And they both have 'man hands,' just like Madonna," Ru quips.

The other judges cackle.

Finally, Ru and the judges have concerns with the way Carmen has styled her jock. "Because your sister is beefy—very masculine—did you ever consider doing something that feminized the body a little bit more?" Ru asks.

Ru sends the queens backstage to "enjoy an Absolut cocktail in the Interior Illusions lounge" while the judges deliberate. They'll decide which two contestants will have to "lip-synch for their lives," with the weaker lip-syncher ejected from the competition.[1]

If anyone shows us that gender can be *performed*, it's the contestants on *RuPaul's Drag Race*. They (for the most part) give their testimonials in men's clothing and then we watch them metamorphose, swiping blush across their faces, donning evening gowns, and strutting confidently in stilettos. Their femininity is more amped up than the typical *Bachelor* contestant's, their lashes stretching out longer than Ashley I.'s. But while their performances are extreme, they're doing what most of us do every day. As the sociologists Candace West and Don Zimmerman have pointed out, we're all socialized to "do gender" from a young age.[2] We may not be on a literal stage getting judged by comedians and reality stars, but we display our maleness or femaleness for an audience of others who have the same understandings of what it means to be a boy or a girl. As RuPaul has exclaimed on the show, "May the best woman win!"

From flouncy little girls to aggressive men, reality TV's larger-than-life characters show us how we've all been groomed to meet certain gender expectations. They expose gender as a social construction that is buffered by questionable assumptions about who is naturally suited for what behaviors and what roles. And they teach us that gender works on two levels: it's something we *perform* every day, but it's also a broader system that stretches over all of our lives and fundamentally impacts the way society operates. Gender is one of our most basic, important, and enduring social categories—and, like race, it's largely something we've created ourselves.

GOING GLITZ

Before we dive into what these programs can teach us about gender, it's important to note the basic sociological distinction between *sex* (biological, anatomical maleness or femaleness) and *gender* (the social meanings, practices, and identities attached to the sex categories "male" and "female"). Now, this distinction is not without its problems, as some individuals are born intersex (their bodies not immediately fitting our definitions of "male" or "female"),[3] and even our ideas about biological sex are influenced by our cultural understandings of gender.[4] But it's an important distinction, nonetheless, for thinking about how we're socialized to think about "male" and "female" in particular ways that are not necessarily tied to inherent traits.

As West and Zimmerman point out, across social situations, most of us consistently "do gender" as either male or female, and we tend to assume that others are doing the same.[5] Indeed, when you first meet a new person, their gender is likely one of the first things you notice about them; it's an assessment we all make routinely and immediately, and it's baked into our English pronouns. When a man sports short hair and wears a tie and blazer, for instance, that affirms our expectations for the male sex category, and we classify him accordingly. Yet we don't *know* his sex is male. In fact, rarely in life do we know anyone's sex for sure, because we're not typically checking out one another's genitals.

While of course there are some embodied cues as to who fits the male and who fits the female sex category (the shapes of our bodies, the sounds of our voices), we also rely on social cues that work in tandem with these biological factors. Certainly, there are some people who disrupt our understandings of gender—for example, androgynous people, cross-dressers, and nonbinary people. (Also known as "genderqueer," nonbinary people express their gender as not exclusively male or female.) But most of us engage in, and expect to see from others, conventional gender performances.

As West and Zimmerman argue, and as *Toddlers & Tiaras* shows us, we are primed to engage in these performances from the time we are very young children. (In fact, most of us are primed even before then, with gender-specific names, clothing, and toys selected for us while we are still in utero.) Because the show generally focuses on "full glitz" pageants, as opposed to "natural" pageants, the trimmings of femininity are even more pronounced, providing a jumbotron view of how kids get indoctrinated into these displays. "Full glitz" entails hairpieces, ornate dresses, faces full of makeup, and manicured nails. As one mom tells us in a testimonial, when you start out in glitz pageants, "you're gonna say, 'Oh, I would never spray-tan my child. I would never allow her to wear false eyelashes.' I have said all of those things, and so far we have done all of those things." Indeed, she puts her five-year-old daughter, Story, in all of these accoutrements; as they're waiting to go onstage, a random bystander tells her that Story is "so pretty."[6]

We've seen how kids illuminate and reproduce the class system; they do the same with the gender system. The sociologist Barbara Risman has argued that "we need to conceptualize gender as a social structure"—that gender, like the economic system or the political apparatus, stretches over us all and exerts immense influence over our lives.[7] Our individual performances stem from, and feed into, that system. While there are a few boys who compete on *Toddlers*, they wear little suits, with nary a false eyelash or a piece of crinoline to be seen. Compare these kids, also, with the boys on *Friday Night Tykes* (Esquire Network, 2014–2017)—which features youth football players who slap on shoulder pads and crunch their helmets together—and we see that childhood is the place where we learn to become gendered beings.

Once we become adept in these performances, we do them throughout our lives. The Kardashian/Jenner sisters preen, fix their hair, exercise, and accessorize. The Housewives shop, gossip, and whisk us through a series of on-air beauty procedures, from manicures to vaginal tightening. And while we may not all be receiving Botox injections in front of camera crews, we move through the world making similar gender-based decisions about how we adorn ourselves, what we put into our bodies, and how we interact with others.

"WE'RE ALL BORN NAKED . . ."

Though we are socialized to participate in these everyday performances, West and Zimmerman point out, we then turn around and justify them as *natural* and *innate*. As reality TV teaches us, we cling to these biological ideas about gender, even in situations where they're clearly being challenged or there's evidence to the contrary.

This brings us back to *RuPaul's Drag Race*.

The show features drag queens who compete in various challenges, runway walks, and lip syncs for a panel of judges, including host RuPaul; the winner receives money, prizes, and the title of "America's Next Drag Superstar." On the one hand, as I've mentioned, this show exposes gender as something that is socially constructed. Recall that, for Judith Butler, drag is an illuminating practice that exposes gender itself as a social fiction. *"In imitating gender,"* she tells us, *"drag implicitly reveals the imitative structure of gender itself—as well as its contingency."*[8] (Fun fact: season nine's Sasha Velour briefly considered portraying Judith Butler for one of the show's challenges!) Also recall that when we "do" gender, we typically confirm others' perceptions of our sex category.[9] The queens on the show—mainly cisgender gay men who put on wigs, eyelashes, ball gowns, heels, and makeup—disrupt this process. Further, there have been some transgender contestants, and there are times when the queens do androgynous drag or "boy drag"—the message being that gender and the physical body are like accessories that can be mixed and matched. As RuPaul tells us repeatedly, "We're all born naked, and the rest is drag."

On the other hand, even *Drag Race* is not immune from our persistent cultural idea that gender is rooted in biology. The queens typically take all sorts of measures to approximate female-sexed bodies. They shave their facial stubble; they "contour" their makeup to create the illusion of feminine cheekbones; they "tuck" (taping back the penis and scrotum, to eliminate the bulge); they put on fake breasts; and they cinch their waists and add padding to create hourglass silhouettes. The judges critique them when they do these things ineffectively. Contestants are praised for being "fish"—that is, looking convincingly like cisgender women. And while RuPaul may repeatedly state that drag is what we *put on* our naked bodies, the celebrity drag queen has also suggested that trans women who undergo transitional surgeries are not welcome to apply for the show, likening such procedures to "performance-enhancing drugs."[10] (As of this writing, there have also never been any cisgender women on the show.) While RuPaul has since apologized for the comment, it reflects how our cultural ideas about the link between anatomy and gender continue to endure, even in places where the boundaries of gender are being pushed. If gender is simply a performance, unlinked to anatomy, then why is "tucking" necessary?

Speaking of nudity, let's return to Shane and Kim from *Naked and Afraid* for a moment. "Can a man and woman survive alone in the wilderness naked and afraid?" the narrator asks in the opening segment of the show, and each episode continually emphasizes that a *man* and a *woman* have been selected for this challenge. With the introduction and the nudity, the show makes a clear nod to Adam and Eve and our notion of two biologically distinct beings. Sometimes, the naked people themselves also promote this notion. For example,[11] after Shane kills the same species of snake that had previously bitten the show's producer, Kim says she doesn't know if she could have even approached the creature.

"Women aren't natural hunters," Shane tells her.

"What do you mean by that?" she asks.

"I think they're [bleep]ing weak. They bitch and moan and complain about every little thing."

Shane's comment tells us a couple of things about ourselves. First, he's demonstrating how we use biological language ("natural") to describe and to legitimate gender differences. Second, this is an instance of dramatic irony, because Shane objectively does much more complaining than Kim on the show. In this way, the show also exposes that these roles are not raw biological certainties.

While *Naked and Afraid* ostensibly focuses on a twosome composed of opposites, it also shows the cracks in this paradigm. The women on the show complicate our conception of a stark male/female dichotomy with their strength, toughness, and ambition. According to one analysis of the show,[12] its female participants are slightly less likely than their male partners to quit. "It was surprising to everybody involved that the steely determination of the women is just unparalleled," one of the show's producers told *Elle* magazine in 2016. "We certainly haven't come up with the answers for it, but it is recognized that, overall, the women seem to be more badass than the men."[13]

One might argue that this happens because the show is picking particularly "badass" women, and that's fair enough, but they're picking particularly tough men as well. These are *all* people who are willing to be left alone in the jungle for twenty-one days. *Naked and Afraid* doesn't prove that women are tougher or stronger than men, nor does it show that there are zero innate differences between males and females. But it does cast doubt on a rigid binary where "male/female" aligns with "tough/weak." Along these lines, it's pertinent that while men (generally speaking) make better time on short runs and marathons, in extreme endurance competitions such as ultramarathons, it's not out of the question for women to perform as well as or better than their male counterparts.[14] The

Naked and Afraid twosome, by calling into question what we thought we knew about male and female bodies and traits, exposes the social fiction of oppositeness that we may take for granted as biological fact.

As Gayle Rubin has pointed out, "opposite sexes" is a misnomer. The two sexes are not "opposed"; the absence of one is not the presence of the other. "Men and women are, of course, different," Rubin has observed. "But they are not as different as day and night, earth and sky, yin and yang, life and death. In fact, from the standpoint of nature, men and women are closer to each other than either is to anything else—for instance, mountains, kangaroos, or coconut palms."[15] (Other scholars, too, have emphasized the similarities between men's and women's bodies. The sociologist Judith Lorber points out that "except for procreative hormones and organs,"[16] they're basically the same.) Clearly, some people are born with penises and some with vaginas, and, yes, there are some people who fit comfortably into our broad characterizations of "masculine men" and "feminine women." But, Rubin argues, that doesn't mean that men and women in general are distinct types of beings, who need to serve fundamentally different social functions. In different ways, *Drag Race* and *Naked and Afraid* each shows us both sides of this: our notion of an innate gender binary as well as the flaws in that notion.

"MADONNA IN THE BEDROOM . . ."

Why are we so eager to believe that our gender practices are logical extensions of our sex chromosomes? We rely on these ideas about gender being rooted in biology because they serve a certain function within society. As Lorber explains, "The continuing purpose of gender as a modern social institution is to construct women as a group to be subordinate to men as a group."[17] Like our controlling images of poor and working-class people, or the racial stereotypes that have their roots in minstrelsy, our long-standing beliefs about women and men as "naturally" different helps to justify the unequal roles we play in the home, the workplace, politics, and the economy. So while scholars like West and Zimmerman aren't telling women to stop wearing nail polish or men to stop using chain saws, they are prompting us to think about how these everyday gender displays can accrue and become meaningful on a broader level. "Doing gender" is not just a senseless performance, but it can have *weight*, sustaining the current power structure.

In an extreme way, *19 Kids and Counting* reveals how our gender socialization of children can potentially have far-reaching consequences. There is a stark division of labor in the Duggar home. This is illuminated in an episode where the boys and girls of the family switch "jurisdictions" for the day.[18] Jurisdictions, as daughter Jill explains, "are the chores we're supposed to keep [*sic*] on a daily basis."

"The girls do a *lot* of work around the house," Jim Bob admits, saying that they're "the ones that actually keep the house going." Indeed, when the kids swap roles, it's clear that the girls regularly do the everyday chores such as cooking, cleaning, and laundry, while the boys have only occasional tasks, such as changing the car's oil.

In this episode, the Duggars allow us to see not only how we all learn to "do gender" from an early age but also how these learned behaviors can translate to the reproduction of inequalities. As we've seen, adult women do more household work and more childcare than men.[19] This is the case in heterosexual marriages even when both partners work outside of the home. According to the U.S. Bureau of Labor Statistics, about 56 percent of married mothers who are employed full-time do some housework on an average day, versus only 18 percent of full-time employed, married fathers.[20] And these asymmetrical household contributions *matter*. They're one factor in the so-called wage penalty for motherhood and wage premium for fatherhood—that is, mothers earn *less* than non-mothers, while fathers earn *more* than childless men.[21] Relatedly, women also have less leisure time than men,[22] and the free time they do have is of lower quality and is more likely to be interrupted by household and childcare demands.[23]

Our notion of men and women as opposite sexes with vastly different attributes and abilities is reflected in the way that men's and women's labor has been organized, particularly within a capitalist context. As the feminist economist Heidi Hartmann has observed, under capitalism, "we are all workers," and women's job is to reproduce the labor force (in a literal, biological sense and in the sense of feeding and caring for husbands and little future workers) as well as to maintain the domestic sphere.[24] In short, women have historically performed all sorts of behind-the-scenes work for which they've received no direct financial compensation. Hartmann links the separation of men's and women's roles to the overall gender power imbalance in society, noting, "Men exercise their control in receiving personal service work from women, in not having to do housework or rear children, in having access to women's bodies for sex, and in feeling powerful and being powerful."[25]

Hartmann's critique of capitalism, and of the breadwinner/homemaker model within it, was published in 1979, and it may strike us as extreme or outdated today. One might argue that we no longer use biologically based arguments to keep women in the home—because women are *not* in the home. As we've seen, the breadwinner/homemaker model is not our dominant one. Many more women are in the workforce now than there were when Hartmann was writing.[26] In addition to the increase in female breadwinners, men are doing more in the home. One study from 2000 found, for instance, that the amount of time men spent on housework had almost doubled since 1965.[27]

But: reality TV shows us how we are still beholden to that model. When schools and day cares closed during the COVID-19 pandemic, for example, women were more likely than men to scale back or terminate their employment in order to attend to their children. "Women do an average of 75% of the world's total unpaid-care work, including child care, caring for the elderly, cooking, and cleaning," one analysis by the *Harvard Business Review* found in September 2020. "As Covid-19 has disproportionately increased the time women spend on family responsibilities, women have dropped out of the workforce at a higher rate than explained by labor-market dynamics alone."[28]

We also continue to define women through their relationships with men. Reality TV seizes upon, and illuminates, these strong cultural associations. This is evident in the bevy of wife-themed reality shows, ranging from *Basketball Wives* and *Married to Medicine* to *Mob Wives* and, of course, *The Real Housewives* franchises. A show like *Wife Swap* works because home is primarily the wives' domain, so we're able to observe how they function in each other's habitats. The term "housewife" may seem like a bit of a relic, perhaps conjuring up images of poodle-skirted pill poppers with bouffant hairdos. Today we're probably more likely to say "stay-at-home mom" or indicate that someone "doesn't work outside of the home," highlighting the importance of domestic labor as work. But the reality genre demonstrates how, whatever terminology we use, we still nudge along the ideas of "men's" and "women's" separate spheres.

Further related to Hartmann's point, the very titles of the *Housewives* shows define women through their heterosexual relationships with men, while is there no reverse equivalent of *Husbands* shows. (To my knowledge, there's been only BET's *Real Husbands of Hollywood*, which was a fictionalized parody of a reality show.) Some of the Black women on shows such as *Love & Hip Hop*, *The Real Housewives of Atlanta*, and *Basketball Wives* are presented as grasping gold diggers. On these programs, the women are often attached to men in the sports and entertainment industries, in a racialized riff on the theme of women being extensions of their male partners.

The concept of women being defined through their connections to their husbands has a long social history not confined to unscripted TV. The anthropologist Claude Lévi-Strauss has traced how, within early kinship systems, women functioned as forms of "sexual property."[29] Our taboo against incest, he has argued, developed as a response to the fact that women needed to be passed across social groups—which could bring solidarity and lead to the formation of political alliances. While we're not usually passing women around like chattel to maintain these alliances anymore, the concept of wives as attachments to their husbands is still prominent, both on unscripted TV and in life. One national survey from 2011, for instance, found that approximately half of Americans thought it was a good idea for states to legally *require* women to change their last names to their husbands' upon marrying.[30] Our TV screens show us how echoes of Hartmann's and Lévi-Strauss's kinship models still move faintly through the cultural ether.

Sometimes, they're not even that faint.

We've observed how Patti Stanger, of "the penis does the picking" fame, uses biological language to justify men's and women's opposite dating roles. She also expects these roles to extend into marriage—something that becomes apparent in the first episode of *The Millionaire Matchmaker*.[31] Here, Patti explains that her male clients want "Madonna in the bedroom, Martha Stewart in the kitchen, Mary Poppins in the nursery," a line she uses repeatedly over the course of the series. She exposes women's role in reproducing the labor force when she weeds out older women from consideration for a date, indicating that her male client is "ready to have babies by Tuesday." While she does value women's intelligence—saying she's looking for "beauty, brains, and class" and "*Maxim* with the Harvard degree"—and she doesn't begrudge women for working outside of the home, she places parameters on that work. For instance, she critiques one woman who introduces herself as "Doctor," saying, "If you lead with your professional foot, the man's ding-dong goes down." A male doesn't want to compete with you, Patti advises the woman. In stating her guidelines so bluntly, Patti shows us the persistence of gender-specific expectations that have real implications for how women and men experience family life.

It may be easy to shrug off the way gender is presented on reality TV because, say, the pageant moms hot-glue things to their kids, or because Patti has silly one-liners about penises, or because there are just so many Duggars. But while these reality stars may be extreme in some ways, they illuminate a system that genders us from the moment we emerge from the biological flume, instructs us to give male and female performances, and then teaches us that these performances are biologically based and should be assigned different societal weight. And most of us are participants. I'm a participant every time I move a lipstick tube to my mouth, keep my opinion to myself in a meeting, bake cookies for my students, and adorn my children. Few of us are painting our boys' rooms pink and putting ribbons in their hair. Few of us are enrolling our girls in youth football. While part of the appeal of shows such as *19 Kids and Counting* and *The Millionaire Matchmaker* might be that the stars are so wacky, they're also the long shadows we have cast.

REALITY TV'S TRANS-ITIONS

To be clear, not everyone on reality TV conforms to retrograde gender stereotypes. The genre also shows us a diversity of gender identities and practices, if we know where to look.

For one thing, we can't ignore that unscripted programming was at the cusp of transgender representation, long before most people had ever heard of a "preferred pronoun." Back in 2005, the Sundance Channel aired *TransGeneration*: a reality show that followed two trans women and two trans men who were attending US colleges. Trans woman Katelynn Cusanelli appeared as a cast member on *The Real World: Brooklyn* in 2008, and since then multiple unscripted shows have focused on trans women (though, interestingly, seldom trans men), including *Becoming Us* (ABC Family, 2015), *I Am Jazz* (TLC, 2015–present), and *I Am Cait* (E!, 2015–2016).

This is not to suggest that trans representations on reality TV have always been peachy. One look at the British show *There's Something About Miriam* (Sky1, 2003)—in which six men competed for the affections of model Miriam Rivera, only to find out that she was transgender in the final episode—provides evidence to the contrary. For years, transphobic slurs were not out of the ordinary on reality TV. On the fourth season of *Project Runway* in 2008, for example, the designer Christian Siriano referred to sloppy garments as "hot tranny messes"; his castmates never challenged the choice of words. For six seasons, *RuPaul's Drag Race* included a segment in which the contestants received video "mail" from RuPaul, the disembodied voice of the host declaring, "Oooh, gurl, *you've got she-mail!*" In addition to this wordplay on the slur "she-male," in 2014 the sixth season of the show included a challenge called "Female or Shemale," in which the contestants viewed a close-up photo of a celebrity and then had to determine whether that person was a "biological woman" (female) or a "psychological woman" (shemale).

But the evolution of reality TV also shows us how much our attitudes about transgender people have shifted over a relatively short period. This is not to suggest that trans people are no longer stigmatized. They still experience high rates of gender-based violence,[32] and they struggle to have their identities validated. The Trump administration, for example, attempted to ban transgender individuals from the military and called for a national definition of "gender" that would make it synonymous with biological sex at birth.

At the same time, there has also been a palpable shift—both on unscripted programming and out in the real world—in terms of how we think and talk about transgender people. While contestants on *Drag Race* still watch videos from RuPaul, the tagline "You've Got She-mail" was retired in season six. And although many other challenges on the show have reappeared across multiple seasons, "Female or Shemale" was relegated to the dustbin of history. Further, there have now been trans-identifying contestants on the show. Beyond the realm of reality TV, in recent years *Harry Potter* author J. K. Rowling has been condemned for her trans-exclusionary views. As of 2019, there were twenty transgender elected officials in the US (up from thirteen the year before).[33] Many major forms of insurance now offer coverage for gender-confirmation surgeries. Gender-neutral bathrooms—while contested—are cropping up across America. A phrase such as "hot tranny mess" would likely *not* fly under the radar on *Project Runway* today, and that tells us something about our evolving dialogue about, and understandings of, people who seem to challenge our ideas about the connection between gender and biological sex.

Reality programs have also played with traditional gender expectations in ways that go beyond trans representation—giving us drag queens, female bodybuilders,[34] and boys who love sewing dresses (*Project Runway: Junior*, Lifetime, 2015–2016). And while many reality programs perpetuate the cultural narrative of men as financial providers and women as domestically oriented, there are also moments when the genre drops the veil and reveals that the heterosexual bread-winner/homemaker model is not a universal, historical truth. I'm not the first to point out that *The Real Housewives* is a misnomer, as a lot of these women are single and/or have paying jobs—and, technically, they're *all* running afoul of the definition by getting paid to appear on the show. And despite the Kardashian/Jenner women's professed devotion to their men and to traditional gender roles in some ways, they are actively reaping the rewards of capitalism—not sitting on the sidelines, as they would within Hartmann's model.

UPSETTING THE APPLE CART?

Before we get too comfortable thinking about reality TV's women as soldiers in a gender revolution, however, it's important to note that one of the things that has allowed women to move into the workforce—both on these shows and in life—is their reliance on *other women*. We've undergone what the sociologist Rhacel Salazar Parreñas has termed a "work transfer system"[35] of domestic labor from one group of women (often white) to another (often people of color). Women still perform many domestic duties—cleaning, childcare, eldercare. On reality shows, if we pay close enough attention, we can spy flashes of the female paid domestic helpers who assist wealthier families in functioning. Tori Spelling may be back to booking acting gigs on *Tori & Dean: Home Sweet Hollywood*, but Patsy's watching little Liam while she auditions. And Beverly Hills Housewife Lisa Vanderpump may be running a restaurant empire, but Rocio's in her bedroom cleaning the closet.

We get one of those glimpses, for instance, on *Tidying Up with Marie Kondo* (Netflix, 2019). On the show, professional organizer Marie Kondo teaches families how to weed out their belongings and streamline their clutter. (To be clear, the affluent Kondo, who doesn't do much of the manual work of the cleaning, is not the domestic worker in this instance.) In the first episode, "Tidying with Toddlers," we meet Rachel and Kevin, who have two young children and who say that they fight about the laundry. Kevin says that he doesn't necessarily expect his wife to do it all by herself, but he also doesn't see why they're currently paying someone else to do it, "because we're perfectly capable of doing those things." The resolution at the end of the episode, though, is that Rachel is now the one doing the laundry—a scenario that aligns with women's broader role in the domestic sphere. But what's also illuminating is their mention of the laundry "helper," who had been coming in to fold their clothes and whom they've now let go. We learn, through Rachel, that the helper is fine with this development, as she wants whatever is best for the family, but we don't actually hear that from the helper because she's referenced but unseen.

Rachel and Kevin's helper, whoever she is, joins a coterie of other workers who occasionally, and usually briefly, sail onto these shows to assist in the home. (There are a few exceptions—for instance, Jeff Lewis's housekeeper, Zoila, who had a major role on *Flipping Out* [Bravo, 2007–2018]). Like Black contestants on *The Bachelor*, they sometimes serve as sounding boards for the central protagonists of these shows, and through these interactions they highlight characteristics of these main characters. On the first season of *The Real Housewives of New York City*, for instance, LuAnn's housekeeper, Rosie, functions mainly as a foil for LuAnn's out-of-touch snobbery. Through their fleeting appearances, they also reveal the network of laborers who linger in the background of our conversations about men, women, and domestic work. They show us that even when women move into the workforce, that doesn't necessarily radically shake the foundation of how we think about men and women and the roles they are suited to perform.

And when women *don't* conform to the roles and expectations that society has laid out for them, they are often pushed back in line, on reality TV as in life. It's no accident that the "bitch" stereotype and "nouveau riche buffoon" stereotype often get applied not just to Black people but to Black *women*. Those at the bottom of the race/gender hierarchy are in danger of upsetting the apple cart of power with their toughness, ambition, or financial success. Reality TV, and pop culture in general, shows us how we seek to maintain the power structure by stuffing such women back down where they "belong." In the classic film *Baby Boom* (1987), for instance, Diane Keaton's high-powered, big-city yuppie character learns the virtues of moving to a rural town, raising a baby, and making apple-sauce. While that movie came out when I was still young enough to believe in Santa Claus, its blueprint is repeated today on numerous Lifetime movies and Hallmark Christmas specials, in which female go-getters ultimately come to appreciate slow, small-town living—and snag men! And on reality TV, silly "rich" (or ostensibly moneyed) women, Black and white, proliferate. By presenting them as buffoonish spectacles, unable to correctly behave like elites, we similarly put them in their place.

THE MEAN JUDGE

I've often heard it said that when it comes to representation, reality TV is an equal opportunity offender. That is, no social group comes away smelling like roses. My response to this is twofold: First, it's important to look not only at *whether* certain groups are portrayed negatively but also *how* they're portrayed, in order to better understand our cultural rifts. And second, straight white men often come away smelling pretty good.

While to some extent we delight in the failures of men on reality TV—for instance, the villain on the gamedoc who finally gets booted and vain and dopey male contestants on *The Bachelorette*—the genre also shows us how we prop up rude and aggressive men in a way we don't really do with women. Perhaps nowhere in reality TV land is this more apparent than in the case of the mean judge. Mean judges such as Simon Cowell and Gordon Ramsay are a staple of competition shows. Simon, a music industry executive who has splashed around from talent show lily pad to lily pad comparing performers to "a baby crying" and "three cats being dragged up the motorway," is one of the highest-paid personalities on TV. His net worth is an estimated $550 million, and he took in $95 million in 2017 alone.[36] Gordon, a celebrity chef who has been featured on well over a dozen reality programs, including the competitive cooking shows *Hell's Kitchen* (Fox, 2005–present) and *MasterChef* (Fox, 2010–present), is similarly known for slinging caustic barbs. He likes to use the word "fuck," mainly in telling chefs on his shows to "fuck off." Some of his favorite epithets are "dickface" and "you donkey." He once threw a fillet at a chef who had ruined it, sneering as he asked, "What are you going to do, get daddy to buy you a new one?" With an estimated net worth of $118 million, by one metric he is the second-richest chef in the world.[37]

Mean judges like Gordon and Simon are able to fit cozily into the mean role, and to profit from it, in part because of *who* they are. If you look at articles and listicles dedicated to the "meanest" or "harshest" or "worst" competition judges, a pattern emerges: they're predominantly white men. Yes, sometimes a person of color and/or a woman sneaks on there. For instance, Janice Dickinson from vintage *America's Next Top Model* makes the cut sometimes, but she also lasted only four seasons of the show, which persisted into its mid-twenties. The harsh judges who have really had legs, though? Gordon Ramsay, Len Goodman, Michael Kors, Nigel Lythgoe, Piers Morgan, Simon Cowell, and Donald Trump. All white men.

This pattern on reality TV mirrors our tolerance for meanness and aggression in real life. There is ample sociological evidence that women and people of color are evaluated more harshly for not playing nice. Aggressive women are rated more negatively than aggressive men,[38] and when women in leadership positions are "autocratic or directive" (i.e., when their leadership is carried out "in stereotypically masculine styles"), they tend to be judged for it.[39] Girls and women are socialized to display communal traits, such as caring and nurturing,[40] and are criticized as unlikable or shrill when they don't conform to these stereotypes.

While Hillary Clinton is a divisive figure, for instance, it is telling that people don't seem to mind her as much when she's *not* seeking power. One analysis found that her popularity plummets when she's running for office,[41] while another found that her approval rating rises when she encounters hardships. As one writer for *Vox* observed in 2016, Americans "like her least when she's ambitious, when she's breaking barriers and engaging in political fights. They like her most when that ambition is thwarted and she's relegated to a more familiar, traditional role."[42]

While we reward Simon Cowell's mean comments with our continued viewership, a hypothetical Simone Cowell might not fare as well. Simon's whiteness likely insulates him, too, as research suggests that we judge people of color more harshly for exhibiting bad behavior. Analyses of sentencing records, for instance, suggest that Black, Hispanic, and Native American defendants receive more stringent penalties than white defendants for the same crimes.[43] One study even found that prospective employers evaluated whites *with* criminal records slightly more favorably than Black applicants *without* records.[44]

Gordon and Simon are able to profit from the mean role, not only through their own efforts but because of their broader social positioning. This is not to say that only men can be terrible (Leona Helmsley) or that the criminal behavior of a nonwhite person has never gone unchecked (R. Kelly). But Gordon and Simon are part of a more general pattern in the types of behavior we are willing to let slide and from which types of people. Another example from real life is actor Jeffrey Tambor (of *Arrested Development* and *Transparent*), who was accused of sexual harassment in 2018. His response was to declare that while he has been "mean" and "difficult" and has yelled at his colleagues on set, he has "never been a predator."[45] This led to a series of think-pieces about how we have gotten to a place where "just" being mean is somehow okay for men like him.[46] What Simon Cowell, Gordon Ramsay, and Jeffrey Tambor have in common is that they are white, male, wealthy, and in positions of power within creative industries.

We've seen how reality stars can capitalize on existing archetypes; however, as the mean judges show us, they can't just inhabit these roles at random. It's easier to slip into the "mean" space if you're already in the "white male creative genius" space. When adults on reality TV engage in behavior that might get a four-year-old booted from preschool, they're not always stigmatized for it, and the instances in which we accept it are synced up with broader circuits of power. Our ideas about which gender is naturally suited for what role, in turn, fortify those circuits, so that our cultural narratives and our gender structure function together in one immense loop.

GENDER ON REALITY TV: IT'S A DRAG

We tell ourselves that men and women are distinct creatures suited to do specific types of things—in our everyday interactions, in the workplace and in the home, and in our broader culture. And unscripted programming lays that all out for us. Not all women on reality TV are homemakers, but they're often shown and discussed in the context of the home—certainly more than their male counterparts. We view men as naturally aggressive and assertive, and we're okay with that—particularly if they're white and already powerful. And we stereotype women as not very smart, as we see on shows such as *Beauty and the Geek* (The WB, 2005–2006; The CW, 2007–2008), which paired up supposed female airheads and smart men to compete in a series of challenges. Perhaps the most notable instance of the bimbo stereotype occurred on *Newlyweds: Nick and Jessica* (MTV, 2003–2005)—a show where singer Jessica Simpson notoriously asked her then husband Nick Lachey whether Chicken of the Sea tuna was chicken or fish.

We also stereotype women as overemotional and crazy, as we see on shows such as *Bridezillas* and in the brawls on *Bad Girls Club* and *Love & Hip Hop*. It is significant that crime-themed reality TV focusing on women tends to highlight the role of emotion in their crimes. This is particularly apparent on *Snapped* (Oxygen, 2004–present), a program that focuses mainly on white female killers. The title itself is gendered; like *Bridezillas*, it reflects our stereotype of females as hyper-emotional.[47] It also suggests that women are not predisposed to commit such crimes; they're simply pushed to the brink. In one episode, for example, forty-six-year-old Cynthia ("Cyndi") George is married to a restaurateur, has seven children, and becomes the prime suspect when her former lover is killed in what appears to be a professional hit.[48] While the victim being gunned down in broad daylight outside of a gas station was jarring, the show explains, the "biggest shocker" of the case was that the trail led to Cyndi. "It was pretty hard to buy that she would do something like this," one of the interviewees recalls. The narrator and interviewees variously characterize Cyndi as a "petite former cheerleader," "very vivacious, very attractive," "young, beautiful," and a "beautiful wife and mother." Beyond this episode, *Snapped* often highlights its protagonists' appearances in framing them as unlikely killers, as though conventional female attractiveness were an inoculant against criminality. The "crazy/emotional woman on reality TV" archetype also proliferated on social media in 2019, when a meme emerged of *Real Housewives of Beverly Hills'* Taylor pointing a finger and screaming, juxtaposed with a photo of a calm-looking cat at a dinner table.

The reality genre demonstrates how these cultural ideas about gender are deeply ingrained, just like our conceptions of class and race. It shows us how gender continues to be one of our most crucial social categories—something that permeates our language, our way of seeing the world, and our evaluations of others. It appears on every form that passes through our hands and every ID we carry. Yet, while gender norms are central to our experiences, they are not inevitable.

And by being *so* over the top, reality TV teaches us that, too.

Going back to Judith Butler's point about drag, she argued that by showing, in an extreme way, that female gender performances don't need to be done by people with vaginas, drag queens aren't mocking women—rather, they're mocking society's idea of gender itself and our notion that it's biologically based.[49] In a similar way, reality TV's extreme bimbos, crazies, and meanies show us the stereotypes about gender that lurk in our culture. By splashing these cartoonish images across our screens, the genre isn't just presenting us with absurd people. It's also showing us the absurdity of these representations and, consequently, *the absurdity of gender as a social construct.* Simply put, reality TV offers us numerous people who are presenting gender in dragged-up ways—only some of whom are literal drag queens.

It's entertaining when RuPaul dons a flowing wig, silly when brides attack people with bouquets, riveting when we're waiting to hear Simon's next cruel zinger, laughable when a voice-over asks, "How could someone so beautiful be a *killer*?" and absurd when sobbing Taylor is juxtaposed with a smirking cat. But this bustling festival of gender stereotyping is not removed from our own lives. Is it any less odd when we believe that only people whose genitals are shaped in a particular way should put on lipstick? Is it any less absurd that we question why a man might want to be a stay-at-home parent or wonder whether a woman has the right comportment to run a country? In the end, reality TV teaches us that the vast majority of us are part of this charade—through our own performances, our expectations of others, and the types of language we use every day to keep this system in place.

9

"Food, a Drink, and a Gay" (Sexuality)

"I'm bisexual, and I [bleep]ing love it!"

A blond woman wearing a tube top and red lipstick declares this enthusiastically, as punchy music plays in the background.

We hear from a few other cast members.

"I am very proud of being bisexual. I think of it as a superpower," a beefy white guy with dark curly hair tells us, smiling.

The upcoming season unfurls for us in a series of short clips: women kissing men, men kissing men, women kissing women.

The words "Come one, come all" flash across the screen in neon.

Squished into one frame for a testimonial, a group of castmates talk to the camera one after another:

"Are you ready, America?"

"'Cause I doubt it."

"Let's [bleep]ing *go*!"[1]

We might sometimes wonder whether reality TV has anything more left to show us. From "seven strangers" in a New York loft, the genre has widened into an expansive landscape, populated by many people outside of the mainstream. Yet when season eight of the MTV dating show *Are You the One?* (2014–present) premiered in 2019, and it featured all people who were attracted to more than one gender, the premise felt groundbreaking to many.

Perhaps, if any television genre were going to stake its claim on sexual fluidity, it had to be reality. Unscripted programming has long been on the vanguard of sexual diversity in some ways. Non-heterosexual characters like Lance and Pedro have been a staple of the genre since the beginning. The LGBTQ advocacy group GLAAD has even lauded the genre for its inclusivity, noting, "As a medium, unscripted television began telling queer and trans stories long before scripted television started to catch up."[2]

Still, this season of *Are You the One?* felt different. Both the show's participants and the journalists who wrote about it suggested that its emphasis on sexual fluidity was a new move. And this tells us something important about how we, as a society, think about sexuality. "Sexuality" is a blanket term used to describe "desire, sexual preference, sexual identity, and behavior,"[3] and when we think about it, we tend to rely on categories, just as we do with skin tone, genital shape, and wallet thickness. We've seen how the concept of "opposite sexes" suggests that our existing gender roles are based in biology and are thereby correct. But the idea that men and women are complementary creatures is also used to reinforce the notion that they are, and should be, naturally attracted *to each other*.[4] In this way, our biological ideas about gender are inextricably linked with our notions about sexuality.

Sexual labels remain central to our culture. Why?

Recall how Michel Foucault argued that by developing procedures to shield children from sex, we in effect sexualize those children. This is part of his broader theory about how we treat sex in our culture. Foucault pointed out that while we might think that sex is a verboten subject, over the past few centuries there's actually been a "discursive explosion" of talk about the topic.[5] That is, we may be puritanical about sex in some ways, but we also talk about it all the time. And we're told *how* to talk about it by powerful social institutions that divide sexual behaviors into various categories, often in efforts to curb or corral them.

The reality genre exposes both sides of this dynamic: the "explosion" and the regulation. From Kim Kardashian's sex tape to the fantasy suites on *The Bachelor*, reality TV is a sexy genre. Yet while it may be a font of sexual diversity (relatively speaking), it also shows us how conservative and reductionist we still are about sex.

REMEMBER: "NIKE!"

In America, sex is taboo but everywhere. It's hemmed in by prohibitions, but in enforcing those prohibitions, we do a lot of thinking and talking about it. I've traced how shows such as *To Catch a Predator* and *Toddlers & Tiaras* illuminate our social understandings of childhood—but they're also a lightning rod for our attitudes regarding sex more generally. The fact that one reality show is ostensibly protecting kids from sexual predators while another is outfitting them in cone bras is squarely in line with our broader cultural ambivalence around sexuality.

Foucault points out that by controlling the ways we understand sex, powerful institutions are able to exert control over *us*. He thought of power as more diverse and diffuse than did someone like Karl Marx, who described how one group directly exerts power over another. Power doesn't stem from just one source, Foucault argued. Instead, major social institutions—such as medicine, the law, the educational system, and religion—use "polymorphous techniques of power."[6] For instance, they affect our attitudes and behaviors by controlling our *language* around sex—our "discourse"—in multiple, sometimes insidious ways.

On reality TV, we can watch sexual discourses wend their way through these institutions, and we can see the results. On *Sex Rehab with Dr. Drew* (VH1, 2009), for example, Dr. Drew Pinsky, a medical doctor, treated celebrities for sexual addictions—showing us the medical establishment's role in distinguishing between normal and pathological sex. And the Duggars are highly conservative about sex, but their lives are a series of procedures (remember: "Nike!") inspired by religion and designed to avoid all but heterosexual, marital, procreative, adult sex. Further, this family has worked through the legal system to promote this singular form of acceptable sex. Son Josh has led at least one rally against marriage equality and has served as the executive director of an organization classified as an anti-LGBT hate group by the Southern Poverty Law Center.[7] The *16 and Pregnant* girls, meanwhile, show us the role of the educational system in promoting ideas about the unacceptability of teen sex and the virtues of abstinence.

Americans may be a bit sexually repressed, but we don't keep sex quiet. We do, however, talk about it in particular ways that sync up with broader systems of power. Marx and Engels have made the point that "life is not determined by consciousness, but consciousness by life."[8] That is, the basic ways that we think about the world are not just a collective pooling of our individual thoughts. While they may differ on the sources of power, Foucault, Marx, and Engels have all described how our belief systems are forged by powerful agglomerations of people with specific agendas.

Just as we do with gender, race, and class, we reinforce our sexual hierarchy by then turning around and falsely perceiving those systems as universal and inherently valid. For instance, we use the idea of natural gender difference to support what Gayle Rubin calls "compulsory heterosexuality"[9]—the idea that men and women are, and should be, biologically attracted to each other only. While heterosexuality may be less "compulsory" now than it was when Rubin was writing in the mid-1970s, our culture remains heteronormative at its core. For instance, same-sex marriage has only recently become legally recognized in the States, and queer people, but not straight people, are expected to "come out" with their identities.

Foucault and others have reflected upon our long history of assigning value to bodies based on their sexual preferences and behaviors and then organizing those bodies accordingly—moving them, for instance, into prisons and mental institutions[10] and ejecting them from our families.[11] And the reality genre highlights how we divide up the world into types of sexual bodies and arrange them in social and physical space. Indeed, while the genre is in some senses inclusive of queer identities, its landscape is stratified by sexual orientation the way it is by race and ethnicity. Just as the African American–centered BET and the Spanish-language network Univision both have original reality shows on their schedules, so, too, are there "gay shows," which cluster on networks such as Logo.

On other networks, producers use multicasting to ensure that their shows are not *too* gay. For example, Amy Shpall, the executive producer of *Work Out* (Bravo, 2006–2008)—a show focused on openly gay Jackie Warner and her crew of personal trainers—has explicitly admitted that Bravo executives asked for some "very straight" men to balance out Doug and Jesse, two gay male trainers.[12] In this way, reality TV—much like the real world, with its gay neighborhoods,[13] gay bars, gay cruises, and gay clubs—has spaces that are explicitly queer oriented but also spaces where queer people have limited entry or are denied. Very few male professional athletes, for instance, are openly non-heterosexual. And it's not likely that we'll have a gay *Bachelor* anytime soon.

THE SEXUAL INVISIBLES

We don't simply place people into boxes—we then assign differential meaning and value to those boxes. Previously, we saw Rubin's argument that we have created a "sexual hierarchy" that coincides with "certified mental health, respectability, legality, social and physical mobility, institutional support, and material benefits."[14] We come to think of marital, reproductive sex as the most "legitimate" form of sex, at the apex of the pyramid. This may be why it's socially acceptable for your coworker to gab about how she's been trying and trying to have a baby with her husband, but not about the queer poly bondage party she attended last weekend (well, depending upon your workplace . . .).

The reality genre casts a bright light on the grid of our sexual landscape. It shows us the importance of these categories we've created and how they impact the stories we tell and the images we see. For instance, it's significant that queer-themed reality shows are nearly always relegated to cable networks, rather than being shown on more mainstream, network TV.

Perhaps *most* telling, though, are the sexual categories that fade into the background of reality TV. For example, a Wikipedia search suggests that while at least eighteen US reality programs have featured a gay man or men as the primary protagonist(s), only about six have featured lesbians in starring roles. (This excludes primarily straight ensemble casts of which queer people are a part.) This difference may reflect the fact that our cultural stereotyping of lesbians and gay men differs markedly.[15] The stereotype of the serious, career-focused lesbian or the earth mother hippie with a zeal for social justice may be less suited for a flashy reality show than the stereotypical image of the flamboyant and hypersexual gay man.

The relatively low visibility of both Asian men and lesbians—both of whom are sometimes stereotyped as asexual—on reality TV also shows us the cultural dominance of the male erotic gaze. That is, what we collectively think of as sexy and enticing is often what is sexy and enticing *to men*. Interestingly, when lesbians do appear on our screens, it's sometimes in highly sexualized ways. *The Real L Word* (Showtime, 2010–2012), one of the few television shows of any kind with a lesbian ensemble cast (and a spin on the scripted series *The L Word*), features a group of conventionally attractive, mainly white women and is objectively part reality TV and part soft-core porn. Similarly, when the Logo channel launched *Curl Girls*, a show about lesbian surfers that aired for one season (2007), it highlighted the women's sex appeal. Its advertising, which featured a cluster of athletic-looking, white (or ethnically ambiguous) women in bikinis, their arms latched around one another, described a "sexy new girl," an "on again–off again, steamy couple," and another character "who'll go topless for her love of shock value."[16] While these presentations of lesbian sexuality may entice women with a sexual interest in other women—*Curl Girls*, specifically, aired on a network geared toward queer audiences—they also likely play to heterosexual male tastes.

So, gender and sexuality are two power systems that work

in tandem to shape what we decide is socially desirable and worth seeing on our screens. Perhaps nowhere is this more evident than on *A Shot at Love with Tila Tequila* (MTV, 2007– 2008). Episode one of the show begins with Tila, a DIY celebrity who first rose to prominence through social-networking sites such as MySpace, writhing around on the floor in lingerie. "You may have drooled over me in my music videos," she tells us, ". . . but what you don't know about me is that I am bisexual!" This pronouncement is punctuated by additional footage of her gyrating in a bikini. We then learn the premise of the show, which is that "sixteen gorgeous straight guys" and "sixteen hot lesbians" will compete for Tila's heart—the tension being that the groups don't initially know about each other.

"This is the first show about lesbians and love," one of the female contestants tells the camera excitedly, reflecting both her unawareness of the show's secret premise and the broader lack of lesbian representation on TV.[17] In the second episode, when the two groups meet and Tila comes out as bisexual, the contestants register shock, but many of the men are smiling and one starts simulating sex with his hips. "I definitely think the women were a little more bothered than the men were," one of the male contestants tells us.[18] Tila has erotic encounters with both men and women throughout the season but ultimately chooses a male partner. Years later, in a YouTube video, she would maintain that she had a boyfriend at the time she filmed *A Shot at Love*, that she was never bisexual, and that she was simply "gay for pay" on the show, suggesting that her performance was manufactured to provoke male desire.[19]

While some of us may recall *A Shot at Love* only dimly, the show was a standout when it aired. According to *The Hollywood Reporter*, 6.2 million viewers tuned in to the first season

finale—at the time, MTV's most watched series telecast.[20] It
has since drawn its share of critiques, as well as multiple analyses in scholarly journals.[21] And while it might be tempting to
think of *A Shot at Love* as a relic from a time when we were
all friends with Tom on MySpace and we thought about sexuality in a more conservative, binarized way, the show's content remains relevant. It still teaches us how we think not only
about female bisexuality but also, more broadly, about the intersection of gender, sexuality, and power in our culture.

A Shot at Love was not a blip; the importance of the heterosexual male gaze in shaping content is still evident when
it comes to female bisexuality. For a sexual minority, bisexual women are relatively plentiful on reality TV, and "girl
on girl" hookups among women of various orientations are
still a staple of the genre. Social scientists have long pointed
out the various ways in which we privilege male sexual pleasure and enlist women in service to that pleasure. Objectification theory, for instance, argues that in contemporary
Western culture, women become the targets of a persistent,
sexualized male gaze that profoundly impacts their life experiences.[22] The notion of men as sexual subjects and women
as sexual objects has been used to explain a variety of contemporary differences between the genders, including the
fact that women have a stronger drive for thinness and that
they disproportionately experience unipolar depression.[23] We
plant the seeds for this divergence early. Even young girls are
socialized to devote more time to physical appearance than
their male peers;[24] one study of elementary school kids found
that girls are "more concerned about dieting and are more
preoccupied with their weight than are boys."[25]

The fact that reality shows appeal to straight male desire
is perhaps curious, since their viewers are more likely to be

women than men.[26] Yet research also suggests that women are socialized to perceive *themselves* through this gaze and to internalize female objectification.[27] In one classic study, for instance, women wearing a swimsuit ate less and performed worse on a math test than did women in sweaters or did men in either attire, even though they knew nobody was watching them.[28]

Yet while a variety of women on reality TV move fluidly between sexual encounters with men and women, bisexual *men* fall squarely within the ranks of TV's "invisibles." Along these lines, *The Real World: D.C.* (MTV, 2009–2010) is particularly revealing, because before season eight of the MTV dating show *Are You the One?* came along, it was one of the few television shows (unscripted *or* scripted!) to include a bisexual-identifying man as a central character. (Interestingly, Norm Korpi from the first season of *The Real World* was described as "bisexual" on the show, though—then and now—he openly identified as gay and is generally considered the first gay participant on the series.)[29] All the more illuminating is the fact that this bisexual man, Mike, shares the screen with bi female cast member Emily.

Both Mike and Emily (the same raised-in-a-cult Emily who later wore pudding on her face on *The Challenge*) are white, conventionally attractive, and barely in their twenties, and both have newly come out when the season begins, but they have markedly different experiences on the show. In the first episode, Emily's sexuality is revealed in a blink-and-you'll-miss-it moment, when her roommate Ashley says, "You're bi, right?" and Emily confirms that she is. Ashley nods and the conversation continues, followed immediately by a talking head of Ty opining that "all the girls here are just so hot." Later, during dinner, when Mike discloses his own sexuality, it receives significantly more attention. "I find out that Mike is bisexual," Ashley narrates in a testimonial. "Oh my God, did that just come out of his mouth? Shocking." In a different testimonial, Emily opines that she's "proud" of Mike for coming out like this, suggesting that it took "a lot of guts."[30] Mike's bisexuality continues to be more of a plotline, and is presented as more problematic, than Emily's throughout the season.

A Shot at Love with Tila Tequila and The Real World: D.C. both provide lessons about our cultural stereotyping of bisexuality and about how those stereotypes diverge and dovetail by gender. Bisexuals, like some gay people, have historically been stereotyped as confused about their sexual orientations and as being promiscuous and incapable of monogamy.[31] Accordingly, Tila is hypersexualized from the first moment she appears grinding in lingerie, and Emily on The Real World describes herself as someone who likes to "have fun" but has problems with romantic commitment. But researchers have also long found that biphobia differs in some ways from homophobia.[32] Bisexual men are often interpreted as "really" being gay people who are afraid to come out, while bisexual women can be perceived as straight women who are simply experimenting.[33] "You're not even comfortable with your own sexuality," Ashley tells Mike; at another point, she refers to him as a "gay guy."[34] And Tila, arguably, is so titillating to the heterosexual male gaze because she is presented as someone who "really" wants a man. She tells us that A Shot at Love "is gonna help me figure out: Do I really like a guy or do I really like a girl?" She chooses a man on the show, and she ultimately comes out as not being sexually attracted to women after all. In cinema, characters with dual sexual attraction are often portrayed as dishonest, emotionally unstable, excessive, and/or criminal,[35] and many of these same stereotypes play out on reality TV. Tila is presented as shady from the beginning of A

Shot at Love, when many of the contestants—particularly the female ones—are hurt by the surprise premise of the show. "It's kind of like a betrayal, in a sense," one woman explains.[36]

The near erasure of bi men from our screens and their treatment as problematic when they do appear demonstrate the specific taboo that lies at the intersection of bisexuality and masculinity. In fact, research has found that college students perceive bisexual men more negatively than they do bisexual women, gay men, or lesbians.[37] Bisexual men also face unique negative stereotyping—for example, the idea that they're the covert purveyors of HIV/AIDS from gay to straight populations.[38] Tellingly, the same research also indicates that straight men rate bisexual men, gay men, and lesbians—but *not* bisexual women—more negatively than straight females do. Perhaps this is unsurprising, as unlike the other orientations, female bisexuality can be perceived as compatible with heterosexual masculinity. Bisexual women are potential sexual partners for straight men in a way that lesbians are not. (Note: This is not to suggest that straight men never see lesbians as potential sexual partners or have never brushed off lesbian identity as "just a phase.") Accordingly, unscripted TV often packages female bisexual eroticism in a way that offers a direct pipeline to male fantasy.

To be clear, bisexual women, gay men, and lesbians do not enjoy full social acceptance. In particular, bisexual women have historically faced rejection from both straight and queer communities.[39] As discussed, we still live in a heteronormative society, where same-sex couples have only recently gained the legal right to marry their partners, and as of 2017 nearly one-third of Americans (32 percent) still opposed that right.[40]

But bisexual men are nearly invisible on these shows, to an extent that the other groups are not, and that teaches us something about ourselves. The erasure of male bisexuals, both from reality TV and from media representations more generally,[41] tells us specifically how we respond to bisexuality as a culture, but it also teaches us more generally about our rabid attachment to sexual categories. "Bisexual," while technically a category itself, messes with our idea of a stark heterosexual/homosexual binary. Bisexual people, and others who do not fit neatly into this dichotomy—for example, pansexuals and asexuals, both of whom seldom appear on reality TV—disrupt our deeply rooted notion of a two-category sexual system, and in doing so, they expose it as a social fiction. (Pansexuality is defined as attraction to people regardless of sex or gender. An asexual has low or absent sexual feelings toward others or desire for sexual activity.) *Male* bisexuality, however, represents a particular threat to straight men because it suggests there isn't a clear boundary between heterosexual and homosexual masculinity. As researcher Mickey Eliason has pointed out, the mere existence of bi men represents "a hidden danger and a direct challenge to the creation of a clear, 'us-them' sexual division."[42] We register a greater dislike of male bisexuals than female bisexuals not only because they're incompatible with heterosexual male desire but also arguably because we perceive them as *a threat to male heterosexuality itself.* And since straight male desire is the primary desire that matters, we then scrub bi men from our screens—to the extent that, as late as 2019, a show about sexually fluid young women *and men* could still make a stir.

"FOOD, A DRINK, AND A GAY"

With guidance from our major social institutions, we decide which sexual categories are "real," sort people into them, and treat those people accordingly. But these categories—like our racial and gender categories—are not inherently "real" at all. In brief flashes, reality TV reveals them to be social fictions.

One linguistic convention within the reality genre, though not unique to it, is the use of "gay" as a noun. We see this mainly on shows featuring straight women and their queer male friends. On *Kathy Griffin: My Life on the D-List* (Bravo, 2005–2010), the comedian came onstage bellowing, "Where my gays at?" and *Tori & Dean* often featured Tori Spelling rhapsodizing about "the gays" in her life. (To be fair, Kathy has received accolades for her LGBTQ activism,[43] and Tori is arguably a "gay icon.")[44] It pops up on other shows as well; on *Jersey Shore: Family Vacation* (MTV, 2018–present), Deena opines at a drag brunch, "Basically, this place has everything I like. Food, a drink, and a gay. Like, my three best things."[45] And the *Real Housewives* programs feature a coterie of ancillary gay male characters, who are often discussed in similar ways. In an episode of *The Real Housewives of Orange County*, for example, Tamra complains that Alexis and Gretchen insist on having "pocket gays" around them at all times to keep them primped.[46] (Note: Tamra didn't coin the term "pocket gay," which *Urban Dictionary* defines as "an extremely short gay person" or "a perfect travel-sized homosexual.")[47]

While these women are technically using "gay" in a grammatically correct way,[48] they're arguably objectifying gay men when they do it. But something else interesting is happening here. If we choose to believe they're using "a gay" in an affectionate way that's self-consciously silly, in these brief moments—whether intentionally or not—they're calling attention to the arbitrariness of that social category itself.

This is not to suggest that same-sex attraction is socially created; indeed, there's compelling scientific evidence that it has a genetic component.[49] But the meanings we apply to various sexual attractions, and the boundaries we draw around them, are socially created. "Gay" is a social construction. The notion of this concept as *a stable category that defines a person and his place in the world* is, in the grand scheme of history, somewhat new. As Foucault has argued, while people have engaged in same-sex eroticism across historical epochs and cultural contexts, in the 1800s, "homosexual became a personage . . . in addition to being a type of life, a life form."[50] This was connected to the criminalization and pathologizing of sexual behavior at that time, as schools, courts, and hospitals solidified the notion of "the homosexual" as a particular *category* of human, rather than simply a facet of one's desire or an aspect of one's behavior. As Gayle Rubin has observed, our sexual desires are now salient in a way that other types of preferences are not: "A person is not considered immoral, is not sent to prison, and is not expelled from her or his family, for enjoying spicy cuisine."[51] We are all constellations of other preferences and genetic traits to which we don't give the same social weight that we do sexuality. Nobody is compelled to "come out" as liking spicy food, or being left-handed, or gravitating toward ska music. Reality TV—with its silly, pseudoscientific taxonomies of gayness—is at once acknowledging that weight and giving a small wink to its artificiality.

SPLASHING IN THE GUTTER

Just as it is central to our culture, sexuality is central to reality programming. The genre, progressive as it may be in some ways, shows us how we clutch social categories and hold them dear to us. Even during the sexual fluidity season of *Are You the One?* many participants still labeled themselves—for

example, "bisexual," "pansexual," "sexually fluid." Some of
the work these categories do in society is simple, practical
work. For instance, they let others know the types of people
we might be attracted to when we go on the dating scene.
They can be affirming, especially for those who are marginalized and looking for community. But they also become a
key source of social inequality, trickling down from powerful institutions with the prerogative to decide which kinds
of desires are legitimate and which are immoral, illegal, and
pathological.

The media itself is one of these institutions and so reality TV, too, participates in these "polymorphous techniques of power." The genre is not without its stereotypical
representations—licentious female bisexuals, beefy gym trainers, *fabulous* fashion designers and wedding planners. The advertisement for the gay male ensemble show *Fire Island* (Logo,
2017), for instance, featured six gay men with well-defined pecs,
in body-clinging bathing suits; one of them was clutching a
tiny dog. And over on the makeover show *Queer Eye* (originally titled *Queer Eye for the Straight Guy*; Bravo, 2003–2007;
Netflix, 2018–present), gay men are presented as a subspecies
of human with a naturally superior "eye" for fashion, grooming, interior decorating, cuisine, and popular culture. From
the absence of male bisexuals to Bravo's campy "pocket gays,"
there's plenty to see on reality TV that helps us learn more
about our conventional norms and understandings relating
to sexuality. More generally, we've seen how the genre represents our conventional values (e.g., what a couple is, what a
family is, what childhood means) and rigid classificatory
schemes (class, gender, race, sexuality) and how it leaves out
some key groups that are also marginalized from broader
society (e.g., poor people, Latinx families, Asian men, bisexual

men). By stereotyping some groups and eclipsing others, these programs not only reflect but also promulgate ideas about which categories—including sexual categories—are real and natural.

But even as it reinforces our system of categorization, reality TV still enables us to see things about sexuality that other forms of media keep hidden. For example, while not all sexual minorities are represented, and while some stereotyping persists even when they are, reality TV has also been praised for diverging from these stereotypes in some instances.[52] Pedro may have been the token gay guy with AIDS on *The Real World*, but the cameras pointed at him daily showed us his multidimensionality—his friendships and conflicts with his roommates, his commitment ceremony to his partner, Sean, his struggle with his health. Upon Pedro's death, then US president Bill Clinton said that the MTV star had given AIDS a very "human face."[53] Richard, while called "a queer" on *Survivor* and while obligated to disclose his sexuality in a way that his straight costars weren't, was not wholly defined through his sexuality either. We likely now remember him not (solely) as "that gay castaway" but as the one whose machinations earned him the final prize. Anecdotally, when I discuss that season with people, many describe him as neither gay nor the winner, but as "the guy who walked around naked." *Queer Eye* may promote stereotypes, but it has also been a massive platform for gay visibility. When it first aired in 2003, it rapidly secured a place in the cultural zeitgeist, garnering "record-breaking ratings for Bravo" (at one point, 3.34 million viewers per episode),[54] an Emmy nod, and endorsement deals and high-profile media appearances for its stars. Even Mike from *The Real World: D.C.* showed us that he wasn't lying to himself or hoodwinking people but was secure in his own bisexual identity, although he chafed under others' mistrust. If anything, Mike was revolutionary in demonstrating that bisexuals can be just as boring as everyone else, as that season is often described as one of *The Real World*'s dullest.[55] (Evidently it outdid *London*!) The sexual diversity within the reality genre is also, to some extent, intersectional. The *Love & Hip Hop* empire, for instance, includes a number of openly gay and bisexual women of color, and the southern working-class family on *Here Comes Honey Boo Boo* embraces its gay uncle.

Our world has changed since Lance was part of *An American Family* in 1971, since Pedro appeared on MTV in 1994, and even since the *Queer Eye* team offered hair product to their first straight male in 2003. This is not to say that queer people are no longer stigmatized or that we aren't still fundamentally a heteronormative culture. As I've argued both in this chapter and elsewhere in this book, they still are and we still are, and unscripted programming illuminates these things. Still, just as it has for trans people, reality TV has been at the crest of a sea change in the way that we think about queer people in the United States. While Barack Obama balked at the concept of same-sex marriage on the campaign trail in 2008, he ultimately changed his initial position—a position that would likely be unthinkable from a Democratic nominee today. (Indeed, an openly gay man, Pete Buttigieg, was a major contender for the Democratic nomination for president in 2019.) *Queer Eye* premiered during the same summer the U.S. Supreme Court issued a landmark decision in *Lawrence v. Texas*, ruling that laws prohibiting consensual homosexual activity were unconstitutional. Since then, the Court has also affirmed the right of same-sex couples to marry (*Obergefell v. Hodges*, 2015) and has ruled that the Civil Rights Act protects gay, lesbian, and transgender employees from discrimination (*Bostock v. Clayton County*, 2020). Significantly, it was a Donald Trump appointee who wrote the Court's majority opinion for the latter—Justice Neil Gorsuch (whom most of my students cannot name).

Reality TV telegraphed these seismic changes that were about to happen to our social landscape when it began to offer us queer possibilities, arguably as early as the 1970s. In doing so, the genre showed us something about *ourselves*— but it also showed us something about *itself*. Racquel Gates has suggested that in some ways, there's more freedom to play around with representation in "the televisual gutter" of reality TV.[56] Because these are "guilty pleasures" that viewers often don't take very seriously, their creators may feel there's less stake in these programs. This, paradoxically, can allow them to stray from mainstream imagery, covering different kinds of people, new kinds of experiences. Its tremendous elasticity and the fact that it's a haven for renegades mean that it shows us parts of humanity that we don't typically get to glimpse. Even though reality TV is a fun-house mirror of our dominant, heteronormative culture, and even as it deals in sexual archetypes, the genre also shows us some possibilities for transcending our deeply entrenched roles and expectations. At the end of the day, tracing reality TV's treatment of sexuality reveals the genre's rich mine of subversive potential.

10

"Bad Boys, Bad Boys" (Deviance)

Adele has been eating couch cushions for nearly twenty years.

"On a daily basis, I probably eat about [an] 8-and-a-half-by-11 piece of cushion," she explains. "I just take little bite-sized pieces and snack on it all day."[1]

Driving in her car, she leans over and extracts some of the pieces from her purse, depositing them into her mouth like popcorn. "The darker cushion—the yellow cushion—it tastes better. It just has a stronger flavor."

Adele attributes the beginning of her cushion eating to her parents' divorce when she was a preteen. "I couldn't control my parents. I couldn't stop them from splitting up. So there was just a lot that I couldn't control, and this was something that I could."

Meanwhile, her habit presents a health hazard, and her family is concerned.

"So now you're thirty, and when you were sixteen I tolerated it, and now it's time to put a stop to it," her mom tells her.

"I want this to be over," Adele affirms, reaching out for her mom's hand across a restaurant table, "and I want help."

We've seen how reality TV exposes the key categories and distinctions that organize our lives. But perhaps the most fundamental distinction in any culture, as illustrated on this episode of TLC's *My Strange Addiction* (2010–2015), is between the acceptable and the unacceptable. We've already gotten a peek at how we try to curb unacceptable behavior, in ways that sync up with other major social hierarchies—class, gender, race, sexuality. Here, we get an eyeful. Unscripted TV is primed to teach us why people step out of line, how we respond to that, why we're drawn to watching them, and what that says about us.

Ultimately, from these shows we learn that while we try to draw this distinction sharply, we all inhabit a hazy space between normal and abnormal. Our ideas about what's normal and what's not are vital to how we treat others and distribute social status. Yet reality TV—both the people on these programs and our viewing of them—chisels away at the boundary between normal and abnormal until it erodes, revealing it to be a social construction rather than a durable, essential truth.

WHAT IS DEVIANCE?

It might be jarring for the layperson to see the terms "deviance" and "deviants" used so casually in this chapter. In everyday life, these words can have a moralistic ring to them. However, social scientists use them in a purely descriptive way: to refer to behavior and people who fall outside of society's norms. (Consider the term "standard deviation" in statistics.)

Scholars of deviance have looked at our misfits, madmen, and other marginalized people, paradoxically to understand mainstream social life.[2] The sociologist Harold Garfinkel, for instance, famously had his students participate in "breaching" experiments, where they would violate commonplace norms—for example, by going into shops and haggling over the price of goods. Through these small-scale, disruptive practices, they exposed our tacit, everyday social guidelines.[3] Reality programming is a rich site for this type of investigation. While its participants are like us in many ways, many of them are also quirky personalities who represent the extremes of human behavior. Through their rule violations, they expose how we socially construct "the normal."

No act is inherently deviant outside of the meaning society gives to it. As the sociologist Howard Becker reminds us, "Before any act can be viewed as deviant, and before any class of people can be labeled and treated as outsiders for committing the act, someone must have made the rule which defines the act as deviant."[4] We may feel that certain activities "just *are*" bad or strange or wrong. But these designations are in fact culturally generated, as they differ across history and context. For example, killing another human may be considered acceptable in times of war or when it applies to state-sanctioned punishment. In fact, while some ideas about what's wrong hold up more robustly across contexts (e.g., incest) than others (e.g., table manners), there are none that apply to every epoch, location, and circumstance.

WHY BE WEIRD?

Why don't deviants just conform? Conformity is certainly easier in some ways. As Émile Durkheim points out, we can incur negative consequences for being deviant, so while it's possible for us to free ourselves from social facts, we can't do it without struggle. Yet he also observes that deviance exists in every society. (Again, note that Durkheim's use of the word "deviance"—and my own use of it—does not imply judgment; it is simply a neutral, sociological term for non-normative behavior.) And while some people may just be

naturally "pathological," Durkheim concedes, there are social explanations for their nonconformity as well.[5]

One way sociologists have accounted for deviance is that
people learn to be nonconforming in the same way that they
learn to conform. In a classic 1953 study of marijuana us-
ers, for instance, Becker found that every element of illegal
drug use has a social component, as one learns the various
meanings associated with pot, how to get it, the procedures
for smoking it, and even how it's supposed to make one feel.[6]
(This is another notable instance of how our ideas about deviance differ historically; Becker's midcentury example may
seem less "deviant" today, as some states move toward legal-
ization of the drug.) The theory of "differential association,"
similarly, suggests that our social environment plays a key
role in whether and how we become deviant. Specifically,
it argues that whether or not we participate in criminal behavior is largely a function of the social networks in which
we're embedded.[7] For example, for some inmates, being a part
of prison networks and learning from those connections—
and not being supplied with alternative networks or skills—
facilitate additional criminal behavior upon their release.
Differential association is one factor that helps to explain why
spending time in prison leads to more lucrative criminal activity upon release.[8]

Because it shows us unusual nooks of society, reality TV is
particularly primed to reveal how deviants are socially created.
Programs involving children, particularly, enforce this notion
that some forms of deviance are taught. The kids who learn
survivalist procedures from their parents and ready themselves
for the world to end on *Doomsday Preppers* (National Geographic, 2011–2014), for instance, fit this bill.

Both the children and adults on *My Big Fat American*

Gypsy Wedding likewise demonstrate how atypical behaviors germinate in particular social environments. On one episode of the show, which purports to show the marriage practices of Romani Americans ("Gypsies"), fourteen-year-old Priscilla is looking for a husband.[9] In its first few minutes, the episode draws a series of stark distinctions between the culture in which Priscilla has been raised and the American mainstream. "Tucked into the shadows of Douglasville, Georgia," its narrator explains, "is a secret community that's home to Romanichal Gypsies." The narrator goes on to assert that the Gypsy way of life is "completely foreign to gorgers: the Gypsy term for outsiders." For example, "Though barely into her teens, Gypsy tradition decrees that Priscilla will soon wed."

"Most fourteen-year-old gorger girls are in school," explains Priscilla, who dropped out at age twelve to do chores and help raise her little brother. "But I'm here cleaning, and that's the way I like it to be."

"Courtship don't start at twenty-five when you're a Gypsy," her mom tells us. "This is her engagement time."

Gypsy girls, Priscilla says, are "raised our lives around" finding the perfect husband, marrying, and maintaining a home. As we've seen, children become little vessels for their parents' cultural values, and that's the case whether those values are middle of the road or off the beaten path. Like the young people on *Breaking Amish*, Priscilla illuminates how different social environments can generate different types of expectations. Teen marriages and truancy may be considered deviant within mainstream American society, but nobody bats an eye within her Gypsy community.

Another sociological explanation for why deviance occurs is that we revert to it when we can't get what we want through typical channels. Strain theory, or the "means-ends" theory of deviance, pioneered by the sociologist Robert Merton, focuses on the misalignment between broad cultural goals—for instance, wealth or fame—and the social mechanisms for meeting those goals.[10] Merton describes the case of the "innovator" who, lacking the (typically but not always economic) means to attain success through legitimate means, attempts to achieve it through deviance.[11] While Merton was writing decades before the first *Real World* season aired, his theory aptly characterizes many participants on reality TV. As we've seen, lots of these people wade into the genre in the hope that its current will propel them forward. The DIY celebrity Cardi B, for instance, who did not have the social connections or education typically necessary to attain wealth, successfully innovated through her use of social media and involvement in *Love & Hip Hop*.

Although Becker and Merton were approaching the origins of deviance from different angles, they both hit upon the idea that these behaviors can't be divorced from social context. While we may presume that weirdness is the result of individual differences—variations in innate temperament—and while it *is* those things, it is not *only* those things. As reality TV's denizens show us, just as the weight of society pushes us to conform, it can push us away from conformity as well. Whether it's the influence of our friends and family or our positions within social hierarchies, our environment powerfully influences where we sit on the spectrum of deviance.

HELP ME IF YOU CAN

When deviance occurs, what do we do about it? Our *response* to deviance is also a social process. Whatever the reason that people engage in aberrant behavior, reality TV teaches us how we fix ourselves and the ones we love. Makeover media has been around for quite some time; in her book *Smart Living: Lifestyle Media and Popular Expertise*, the media scholar Tania Lewis traces its appeal from etiquette manuals in Victorian England to the emergence of men's magazines such as *Playboy* and all the way into reality TV land.[12] Today, transformation shows have become a major subgenre of reality TV. At any given moment, you can sink into your couch, aim your remote, and learn how to repair your face, your wardrobe, your house, your kids, your marriage, your diet, or your car.

These "fixing" shows demonstrate what we consider to be wrong and how we react to that perceived wrongness. Erving Goffman explains that, generally, we have socially prescribed ideas about what's "ordinary and natural" for various types of people in society—that is, we make certain assumptions about what the people around us "ought to" be.[13] When people don't fit into those categories, we think of them as deviants. While we're all likely familiar with the term "stigma"—coming from the Latin word meaning a mark on one's body—Goffman defines it in a specific way, as "an attribute that is deeply discrediting."[14] When we find that a person does not meet our standards for what's acceptable, she gets "reduced in our minds from a whole and usual person to a tainted, discounted one."[15]

Many different lifestyle makeover programs illuminate the discrediting process. These shows tend to uncover a stigma—Adele's cushion eating, for instance—and demonstrate how it might be remedied. The TLC show *Hoarding: Buried Alive* (2010–2014), for instance, highlights people who have amassed significant clutter in their homes, to the point where it has become a hygiene issue. On one episode, the narrator informs us that "many people who hoard keep their disorder a secret, even from their friends and family," and that "Judy has a secret that's been growing harder and harder to keep."[16] Judy ultimately reveals her mess to a professional organizer, a therapist, the TLC cameras, and the viewing public.

One of the ways that people deal with their own deviance is by attempting to correct the undesirable attribute, Goffman observes.[17] This is the main premise of *Hoarding* and other lifestyle-makeover shows. But it's not only the deviants who are invested in this correction but also the other people in their lives. When we interact with others and sort them into categories, in the way that Goffman describes, we feel discomfort with those whom we cannot easily plunk into the "normal" bucket. This discomfort is highlighted in "mixed" scenarios, like the scenes on *Hoarding*, where deviants and "normals" (as Goffman characterizes them) come into contact.[18] Goffman's point about these "mixed" encounters hints at why we may become invested in fixing deviants: they seemingly disrupt the standard rhythms of everyday life. It also suggests one appeal of these shows: they enable us to observe people like Adele and Judy from the cool remove of our couches, avoiding the unease we might derive from personal contact.

DOCILE BODIES IN *LOCKDOWN*

We identify deviant bodies, and we try to tame them. We do this in cooperation with individual experts and through large-scale institutions that are invested in maintaining social order. We've previously traced Michel Foucault's argument that powerful social institutions have historically controlled our discourse about what's normal and what's not. The medical establishment, for example, keeps up an ongoing narrative about which bodies are appropriate and which need to be fixed. Self-help reality TV, accordingly, is chockablock with health-care providers, from psychiatrists to dermatologists to gastroenterologists.

Another institution that defines and reinforces our notions about deviance is the law. The reality TV landscape, teeming with portrayals of the justice system, shows us its power to pinpoint and control deviance. One episode of the show *Lockdown* (National Geographic, 2007), for example, takes us into Oak Park Heights correctional facility in Minnesota. Oak Park houses "inmates so violent they can't be controlled elsewhere," according to the narrator, and the program highlights how the facility takes these men's bodies and renders them docile.[19] In one scene, a prisoner getting a haircut is wearing multiple sets of shackles and is accompanied by three guards. "The heavy restraint system reduces the inmate's movement and ability to attack," we are told. Yet while prisons do apply physical force to keep unruly bodies in line, they don't keep every inmate shackled at all times or aim guns at them around the clock. Instead, as Foucault observes, prisons, like all institutions, must use "polymorphous techniques of power" to curb potential deviance.[20]

Prisons are constructed in specific ways to contain, control, and surveil their inmates. Indeed, one of the primary purposes of these institutions is to separate criminal bodies from the rest of society.[21] On *Lockdown*, we learn that Oak Park Heights is a "fortress-like compound" with five-story walls and a master switch that can be flipped at any time to "lock the entire complex down." The larger enclosure of the prison is also divided into multiple smaller areas through "partitioning,"[22] as Foucault calls it, to control the flow of bodies through the structure. At Oak Park Heights, "numbers are power," and the men are "segregated into small groups for maximum control." The inmates are frisked as they move from space to space, and only a few can have recreation time at once. Detailing the birth of the modern prison, Foucault explains that specific places within the structure "were defined to correspond not only to the need to supervise, to break dangerous communications, but also to create a useful space."[23] *Lockdown* takes us on a tour through these "functional sites,"[24] including the recreation area, the cafeteria, and the high-security segregation unit. Finally, Foucault observes that bodies are made docile through the use of "time-tables"—schedules that "establish rhythms, impose particular occupations, [and] regulate the cycle of repetition."[25] Oak Park Heights controls its inmates by shuttling them with precision to various locations throughout the day. Even their bodily functions are subject to specific rhythms. The showers may be used only every twelve hours, and the toilets can be flushed only twice per use. The prison, in sum, maintains order by controlling what people do with their bodies.

Lockdown teaches us not only how prisons employ various techniques to curb deviance and to enforce conformity but also how various other institutions use these same mechanisms. As Foucault points out, social institutions keep our bodies in line essentially from the time we are old enough to respond to them. Elementary school students, for instance, eat lunch during a certain interval each day, travel from place to place in a straight line, sit in assigned seats, and must request permission to use the bathroom. Hospitals, the military, and even theme parks direct the movement of humans via similar mechanisms. Programs such as *Lockdown* demonstrate how we're all embedded within powerful institutions that control our activities—and how they make our bodies docile, often without anyone even putting their hands on us.

WHY DO WE LOVE BAD BOYS?

Lockdown is just the tip of the iceberg when it comes to reality programs focused on the justice system. Some of these shows have had remarkable staying power. Before it moved to Lifetime, *America's Most Wanted* (Fox, 1988–2011, 2021–present; Lifetime 2011–2012)—which showed crime reenactments and provided information about at-large fugitives—was the longest-running show on the Fox network.[26] The small-claims-court show *Judge Judy* (CBS, 1996–present) has been on the air for about a quarter century. *Cops*, on television for more than three decades, was the longest-running prime-time show in the United States when it was canceled.[27] True crime programs such as *Tiger King* (Netflix, 2020) and podcasts such as *Serial* (WBEZ, 2014–present) are immensely popular. Over in scripted TV land, *Law & Order* ran for twenty years (NBC, 1990–2010), with one of its spin-offs, *Law & Order: SVU*, enduring for even longer than the original (NBC, 1999–present). We like to consume media about these topics. Why, and what does that say about us?

One thing it tells us is simply that the justice system is a large part of our lives. The US houses one-quarter of all inmates in the world, even though we're only 5 percent of the global population.[28] We incarcerate more people per capita than any other country; currently, nearly 2.3 million people are being held within our criminal justice system.[29] This system has also become more a part of our lives in recent years. The number of people in US prisons and jails has increased 500 percent over the last four decades. In fact, today the number of people in prison for drug offenses *alone* exceeds the total number of people who were locked away for any crime in 1980.[30] And the number of people embroiled in the criminal justice system is much higher if one considers not just current inmates but also those on parole or probation; in 2015, according to the Bureau of Justice Statistics, about one in thirty-seven adults in the US fell into this category.[31]

A lot of us are moving through the legal system at any given time. And we have a lot of "crime and punishment"–type shows. Entire networks, such as Court TV and Investigation Discovery, are built around our systems of justice. We're called for jury duty, pulled over for speeding, and stopped at checkpoints. We file police reports when we have fender benders. So perhaps there are so many reality shows about the law for the same reason there are so many about families: it's a major social institution in which nearly all of us participate, to varying degrees.

Some of the elements of reality TV that appeal to us in general are also relatively pronounced in these types of shows. The sociologist Charles Tilly has argued that human minds respond particularly well to "standard stories," or "sequential, explanatory accounts of self-motivated human action."[32] Standard stories are central to our lives, as the underpinnings of fables, sitcoms, plays, novels, and even the narratives that juries piece together during deliberation.[33] Similarly, law-oriented reality programs often provide clear heroes and villains, straightforward and sequential narrative structures, and moral reductionism. For instance, broad cultural notions about normalcy and deviance (and about gender and criminality) were distilled in the *Cops* theme song, which asked, "Bad boys, bad boys, whatcha gonna do? Whatcha gonna do when they come for you?" Perhaps we find succor in seeing these "bad boys" identified, contained, and brought to justice.

The standard stories on justice TV also unfold in ways that reinforce narratives about race, class, and gender that are familiar and cozy. When Patricia Hill Collins wrote about controlling images, she specifically connected these images to Black men's perceived criminality and hypersexuality and to their overrepresentation in the prison population.[34] While the justice system touches most of us in some way, poor communities and communities of color are considerably more policed,[35] and involvement in the system is highly patterned by race. Black men are six times as likely to be incarcerated as white men, and Hispanic men are more than twice as likely to be incarcerated as non-Hispanic white men.[36] In eleven US states, at least one in twenty Black men is behind bars.[37] While one might argue that perhaps people of different races commit crimes at different rates, multiple studies have shown that even when rates of criminality are similar, white people are less likely to come under the auspices of the law.[38] And when convictions occur, as discussed, sentencing can also differ by race.[39]

These types of programs not only display our ideas about race and deviance but also help to perpetuate them. It seems unlikely that most people who watched *Cops* were social science nerds like me, riveted and repulsed by what the show had to teach us about broad inequalities. Rather, they tuned in to watch a clash between two groups: the police (who were generally portrayed positively) and the suspected perps (who were generally not). On *Live PD*, the underlying "standard story" was even more nakedly visible. In each episode, footage from the patrols was interspersed with cuts to a studio, where we watched commentators—most of whom had worked in law enforcement themselves—respond to the action. In this way, the show often resembled a sporting event where the viewer was clearly meant to root for the cops. On one episode, for instance, while an officer is questioning and cuffing a suspect, the main commentator describes how that officer had previously been shot in the line of duty: "She is a real hero."[40]

Tellingly, research suggests that viewing crime-related reality programming improves white people's—and *specifically* white people's—attitudes toward police.[41] Not all of the perps on *Cops* are men of color; the drug-addled poor white person is also a regular character. But there's a reason these standard stories about heroes and villains seem to resonate more with white audiences, who may more comfortably identify with the law enforcement figures than with the stereotypical criminals: dark skinned, male, and lower-class.

TOWNSPEOPLE WITH TORCHES

So, law-and-order programs may resonate with us strongly because they—like other reality TV shows—reinforce our comfortable national narratives about race, gender, class, respectability, and how bodies should be organized and contained. But what is it about deviance and *deviants*, in particular, that engages our interest? While Goffman suggests that we may try to fix deviants in order to allay our own discomfort with them, and while this is certainly true, we also benefit from their existence.

Recall that a fundamental puzzle, for Émile Durkheim, was social cohesion. What's to prevent all of society's self-interested, autonomous individuals from scurrying off into their own directions and refusing to cooperate with one another? For Durkheim, society was a giant, complex organism with different parts, each component serving a different societal function.[42] Looking through the lens of this theory, we might be inclined to interpret deviance as something dysfunctional—an indicator that the organism is sick. But as Durkheim points out, crime isn't just something that happens when a society needs a tune-up. On the contrary, it's a feature of *every* society. This is curious, he ventures, since humans have been developing mechanisms to eliminate deviance throughout history. Theoretically, we should have gotten pretty good at it by now. And, again, he doesn't think that deviance persists just because there will always be people naturally predisposed to it (though he doesn't deny this). Rather, he argues that we *need* deviance in a way. The presence of deviance doesn't mean that society is breaking down; it means it's working correctly.[43]

For Durkheim, deviance shores up our notions of what's normal and, in doing so, reinforces our social cohesiveness. Like townspeople in an old horror film chasing after a monster with their torches, we are bonded in our collective rejection of the ones who do not belong. This has always happened, Durkheim suggests, and will always happen. In fact, if we were a society of saints, we would simply redraw the boundaries of acceptability so that some of our members might still be cast as deviant.[44]

Why are we pulled toward reality programs with cushion eaters, Gypsies, bar brawlers, and killers? Because we're drawn to the spectacle of deviance, and we always have been. That's the premise behind the freak show—a form of entertainment that arose in the Colonial period, was popular in the nineteenth century, and continues even today.[45] The freak show rested on clear-cut ideas about normalcy and deformity, displaying the latter as spectacle.[46] We see shades of this today on unscripted TV, where deviant bodies are presented to us as curiosities: the conjoined twins on *Abby & Brittany* (TLC, 2012), the gushes of facial pus on *Dr. Pimple Popper*, and the array of programs starring little people. These include, but are not limited to, *Little Chocolatiers* (TLC, 2009–2010), *The Little Couple* (TLC, 2009–present), *Little People, Big World* (TLC, 2006–present), *Little Women: Atlanta* (Lifetime, 2016–present), *Little Women: Dallas* (Lifetime, 2016–2017), *Little Women: LA* (Lifetime, 2014–present), *Little Women: NY* (Lifetime, 2015–2016), and *Our Little Family* (TLC, 2015).

But reality programs also allow us to rubberneck at a wide range of human deviance beyond the physical body. As we know, many viewers tune in for the enjoyment of discussing the action with others.[47] When we watch to make points of contact with other people, reality TV serves a communal function. Our water-cooler conversations about *Hoarding: Buried Alive* may seem like frivolous chitchat, and we might not want to lend them much social weight. But these moments of shared culture accumulate and contribute to our social cohesiveness. Our viewing, then, works on dual levels that are seemingly paradoxical: we gravitate toward reality stars because we identify with them, but they also reinforce our social solidarity when we collectively reject them.

Some viewers lean, and some programs lend themselves, more toward the former or toward the latter. One fan of *Keeping Up with the Kardashians* might identify with Kylie, while another enjoys gossiping about the ever-changing topography of her face. For many of us, it's a mix. And many reality TV participants, like the Kardashian/Jenners, nestle in a space between deviant and acceptable. They are rarely *just* one or the other.

And neither are we.

These characters are versions of ourselves who go too far.

Through our viewing, we are able to draw and redraw the boundary between acceptable and unacceptable and place ourselves on the correct side. But perhaps we're so invested in curating that boundary precisely because we know it's so messy and unstable. As sociologists have long observed, few of us can say we've *never* engaged in deviance. Edwin Lemert, for instance, distinguished between "primary" deviance, which is practiced by people who are basically conformists, and "secondary" deviance, wherein the deviance is persistent, with a negative label applied to the doer, who often internalizes it.[48] In the case of primary deviance, we often explain away the behavior as being "situational" or "as functions of a socially acceptable role."[49] (Drinking to excess while in college is one classic example.) Indeed, *most* of us have engaged in deviance at some point or another, if only because some situations present a deviance catch-22. Driving at least a few miles above the speed limit on a major highway, for instance, is commonplace and expected but also illegal; we're deviant if we perform this act and deviant if we don't.

Many of us have messy homes. Many of us have technically violated the law. And while we don't all binge on couch cushions, some of us have been known to polish off a whole sleeve of fudge-stripe cookies in one sitting (hypothetically). Although gorger girls may not drop out of school to cook, clean, and get married, we, like Priscilla, also live in a culture where women still are the primary caretakers of children and do a disproportionate amount of domestic work. As we've seen throughout this book, reality TV confronts us with an array of peculiarities that are simultaneously anathema and known to us in muted form. Just as these shows enable us to map out the terrain of normalcy, they also caution us against making such clear-cut distinctions.

CRAP HIERARCHY

Reality stars are not just deviant and neither are we, but they *are* deviant and so are we. They remind us that deviance exists on a spectrum and that our understanding of what is acceptable changes across social contexts. This concept applies to our viewing of reality shows as well.

Is watching reality TV a "deviant" act? Yes, and no. As we've seen, one of the contradictions of the genre is that it's both highly popular and somewhat taboo. Recall the study that found that "people have a negative view of the impact of reality TV," although 77 percent of respondents said they watched at least one reality show from the list included in the survey "sometimes or frequently." The respondents' viewing of these shows "belies [their] disdain for the genre," the researchers concluded, as "the reputation of reality programming does not appear to have substantially interfered with viewing behavior."[50]

But as far as guilty pleasures go, some reality programs seem a bit guiltier than others. At the apex of legitimacy are the cooking and home decor programs that pervade waiting rooms across America. When a new mom-friend, for instance, confessed her love for the Chip and Joanna Gaines home remodeling show, *Fixer Upper* (HGTV, 2013–2018), I couldn't help wondering if she would have been as candid about an affinity for *Snooki & Jwoww*.

Recall that a major distinction between documentaries and reality television is that the former is educational in nature while the latter is intended mainly to entertain.[51] But there is slippage between these categories, as documentaries also seek to entertain and some reality shows, at least nominally, attempt to educate. The term "edutainment," applying to children's shows that amuse and also teach, highlights this false dichotomy. And reality shows teach us all types of things: what a modeling "go see" is, how to prepare a home for sale, how to get a new product to market. They imbue us with new vocabularies, from the "tucks" and "fish" on *RuPaul's Drag Race* to the "molecular gastronomy" of *Top Chef*. I learned the best way to crack an egg from *Snooki & Jwoww*, and it's because of Vicki from *The Real Housewives of Orange County* that I roll my clothes when packing for trips. Indeed, before the network became known for its polygamists, sextuplets, and little people, TLC was an acronym for "the Learning Channel."

It seems that the more closely reality TV resembles its documentary ancestors—that is, the more it overtly seems to *teach* us—the more it takes on the halo of legitimacy. One study of college students found that they distinguished between "good" and "bad" reality TV. The former label belonged to programs that "give the viewer useful ideas or advice; give people a second chance; are entertaining or funny; and can be applied to the viewer's actual life."[52] One facet of a show like *Bad Girls Club* that catapults it into the "ratchet" zone is that it points to its participants' ill behaviors but does not particularly focus on their improvement. Other research similarly suggests that viewers do not evaluate all reality TV equally but make assessments about the relative value of various subgenres. As one respondent told the British communications researcher Annette Hill, when it comes to reality TV, there is "crap I would never watch, crap I might watch, and then crap I would definitely watch."[53]

Still, it's "crap." Even if the acceptability of these programs does vary, there's a reason people refer to the genre, writ large, as "guilty pleasure" TV. We reserve that label for a particular range of cultural pursuits. We likely wouldn't call attending a

Shakespearean play or reading Proust a "guilty pleasure," so why are we guilty about this?

There are a variety of possible answers to that question. Perhaps the most obvious is that it's nonredeeming; aside from the occasional educational nugget, we don't "get" anything from these programs. Yet professional sports don't have intellectual value either, and we don't regularly refer to them as "guilty pleasures." There are other potential reasons for our disdain for reality TV: because it's populated by real people behaving in "low-class" ways and it's important to us to keep taste hierarchies intact; because, unlike sports, it's a genre associated more with female viewership than male[54] and we tend to devalue cultural products geared toward women (e.g., "chick flicks," "chick lit"); or maybe because we just like to feel guilty about things—a propensity that perhaps illuminates our country's charred but intact religious foundation. Not to mention, reality TV arguably *does* have value. In this very book, we've toured the genre like a museum, stopping to peer at its various artifacts, examining the things that they do for us and the various facets of our culture that they reveal.

But a large reason we feel this way about reality TV likely has to do with the types of people who populate these worlds. Even if we're gathering our torches as we tune in to *The Bachelor*, we may still feel contaminated by the monster's stigma. Athletes, conversely, are doing something socially laudable. When we watch sports, wearing our favorite players' jerseys and bonding with others in our support for "our" teams, we don't become implicated in unacceptable behavior. There's a stink to reality TV that has never quite worn off, no matter how many people watch or how much the genre becomes a part of contemporary life. And maybe we're reticent to admit we watch these shows because we think their participants' behavior reflects on us—and maybe because we *know* that it does.

CRACKING THE LOCKS

Unscripted programming cracks the locks and thrusts open the places in ourselves that we keep hidden, both individually and as a society. One way it does this is by showing us the people who run amok of our norms, why they do that, and how we attempt to yank them back into the fold. It reveals the "polymorphous techniques" we use to curb deviance, via loved ones, individual experts, and behemoth institutions. It teaches us *whom* we view as legitimate but also how those views are fundamentally shaped by our culture. And it reveals that these views, while socially constructed, are still "real" in the sense that they are vital to our lives, impacting how we distribute societal power, treat others, and experience the world ourselves.

These programs offer us things and people ostensibly in need of fixing, from kitchen islands to inmates. But they also show us people who push back against society's norms. The genre shows us how conservative we remain, illuminating the social repercussions for stepping out of line. But on the flip side of that, it highlights humanity's heterogeneity. And, to be fair, reality TV doesn't try to fix us all—nor does it try to. On *Nailed It!* (Netflix, 2018–present), for instance, which humorously features everyday people attempting to re-create bakers' masterpieces, there's an exuberance about failure, a sense that we're all laughing together at our inability to measure up.

By presenting caricatures of our own oddities, these programs demonstrate how society sets parameters for normalcy and how we all move in and around those barriers, which are changeable and nuanced. Ultimately, the genre exposes the muddiness of distinctions that we may perceive as crisp and clean. The boundaries that we draw between the normal and the freaky aren't "real" in any universal sense. And the monsters we reject are not as different from us as we'd like to believe. We're all just a bunch of fudge-stripe cookies away from being in the wrong category.

Reality TV is both a guilty goody and a nutritional bite, nestling in the crook between normalcy and deviance—just like its participants and just like us. And while the "freaky" undercurrent of reality programming remains strong, reality stars are more than *just* sideshow. Some of them are also our main attractions. They're flash points for our desires, behaviors, and peculiarities. And for a while, one was running our country.

Conclusion

And it's true we are immune
When fact is fiction and TV reality
—U2, "Sunday Bloody Sunday"

President Donald Trump sits behind his desk in the Oval Office grinning toothily, hands clasped together, signature hair swooped across his scalp. To his side, between the president and the American flag, stands Kim Kardashian, her extensions cascading in thick curtains over her shoulders. "Great meeting with @KimKardashian today, talked about prison reform and sentencing," reads the president's accompanying tweet.[1]

This is not a scene from a reality show. In May 2018, many major news outlets covered this real-life meeting between the two reality show dynasts, one of whom was then helming the most powerful country in the world. As reality TV has seeped into the cultural ether, perhaps it was only a matter of time before it infiltrated politics, too.

The combination of these two worlds may appear jarring at first. Sometimes reality TV seems to be a space apart from politics. While we might expect the genre, with its fast production turnarounds and its focus on real people grappling with today's problems,[2] to be an ideal platform for the political, reality shows seldom cross into that realm.[3] For instance, while the contestants on *The Bachelor* are ostensibly searching for their future spouses, we don't ever hear them discuss their stances on abortion, immigration, or gun control. Perhaps these particular people are simply unconcerned with politics—something the "Virgin Hunk" *Saturday Night Live* skit implies when the narrator states that the star "has to choose between thirty women who didn't vote." It's also likely that these shows don't want to alienate viewers, whose ideologies may not coincide with those of their stars.

Perhaps the creators of these programs also suspect that we're not interested in ingesting our guilty goodies with a side of politics. When *The Real Housewives of New York City*, for example, included a plot arc about the 2016 presidential election, viewers crowded onto online message boards to register their fatigue. "We come here for the Botox injections and slurring fights," the consensus seemed to be, on the boards that I follow; "we don't want to relive this national moment via reality TV." Subsequent *Housewives* episodes focusing on antiracism protests and clashes over mask wearing during the COVID-19 pandemic went on to evoke similarly weary sentiments.

And perhaps it's not a coincidence that our seat of political power seems to be where reality shows go to die. The Washington, DC, iteration of *Housewives* lasted just one season, and the capital city's *Real World*, as discussed, is considered one of the more boring. "When we did the D.C. season, in all the excitement of Obama coming in and young people being engaged—it landed with a big thud," Jonathan Murray has explained. "When we talked to our viewers, [they said] they didn't tune in to *The Real World* to watch a discussion of religion, which they saw as esoteric. They said if they wanted to watch that, they would watch CNN."[4] Murray's comment is particularly interesting given that in the early years of the show, *Real World* cast members *did* talk about these kinds of issues. On one episode from the first season, for instance, the roommates attended two political rallies, ramping up to the 1992 presidential election.[5] Perhaps this difference between then and now reflects the genre's increasing divergence from the documentary format and our shifting sense of what we expect these shows to offer us.

Yet in other ways—as the Oval Office tweet suggests— these two types of media spectacle are intensely intertwined, even if we don't often see that on our screens. Out here in the real world, unscripted entertainment has long been connected to politics, arguably dating back to Richard Nixon's 1968 *Laugh-In* appearance and Bill Clinton tooting his saxophone on *Arsenio* in 1992. In a book published while I was in preschool, the culture critic Neil Postman bemoaned the eclipsing of political life and show business and its deleterious impact on public discourse. He discussed, for instance, how we had elected actor Ronald Reagan to the presidency and how George McGovern and Jesse Jackson had both hosted *Saturday Night Live*.[6]

Today, the figures from reality TV are thoroughly unmoored from our screens, infusing our social media and moving within our political infrastructure. Sean from *The Real World: Boston*, for instance, served as a district attorney in Wisconsin from 2002 to 2010. He's married to Rachel from Pedro's season of *The Real World*, who has been a commentator on *The View* and Fox News. In 2011, Snooki tweeted at President Obama regarding his raised tax on tanning beds—a tweet to which Arizona senator John McCain responded supportively.[7] In 2016, Omarosa Manigault Newman joined the Trump campaign as director of African American outreach, later serving as an aide to the president and then returning to *Celebrity Big Brother*. In 2018, Minnesota state representative

Drew Christensen drafted a bill to ban *Bachelor* star Arie Luyendyk Jr. from the state after he jilted Minnesotan Becca Kufrin on the show.[8] Leading up to the 2020 presidential election, Cardi B interviewed Joe Biden about his proposed policies. And moving beyond the US, sometimes the connection between the genre and political life can be even thornier. Reality TV in the Arab world, the communications scholar Marwan Kraidy has pointed out, "is so controversial that it has triggered street riots, contributed to high-level political resignations, compelled clerics to issues hostile fatwas, and fanned transnational media wars."[9]

We can't know if Donald Trump would have been successful in his presidential bid if he hadn't sat behind a desk on *The Apprentice*, wearing a power suit and barking orders. One thing is certain, though: while the connection between politics and unscripted programming long predated and existed apart from him, Trump was particularly adept at exploiting that connection. His self-branding efforts rivaled those of the Kardashians. In addition to his signature hair and catchphrases (e.g., "You're fired!," "#sad"), he regularly used the political mic to bring attention to his various properties. As an NPR headline during his 2016 campaign succinctly explained, "Trump Often Uses the Campaign Spotlight to Promote His Own Brand."[10]

From the early days of his campaign and throughout his presidency, Trump also drew upon the key conventions of reality TV to his benefit. He used broad characterizations (the Fraudulent Media), mobilized controlling imagery that perpetuated demographic stereotypes (the Bad Hombre, the Nasty Woman), and relied on standard stories with simplistic plots and clear villains (China is to blame for the novel coronavirus). He successfully used a multiplatform approach;

his tweets will live in infamy. Unable or unwilling to remain silent, he chattered over his debate opponents in the manner of a Real Housewife on a reunion special. He also employed cliff-hangers and big reveals—as when, after an earlier teaser via Twitter, he unveiled his first Supreme Court pick. Later, his announcement of his second pick, Brett Kavanaugh, aired on ABC between *The Bachelorette* and the reality dating series *The Proposal*: a lineup primed to evoke parallels between these two types of spectacles. (One *Huffington Post* writer characterized the evening as "a nauseating turducken of reality pageantry.")[11] Also like the reality genre, Trump mobilized stereotypes about women and people of color in order to provide entertainment and to provoke emotion from his audience. Throughout his tenure in the White House, he was a shit-stirring *divide et impera* personality, fomenting conflict between two halves of a divided nation. His penchant for drama endured right up until the twilight of his presidency, when he incited an attack on the U.S. Capitol.

The Trump presidency seized upon our wariness about what's really real—a wariness that is common to our consumption of both politics and unscripted programming. Trump capitalized on our uneasy relationship with reality in an era of "fake news," "alternative truth," doctored footage, QAnon, and social media bots. These days, questioning verifiable facts isn't just for tinfoil-hat conspiracy theorists chattering on about faked moon landings and grassy knolls. This kind of thinking continues to shift into the mainstream, as otherwise seemingly normal folks—our mailmen, our teachers, our cousins—click and share memes about Democrat-led child sex-trafficking rings and microchips in our vaccines.

Of course, Trump was far from the first human to call into question our objective experience of reality, as any compendium of ancient philosophy would demonstrate. He was also hardly the first to blur real life and spectacle. In his 1998 book, *Life: The Movie*, the journalist and film critic Neal Gabler argued that life and art were now interchangeable. "Every day the life medium generates new episodes," he went on to explain. "Every day someone finds more inventive applications for its use."[12] While Gabler was reacting to events such as the O. J. Simpson trial and Princess Diana's death, today the thick intergrowth of fiction and truth confronts us everywhere. Although we can't lay this development at the feet of Trump or reality TV writ large, the fact that a reality star was installed in the Oval Office is crucial evidence of our continued synthesis of art and life. Indeed, Trump's ability to blur the two may have been buffered by our decades of watching reality TV. The genre has taught us to pair a heavy dose of skepticism with our ostensibly unscripted, "real" content.

But another thing that reality TV and Trump's rhetoric had in common was that consumers never had to believe they were "really real" in order to gravitate toward them. Much has been written about Trump's tenuous relationship with truth. In 2021, *The Washington Post* estimated that over the duration of his presidency, he made 30,573 "false or misleading claims."[13]

But fact-checking didn't stem the tide of these statements; indeed, as the *Post* pointed out, "nearly half" of these claims came in the final year of his presidency. Nor did fact-checking destabilize Trump's base, because people did not necessarily need to believe what he said in order to support him. As the communications theorist Dana Cloud points out, Trump's devotees took him "seriously" but not "*literally*": "His language is keyed to produce a feeling rather than make a convincing argument. . . . Part of being credible is resonating with the lives and struggles of one's audience."[14] Along similar lines, the media scholar Misha Kavka has pointed out that reality TV "works at the level of *feeling* rather than cognitive content."[15]

The people who watch reality TV don't need to view it as a pure mirror of life in order to enjoy and connect with it. "Although reality TV whets our desire for the authentic," Murray and Ouellette point out, "much of our engagement with such texts paradoxically hinges on our awareness that what we are watching is constructed and contains 'fictional' elements."[16] The shows themselves sometimes drop hints about their own artificiality. In the final episode of *The Hills*, for instance, the cameras pulled back to reveal the production set. Its participants have since disclosed that various situations on the show were staged.[17] These revelations hardly amounted to a scandal, and *The Hills* was even rebooted years later. A subgenre of reality TV explicitly plays with notions of what's real, with shows such as *Joe Millionaire* and *I Wanna Marry "Harry"* built on false premises that are ultimately exposed as such. On the flip side, scripted shows deploying some of the conventions of reality TV (*The Office*, *Parks and Recreation*, *Modern Family*) have woven together reality and unreality in an opposite way. Even the initial packaging of *The Real World* as a "true story" suggested that it existed somewhere between life and art. It was real, but with a narrative arc.

Personally, I enjoy looking for the "really real" moments in reality TV, the smudges in the gloss. When Kim goes off on Khloé and you get the sense she means it. When the Housewives haul out one another's real-life text messages to read during their reunions. When the kids on these shows say things that are offbeat and off-brand. When a participant on *What Not to Wear* gets so worked up that the usually polished hosts start glancing nervously at the cameras and reminding her it's only a TV show. Like a superfan searching for Easter eggs in a *Star Wars* movie, I find satisfaction in being able to recognize and acknowledge those moments. Though others may not share that particular pleasure, many of us are now savvy about how these cultural products are generated; yet that's almost incidental to our enjoyment of the genre. We respond to it "at the level of *feeling*," and maybe that's why we don't see much about politics *on* reality TV. Despite its serious and teaching moments, it's primarily about pleasure after all.

WHAT REALITY TV SAYS ABOUT US

Though we may watch it for fun, reality TV exposes sobering truths. The insights that we can draw from the genre run the gamut from the micro to the macro; it teaches us about ourselves as individuals and as groups and institutions and about the broad structures of power that overlay our lives. These programs show us social facts—Durkheim's forces that press upon us and from which it is difficult to wiggle free. They reveal how we splice the world into categories and then afford those categories differential social goods: money, health, respectability, power. They show us how we then advance particular cultural narratives to make these categories seem natural and right. They show us the narrow parameters we use to delineate legal marriage, real families, authentic childhoods, correct bodies, acceptable tastes, good girls, and legitimate sexual orientations. By watching these seemingly trivial programs about partyers, overeaters, and vaginal rejuvenators, we can see how those in power benefit from our validation of the status quo.

Americans have long been concerned with the erosion

of "traditional" values, and one might expect reality TV's outrageous misfits to be at the leading edge of that erosion. But while conservative groups would be unlikely to endorse most of these shows, they're havens for some of the most old-fashioned values that pulse through contemporary American society. They show us how steadfastly we cling to conventional ideas about, for instance, families, marriages, sex, women's roles, Black bodies, and queer people.

And here, too, reality TV and Donald Trump align. Both have relied on conservatism repackaged as outlandishness. Trump came onto the political scene as the man who wasn't a career politician—the flashy showman who would do things differently, who would "drain the swamp." But far from being a renegade, he capitalized on and crystallized the ideologies that have long loomed large in American culture. For example, while other contemporary presidents more quietly embraced xenophobic and racist policies (e.g., antidrug laws that have led to the mass incarceration of Black and brown people), Trump moved to ban immigrants from "shithole" countries, denied the very existence of systemic racism, and, when Nazis clashed with anti-Nazi protesters in the streets of Charlottesville, told the press that there were "very fine people, on both sides." And while prior presidents have embraced retrograde ideas about gender, Trump was caught on tape boasting about grabbing a woman's genitals. Both Donald Trump and reality TV have dazzled us using dramatics that are at once entertaining and pedestrian. They offer us extreme strains of the values that already course through our national veins.

In demonstrating these narrow-minded views of the world, in some ways the reality genre mirrors the worst of ourselves. We sustain inequalities through the stories we tell, and we pass on these beliefs and practices to our kids. We manipulate others and allow ourselves to be manipulated by them. We buy lots of stuff, and we focus on those material possessions as the pathway to bliss. We overindulge. We sexualize children, laugh at poor and fat people, and render some segments of the population invisible. These programs demonstrate how centuries-old stereotypes still thrum within our culture like a meaty heart. They take the little oozing bundles of our racism, our sexism, and our heteronormativity and lay them at our feet. In the wild curvatures of the fun-house mirror, we are ourselves but uglier, more grotesque.

The fact that we want to *view* this particular content shows us things about ourselves as well. First, though we may feel we live in a time of increasing isolation, we're still fundamentally social animals. In Durkheim's time, people bonded over shared interests, beliefs, and rituals—and we still do those things today. While reality TV is not solely responsible for our cohesiveness as a society, the genre is one strand in the thick ropes of culture that bind us together. Second, the fact that we want to watch those ugly curvatures suggests that we crave clear-cut categories and distinctions. As Trump's popularity has shown us, we are soothed by simple stories about social hierarchies that are rooted in nature and individual effort. Even in the face of contrary evidence, we want to believe in firm boundaries—between childhood and adulthood, male and female, queer guy and straight dude, crook and saint. We're comforted when the genre shows us people who have gone out of bounds and are yanked back in—whether they're aggressive women, wealthy people of color, tacky dressers, or murderers.

Indeed, the fact that reality TV is arguably offensive a lot of the time, while at the same time presenting itself as "real," enables it to reveal our cultural stereotypes in a way that other genres are too timid or polite to show us. And we have a voracious appetite for them. While other cultural products teach us things about ourselves as well, reality TV does this on a vast and unprecedented scale. Perhaps more than any other medium, it shows us the breadth of human experience. Even in its gaps, we can spy glints of who we are.

Still, while some of our most retrograde values flow through these programs, *they don't always, and they don't have to*. Like any entertainment medium, unscripted programming has the capacity to evolve. We've seen how it has popped from its documentary roots, thrusting zanier and zanier cast members into increasingly convoluted and provocative scenarios. But these shows can also keep pace with our social consciousness. In 2020, for example, some cast members on the Bravo show *Vanderpump Rules* were fired for falsely reporting a Black castmate to the police, while others were given the ax for their racist tweets.[18] That same year, CBS announced that, moving forward, at least half of the participants on its reality shows would be people of color and that the network would be allocating at least a quarter of its annual development budget for reality programming to those programs created or co-created by people of color.[19] While we may skeptically view such efforts as unsubstantial lip service, and while the genre continues to promulgate racial divisions and stereotyping in a variety of ways, these examples nonetheless reflect a departure from how reality TV shows' creators have dealt with racism, and with inclusion, in the past.

Indeed, many aspects of reality TV make it inherently well suited for showing us *new* ways of living, thinking, and organizing our worlds. As we've seen, this is particularly true for some of the more marginal shows, the ones most squarely located in Racquel Gates's "televisual gutter." We may perceive these shows as less mainstream or give them less attention than their counterparts in the genre for a variety of reasons—because they are "Black shows," or "gay shows," or niche cable shows on far-flung networks. While these designations themselves reflect our long-standing social inequalities, there can be a kind of freedom in not being taken too seriously. These programs, in particular, hold the potential to scribble wildly outside the lines.

So, all is not lost. Reality TV doesn't just teach us that we're awful. While on the one hand these shows demonstrate the durability of social categorization and the insidious tenacity of the narratives that support them, on the other hand they also reveal the tremendous diversity of our experiences and our own ability to push back against societal constraints. Reality TV was the canary in the coal mine when it came to gay representation. It's given Black women and trans people a platform in ways that scripted TV has not. It's shown us some new possibilities for families and gender expression. Its educational value lies not only in showing us how intractable we are but also in its potential to offer us a different snapshot. And personally, I probably wouldn't be such a fan if I didn't believe in that potential.

Throughout its history, the genre has shown us types of people we don't often see on scripted TV. And while their representations can be problematic, these stars also use their creativity and tenacity to work within, expose, and finagle their own stereotyping. When we view it with a sociological imagination, reality TV reveals the immense power of social structures, institutions, and cultural narratives to constrain us. But it also shows us how our past doesn't have to define us—or else we would always remain the same. Often on the vanguard of new social and technological developments, from changes in marriage to multiplatform branding, the genre reveals how we feel the pressure of societal expectations but also how we move around under that pressure, putting our heads down and plunging forward. While the mirror magnifies our flaws, it also showcases the extreme arcs of our beauty, how we move, and how we evolve.

THE REALITY OF REALITY TV

When I tell people that I teach a college class on the sociology of reality TV, they often ask, "Is it about how the shows are all fake?" The class isn't about that, though it doesn't ignore the fact that reality shows—casted, curated, manipulated, edited, and packaged—bear the smudgy thumbprints of their creators. They're just like any other cultural products in that sense.

Still, the question of whether reality shows are "really real" misses the mark and does a disservice to what these shows can actually teach us. In the end, unscripted programming teaches us that *all* reality is socially constructed. The genre exposes how we make designations about what is "real"—designations that we then turn around and perceive as universal and innate. In its raw and heightened portrayals of the norms we create and pass down to our children, it peels back our collective skin and shows us, bloody and messy, the things that we value, who gets to be seen as real, and who doesn't stand a chance. But then it rears back and shows us that what it means to be "real" is, in fact, ambiguous. Once we peer into the face of that ambiguity, we're better able to see the unstable social fictions that more broadly dominate our lives.

What we experience as reality, often, is not universal and static but a shifting amalgam like Countess LuAnn. Who and what get to be seen as legitimate? Who takes a seat within the core of society, and who is confined to the margins? What constitutes an authentic family or a real childhood? Who's allowed to be mean? How do we think about women and sexuality and racial minorities and wealth and our own bodies and what's tasteful and what's not? Reality television teaches us how the categories and meanings we use to organize our worlds are built on unsteady ground. These designations are "real" in the sense that they have significant repercussions—how high we ascend in the educational system, how much we earn, where we live, how healthy we are, how much other people respect us, and when we die. They're real in terms of how we think about our own identities. But they aren't "real" in the sense of historically transcendent and immutable. Ultimately, the genre exposes how *our "reality" is largely a social reality—something humans created.*

Furthermore, if we learned anything from Donald Trump's tenure in the White House, it's this: one thing that's "really real" about unscripted programming is its impact. Not only did starring on *The Apprentice* perhaps help propel Trump to the White House, and not only did the president employ techniques from the genre to buffer his popularity, but his presidency arguably *became* a reality show. Ultimately, during the waning days of his administration, we watched in real time as he whipped his followers into a lather. Windows were shattered, lives were lost, and the event left an indelible mark: in a historic move, Trump was impeached for a second time. Trump's role in the insurrection at the Capitol was a particularly extreme example of the consequences that can ensue when entertainment and reality are indistinguishably fused in an ouroboros.

But as we've seen, by looking at such extreme examples,

we can better understand social processes that are happening more regularly on a smaller scale. And the Trump presidency has been far from the only reality show to have social repercussions. The genre has influenced disparate areas, ranging from teen pregnancy rates to prison reform and the genesis of "Instagram star" as a profession. Some scholarship has drawn connections between the genre and surveillance culture. Mark Andrejevic, for example, has observed that reality TV "works neatly as an advertisement for the benefits of submission to comprehensive surveillance in an era in which such submission is increasingly productive."[20] Reality TV isn't solely responsible for this culture, but it arguably functions as a tool of this culture and as a key site where we can see this surveillance happening. Notably, Andrejevic made this claim back in 2004—on the cusp of Facebook (2004) and before Twitter (2006), before Edward Snowden and WikiLeaks and Russian bots and the DNC email hack and the online algorithms that know women are pregnant before their families do.[21] Today, we live our lives publicly in unprecedented ways, not only primed for our own surveillance but also actively participating in it in a plurality of ways. As Kim Kardashian has pointed out, when asked about the media's objectification of women, "Even if I'm objectifying myself, I feel good about it."[22]

Though we're not all storming the Capitol with zip ties in hand, there are other connections between the material on these shows and how we engage with the world. One study of nearly five hundred adolescents over three years found that girls who watched *Temptation Island*, *The Bachelor*, or *Joe Millionaire* were more likely to communicate with one another about sexuality and that boys who watched were more likely to be sexually active.[23] Other research has found that watching programs such as *Real Housewives*, *16 and Preg-*

nant, and *Keeping Up with the Kardashians* was connected to young adults' ideas about gender and relationships. For instance, "heavy viewers" of these shows "were more likely to think females in the real world engage in inappropriate behaviors (e.g., arguing, gossip) more than males."[24] These viewers were also more likely to overestimate the extent to which real-life romantic relationships involve conflict.[25] Another study found that people who heavily consumed TV shows, like *Keeping Up with the Kardashians*, "that valorize and regularly portray wealth, fame, and luxury" are "significantly more materialistic and anti-welfare than lighter consumers."[26] Viewers of reality TV are more likely than nonviewers to have one-night stands;[27] to use tanning lamps and to tan outdoors;[28] to drink alcohol;[29] to go hot-tubbing on dates;[30] and to engage in online activity such as blogging, video sharing, and social media use.[31]

While correlation is not causation—that is, maybe the *types* of people who gravitate toward hot tubs and tanning lamps are also the types of people more likely to enjoy reality TV—it's not out of the question that the genre also encourages such behaviors. One study of college students, for instance, found that some men watch reality programs in order to learn more about dating.[32] In another study, viewers explicitly said that makeover TV had induced them to consider plastic surgery.[33] Other research, discussed throughout this book, has directly shown causal links between these shows and the lifestyles and values of the people who watch.[34]

And perhaps none of this is surprising, as media psychologists have long demonstrated that the TV we watch contributes to our beliefs about the world. "Cultivation theory," an approach to media established by the communication scholar

George Gerbner, argues that "the more time people spend 'living' in the TV world, the more likely they are to believe social reality is congruent with TV reality."[35] Unscripted programming is now nearly half of that TV.[36] It would be astounding if it *hadn't* impacted our lives. Love it or bemoan it, gobble it up or wrinkle your nose and push it away, it's a part of us now. It is an echo of our culture, but it's also *potent*, moving us in various ways. And it can actually impact us for the better. The ethicist Deni Elliott has argued, for instance, that despite its problems, reality programming can be used as a tool for greater inclusivity. Through this genre, people can look into lives different from their own, better understand their own values, and engage in democratic action.[37]

Now, to be clear, none of this gets into the ethics of the *production* of these shows. As a viewer, I don't feel good when *Bachelor* contestants are filmed too drunk to stand or when true crime programs mine entertainment from survivors' pain. And the filming process can be brutal to the crews as well as the performers on reality TV. As we know, these relatively low-budget productions tend not to employ paid actors or unionized crews—a context potentially ripe for exploitation. For instance, programs such as *Top Chef, The Real Housewives of Orange County, The Bachelorette*, and *Big Brother* continued to film during the height of COVID-19. As one field producer who had worked on popular reality shows told *Vanity Fair* in September 2020, "Producers and crews already have been treated like they're expendable in this industry since it started. COVID is just another hoop for production companies and networks to navigate through as cheaply and as quickly as they possibly can."[38] While morality is not the topic of this particular book (recall Simmel's point about how sociology does not "complain or condone"), it is important to look at the assembly and dissemination of these shows with—at the very least—a critical ethical eye.

Still, we've seen how the genre gives voice to people who might not otherwise have a platform. More broadly, Kathryn Lofton suggests that one reason we should care about popular culture is that while it can catalyze disaster, as in the cases of the propaganda historically deployed by fascists, it can also enable meaningful social change.[39] By magnifying our faults, reality TV can spur us to behave differently. When Julie first stepped out of that cab and into that loft in New York City, she became part of something that would alter our lives. This genre has been our background noise, for many of us, since childhood; we sway with its rhythms, which have grown progressively louder and don't promise to go away.

As a final note, it is my hope that this book has inspired you to stop and listen more closely to that music—to think about not only the dynamics of these programs but also those at work in other media and in our everyday lives. To interrogate what purpose they serve. And to understand that sometimes the better question is not what's "really real" but how our existing notions of what's real and true are generated. Because while this guilty pleasure is demonstrably unhealthy for us in some ways, it's also a site for deep reflection about who we are as a culture, the places we've been, and where we want to go next.

Notes

Complete bibliographic information can be found in the References section.

INTRODUCTION

1. Kaufman 2018, 21.
2. Johnson 2000.
3. Bell 2010, 8.
4. Dehnart 2018.
5. Koppel 2001.
6. Statista 2016.
7. Lundy, Ruth, and Park 2008.
8. Gerbner 1969; Signorielli and Morgan 1996, 117.
9. Gerbner et al. 1986.
10. Gerbner et al. 1986, 18.
11. Montemurro 2008, 84.
12. Butler 1999, 175–76.
13. Becker 1963; Durkheim [1895] 2002; Epstein 1994; Goffman [1961] 2017.
14. Domoff et al. 2012, 993.
15. Kearney and Levine 2015.
16. Corner 2002.
17. Murray and Ouellette 2009, 4.
18. Huff 2006, 10.
19. Lenig 2017.
20. Pozner 2010, 281–82.
21. Kaufman 2013.
22. Pozner 2010, 285.
23. Lenig 2017, 3.
24. Montemurro 2008; Murray and Ouellette 2009.
25. Blickley 2018.
26. Bignell 2005; Biressi and Nunn 2005; Cummings 2002; Holmes and

Jermyn 2004; Kavka 2012; Kilborn 1994; Montemurro 2008; Murray 2004; Roth 2003.
27. Kilborn 1994.
28. Nabi et al. 2006.
29. Calvert 2000.
30. Lundy, Ruth, and Park 2008; Papacharissi and Mendelson 2007.
31. Lenig 2017, 12; Papacharissi and Mendelson 2007.
32. Stefanone, Lackaff, and Rosen 2010.
33. Edwards 2013.
34. Kaufman 2018, 102.
35. Kaufman 2018, 164.
36. Horton and Wohl 1956.
37. Punyanunt-Carter 2010.
38. Rose and Wood 2005, 284, drawing on Baudrillard 1983.
39. Deery 2004, 1.
40. Deery 2012, 2.
41. Plaugic 2017.
42. Kaufman 2018, 225.
43. Deery 2012, 2.
44. Thomas and Swaine Thomas 1928, 572.
45. Abt and Mustazza 1997; Gamson 1998; Grindstaff 2002.
46. Arnovitz 2004.
47. Brown 2016.
48. Kaufman 2018.
49. Papacharissi and Mendelson 2007.
50. Adalian 2011.
51. Obama 2018.
52. Lofton 2017, 21.
53. Simmel [1903] 1971, 339.
54. Lundy, Ruth, and Park 2008.

1. "DON'T BE ALL, LIKE, UNCOOL" (THE SELF)
1. *The Real World* 1992a.
2. Mills 1959.
3. Durkheim [1901] 1982, 52.
4. Durkheim [1897] 1951.
5. Mills 1959, 3.
6. Ouellette and Hay 2008; Weber 2009.
7. Simmel [1903] 1971, 329.
8. *Breaking Amish* 2012.
9. Simmel [1903] 1971, 326.
10. Durkheim [1901] 1982, 56.
11. Chudnofsky 2013.

12. Cooley 1922, 184.
13. Goffman 1959.
14. Murray and Ouellette 2009, 2.
15. Suggitt 2018.
16. Turner 2006.
17. Davis 2017; see also Warner 2015.
18. Pickens 2015, 41.
19. Kaufman 2018, 164.
20. Edwards 2013, 20.
21. *The Real Housewives of New York City* 2008.
22. *The Real Housewives of New York City* 2015a.
23. Gold 2015.
24. Dodes 2018.
25. *The Real Housewives of New York City* 2015b.
26. Rouse 2015.
27. *The Real Housewives of New York City* 2018.
28. Dodes 2018.
29. West and Zimmerman 1987, 128.
30. Valenzuela, Halpern and Katz 2014.
31. Goffman 1959.
32. Mead [1934] 1994.

2. "HERE FOR THE RIGHT REASONS" (COUPLES)

1. *The Bachelor* 2015.
2. Parker 2020.
3. Porter 2019.
4. Moors et al. 2013.
5. Krueger, Heckhausen, and Hundertmark 1995; Byrne and Carr 2005.
6. Bailey 1989.
7. Bailey 1989, 98.
8. *The Bachelor* 2014.
9. McNearney 2017.
10. Eastwick and Finkel 2008.
11. Cleveland, Fisher, and Sawyer 2015.
12. Bailey 1989, 94.
13. Fein and Schneider 1995.
14. *The Millionaire Matchmaker* 2008.
15. Bailey 1989, 87.
16. Wade 2017.
17. Bogle 2008; England and Thomas 2006; Wade 2017.
18. England and Thomas 2006, 147.
19. Yapalater 2016.
20. Yapalater 2016.

21. E. Johnson 2016.
22. Cato and Carpentier 2010.
23. https://www.youtube.com/watch?v=rjPVo564uxE.
24. Gardner 2012.
25. Ahmed and Matthes 2016; Durrheim et al. 2005; Gopaldas and Siebert 2018.
26. Dubrofsky 2006, 39.
27. Geiger and Livingston 2018.
28. Geiger and Livingston 2018; Michael et al. 1994; Wilcox and Wang 2017.
29. Ryan and Bauman 2016; Williams and Emamdjomeh 2018.
30. Fiore and Donath 2005; Lin and Lundquist 2013.
31. Bialik 2017.
32. Aurthur 2017.
33. Coontz 2005, 5–6.
34. Cherlin 2004.
35. Cherlin 2004, 851.
36. Cherlin 2009.
37. *90 Day Fiancé: Happily Ever After?* 2018.
38. Hagi 2017.
39. Roca 2017.
40. Longo 2018, 469.
41. Longo 2018, 469.
42. Pearce, Clifford, and Tandon 2011.
43. Longo 2018, 487.
44. Rubin 1999, 151.
45. Wang and Parker 2014.
46. Edin and Kefalas 2011.
47. Cherlin 2004, 848.
48. *Love Is Blind* 2020.
49. Kerr 2019.
50. R. Johnson 2016.
51. Lawless and Italie 2020.
52. Bialik 2017.

3. "NOT HERE TO MAKE FRIENDS" (GROUPS)

1. *Survivor* 2000a.
2. Simmel 1964, 22.
3. Simmel 1964, 134.
4. *Naked and Afraid* 2013.
5. Simmel 1964, 136.
6. Simmel 1964, 156.
7. *Survivor* 2000b.

8. Simmel 1964, 134.
9. Simmel 1964, 134.
10. *Top Chef* 2007.
11. Durkheim [1897] 1951.
12. Durkheim [1901] 1982, 52–53.
13. Durkheim [1901] 1982, 53.
14. Colicchio 2007.
15. Schneider 2018.

4. "KIM IS ALWAYS LATE" (FAMILIES)

1. *Keeping Up with the Kardashians* 2007.
2. Spector 2015.
3. Lofton 2017, 186.
4. Goode 2006, 18.
5. Goode 2006, 19.
6. *Keeping Up with the Kardashians* 2007.
7. Cherlin 2004.
8. Amato et al. 2007; Cherlin 2004, 2009; Coontz 2005.
9. Thornton and Young-DeMarco 2001.
10. Amato 2007, 207.
11. Cherlin 2004.
12. Cherlin 2004.
13. *Sister Wives* 2010.
14. *Sister Wives* 2016.
15. Hays 1996.
16. Hays 1996, 20; drawing on Whiting and Edwards 1988.
17. Hays 1996, 27.
18. Coontz 2000, 288.
19. Hays 1996, 29.
20. Yahr 2014.
21. Whiting 2013.
22. Duh 2017.
23. Ghahremani 2012.
24. Alvarez 2018.
25. France 2018.
26. *Celebrity Wife Swap* 2012.
27. Hays 1996, 21.
28. *Supernanny* 2005.
29. Lareau 2002, 747.
30. Crimesider Staff 2015.
31. Gates 2017.
32. Gates 2017.
33. Gates 2017.

34. Dunn n.d.
35. Harris-Perry 2011, 114.
36. PBS n.d.
37. Muñoz 1998.
38. Weston 1997.
39. Flores 2017.
40. Hurtado 2018.
41. Engstrom and Semic 2003, 145.
42. Pew Research Forum 2015.
43. Cherlin 2010.
44. Cherlin 2004, 853.
45. Edwards 2013, 5.
46. Popenoe 1993.

5. "SPARKLE, BABY!" (CHILDHOOD)

1. *Toddlers & Tiaras* 2009b.
2. Mintz 2010.
3. Mintz 2010.
4. Mintz 2010, 65.
5. Mintz 2010, 58.
6. Mintz 2010, 58.
7. Mintz 2010, 58.
8. Hays 1996, 20.
9. Hays 1996, 24.
10. Hays 1996, 40; citing Vincent 1951, 205.
11. *Toddlers & Tiaras* 2011b.
12. *Toddlers & Tiaras* 2011a.
13. *Chopped Junior* 2016.
14. Fair et al. 2009.
15. Bannon 2008.
16. Duggar et al. 2014, 92.
17. Mitovich 2015.
18. Brückner, Martin, and Bearman 2004, 249.
19. Terry-Humen, Manlove, and Moore 2005.
20. Jaffee et al. 2001.
21. Schalet 2006, 132.
22. Schalet 2006.
23. Guttmacher Institute 2019.
24. Sexuality Information and Education Council of the United States 2018.
25. Stanger-Hall and Hall 2011.
26. Foucault 1990, 27.
27. Kane 2006, 162–63.

28. *16 and Pregnant* 2010.
29. Kirby and Lepore 2007.
30. Kost and Henshaw 2014.
31. Mintz 2010, 59.
32. Mintz 2010.
33. Bourdieu 1984.
34. Bourdieu 1986.
35. Davis-Kean 2005.
36. *Child Genius* 2015a.
37. Lareau 2002, 747.
38. *Child Genius* 2015b.
39. McBee 2006.
40. Lareau 2002, 747.
41. Levey Friedman 2013, 92.
42. Levey Friedman 2013, 92.
43. *Dance Moms* 2012a.

6. "I QUESTION YOUR TASTE LEVEL" (CLASS)

1. *Toddlers & Tiaras* 2012.
2. Deery 2012, 4.
3. Kraszewski 2017.
4. Marx and Engels [1848] 1994.
5. Marx [1852] 1994.
6. *Undercover Boss* 2012.
7. Marx 1867.
8. Marx and Engels [1846] 1994.
9. Weber [1922] 1968.
10. Harris Insights and Analytics 2014.
11. https://www.youtube.com/watch?v=5YMV05HosIo.
12. Weber [1922] 1968.
13. Harris Insights and Analytics 2014.
14. Mejia 2018.
15. Collins 1990.
16. *Here Comes Honey Boo Boo* 2012.
17. Bloomquist 2015, 412.
18. Lena 2019, 119.
19. Lena 2019, 121.
20. Lenig 2017, 164.
21. Deadline Team 2013.
22. Skeggs, Thumim, and Wood 2008, 9.
23. Allen and Mendick 2013, 469.
24. Calvert 2000; Nabi et al. 2006.
25. Lena 2019.

26. Zulkey 2012.
27. Poniewozik 2012.
28. Bourdieu 1986, 48.
29. Glasser, Robnett, and Feliciano 2009.
30. Czerniawski 2012.
31. Czerniawski 2012, 130.
32. Wegenstein and Ruck 2011.
33. Allen and Mendick 2013, 462; see also Skeggs 2009.
34. Weber 2009, 79.
35. Bourdieu 1984, 99.
36. *Project Runway* 2019b.
37. *Project Runway* 2019a.
38. Weber [1904] 2012.
39. Conley 2017, 107.
40. Lenig 2017.
41. Bourdieu 1984, 101.
42. *The Real Housewives of Beverly Hills* 2011.
43. *The Real Housewives of Beverly Hills* 2012.
44. *Duck Dynasty* 2012.
45. Umstead 2013.
46. Katz 2016.
47. O'Connor 2013.
48. Jennings 2019.
49. Lena 2019; see also López-Sintas and Katz-Gerro 2005.
50. DiMaggio 1987, 444.
51. Peterson and Simkus 1992.
52. Lena 2019, 6–7; see also Peterson and Kern 1996.
53. Lundy, Ruth, and Park 2008; Papacharissi and Mendelson 2007.
54. Lundy, Ruth, and Park 2008.
55. Nussbaum 2016.
56. *The Real Housewives of New York City* 2015c.
57. de Moraes and Bloom 2014.
58. Maglio 2018.
59. Robehmed 2018.
60. Casserly 2011.
61. Lena 2019.
62. Lena 2019, ix; see also Johnston and Baumann 2007.
63. Maglio 2018.
64. Lena 2019.
65. Bourdieu 1984, 110.
66. Kochhar 2018.
67. Clark 2015.
68. Carnevale et al. 2019.

7. "WHO GON' CHECK ME, BOO?" (RACE)

1. *The Real Housewives of Atlanta* 2009.
2. Thomas 2005.
3. Lefebvre [1991] 2014, 289.
4. Bureau of Labor Statistics 2019.
5. Sakala 2014.
6. Wagner 2017.
7. Massey and Denton 1993.
8. Massey and Denton 1993.
9. Wilkerson 2020, 17.
10. Gates 2018, 147.
11. Kaufman 2018, 103.
12. Quinn 2017.
13. Harris 2015, 26; Palmer-Mehta and Haliliuc 2009; Pozner 2010.
14. Bloomquist 2015, 411.
15. Blistein 2018.
16. Simon, Sidner, and Ellis 2019.
17. Framke and Abad-Santos 2015.
18. Teeman 2018.
19. *The Challenge: Battle of the Exes* 2012.
20. Morrissey 2012.
21. Coleman 2014.
22. Palmer-Mehta and Haliliuc 2009, 89–90.
23. Simien 2014, 43.
24. Crenshaw 1989.
25. McCall 2005.
26. Smith-Shomade 2002.
27. Lemons 1977, 104.
28. Lemons 1977, 102.
29. Palmer-Mehta and Haliliuc 2009, 91.
30. *The Real World* 1993.
31. Orbe 1998, 35.
32. Collins 2004, 56.
33. Campbell et al. 2008.
34. *I Love New York* 2007.
35. West 2018, 148–49.
36. Allison 2016, xxi.
37. Allison 2016, xxii.
38. Adelabu 2015; Harris 2015.
39. Collins 1990.
40. Pager and Karafin 2009, 70; citing Kirschenman and Neckerman 1991; Moss and Tilly 2001; and Wilson 1996.
41. Bertrand and Mullainathan 2004.

42. Wilson, Hugenberg, and Rule 2017.
43. Hegewisch and Hartmann 2019.
44. Anderson 2018.
45. Xu et al. 2018, 10.
46. Lemons 1977, 102.
47. Harris 2015, 20.
48. *Married to Medicine* 2013.
49. hooks 1981, 55.
50. *America's Next Top Model* 2004.
51. *America's Next Top Model* 2005a.
52. *America's Next Top Model* 2005b.
53. Crenshaw 1989.
54. Ettachfini 2019.
55. Dubrofsky 2006.
56. Dehnart 2007.
57. Dehnart 2018.
58. Lichter and Amundson 2018.
59. Park et al. 2015.
60. Lichter and Amundson 2018; Park et al. 2015.
61. Flores 2017.
62. Fernandez 2013.
63. Lichter and Amundson 2018, 70.
64. Smith-Shomade 2002.
65. Jenkins 2017, 77.
66. Tejada 2017.
67. Pew Research Center 2015.
68. Wong et al. 2012.
69. Wang 2010, 404.
70. López, Ruiz, and Patten 2017.
71. Hamamoto 1994, 4.
72. *Students for Fair Admissions, Inc. v. President and Fellows of Harvard College* 2018.
73. Simien 2014.
74. Allison 2016, xxi.
75. Boylorn 2008, 430.
76. Gates 2018.
77. Warner 2015.
78. Grossman 2012.
79. *Dance Moms* 2012b.
80. DuBois 1903, 2.
81. Gamson 1998, 19.
82. Whiting, Campbell, and Pearson-McNeil 2013, 16.
83. Whiting, Campbell, and Pearson-McNeil 2013, 17.

84. Allison 2016, xxiv.
85. Brown Givens and Monahan 2005.
86. https://en.wikipedia.org/wiki/Controversy_and_criticism_of_Jersey_Shore.
87. Conley 2017.
88. Gonzalez-Barrera and Lopez 2015.
89. Gates 2017.
90. Fernandez 2013.
91. *Snooki & Jwoww: Moms with Attitude* 2019.
92. *Snooki & Jwoww: Moms with Attitude* 2019.
93. Cillizza 2019.
94. Mill and Stein 2016.
95. Ignatiev 2012.
96. Conley 2017.
97. Thomas and Swaine Thomas 1928, 572.

8. "WE'RE ALL BORN NAKED . . ." (GENDER)

1. *RuPaul's Drag Race* 2011.
2. West and Zimmerman 1987.
3. Intersex Society of North America 2008.
4. Laqueur 1990.
5. West and Zimmerman 1987.
6. *Toddlers & Tiaras* 2009a.
7. Risman 2004, 429.
8. Butler 1999, 175, emphasis in original.
9. West and Zimmerman 1987.
10. Framke 2018.
11. *Naked and Afraid* 2013.
12. Biegert 2017.
13. Weber 2016, quoting Kristi Russell.
14. Brown 2017; Praderio 2018.
15. Rubin 1975, 179.
16. Lorber 1994, 37.
17. Lorber 1994, 33.
18. *17 Kids and Counting* 2008.
19. Cleveland, Fisher, and Sawyer 2015.
20. United States Bureau of Labor Statistics 2008.
21. Anderson, Binder, and Krause 2002; Avellar and Smock 2003; Budig and England 2001.
22. Mattingly and Bianchi 2003.
23. Bittman and Wacjman 2000.
24. Hartmann 1979, 3.
25. Hartmann 1979, 14.

26. Toossi and Morisi 2017.
27. Bianchi et al. 2000.
28. Mahajan et al. 2020.
29. Lévi-Strauss [1949] 1994.
30. Hamilton, Geist, and Powell 2011, 157.
31. *The Millionaire Matchmaker* 2008.
32. James et al. 2016; Wirtz et al. 2020, 227.
33. Victory Institute 2019, 5.
34. *My Strange Addiction* 2010.
35. Parreñas 2001, 78.
36. Garrity 2019.
37. Stokes 2018.
38. Barber, Foley, and Jones 1999.
39. Eagly, Makhijani, and Klonsky 1992, 3.
40. Eagly and Karau 2002; Heilman et al. 2004.
41. Doyle 2016.
42. Nelson 2016.
43. Steffensmeier and Demuth 2000; Everett and Wojtkiewicz 2002.
44. Pager 2003.
45. Abramovitch 2018.
46. Holmes 2018; Leah 2018.
47. Toffel 1996.
48. *Snapped* 2011.
49. Butler 1999, 175–76.

9. "FOOD, A DRINK, AND A GAY" (SEXUALITY)

1. *Are You the One?* 2019.
2. GLAAD 2019.
3. Conley 2017, A-11.
4. Rubin 1975.
5. Foucault 1990, 17.
6. Foucault 1990, 11.
7. HRC staff 2015.
8. Marx and Engels [1846] 1994, 15.
9. Rubin 1975, 179.
10. Foucault 1990.
11. Weston 1997.
12. Himberg 2014, 296, citing personal communication with Amy Shpall.
13. Greene 2014.
14. Rubin 1999, 151.
15. Geiger, Harwood, and Hummert 2006; Herek 1984; Vaughn et al. 2017.
16. Riese 2019.
17. *A Shot at Love with Tila Tequila* 2007a.

18. *A Shot at Love with Tila Tequila* 2007b.
19. https://www.youtube.com/watch?v=mWLVXWLN4-s.
20. Nordyke 2007.
21. For example: Callis 2014; Richter 2011; Suhr 2012.
22. Fredrickson and Roberts 1997.
23. Fredrickson and Roberts 1997.
24. Rivers, Barnett, and Baruch 1979; Duckett, Raffaelli, and Richards 1989.
25. Phares, Steinberg, and Thompson 2004, 421.
26. Statista 2019.
27. Martins, Tiggemann, and Kirkbride 2007, 634.
28. Fredrickson et al. 1998.
29. France 2017.
30. *The Real World* 2009a.
31. Eliason 1997, 318.
32. Bennett 1992.
33. Callis 2013.
34. *The Real World* 2009b.
35. Garber 1995.
36. *A Shot at Love with Tila Tequila* 2007b.
37. Eliason 1997.
38. Eliason 2000, 149.
39. McClean 2008.
40. Pew Research Center 2017.
41. Callis 2013.
42. Eliason 2000, 149.
43. Associated Press 2018.
44. Groom 2008.
45. *Jersey Shore: Family Vacation* 2018.
46. *The Real Housewives of Orange County* 2011.
47. https://www.urbandictionary.com/define.php?term=pocket+gay.
48. https://www.merriam-webster.com/dictionary/gay.
49. Sanders et al. 2015.
50. Foucault 1990, 43.
51. Rubin 1999, 171.
52. Kavka 2008, 130; see also Pullen 2006.
53. Muñoz 1998, 154, quoting Bill Clinton.
54. Advocate.com editors 2004.
55. Morrissey 2010.
56. Gates 2018, 150.

10. "BAD BOYS, BAD BOYS" (DEVIANCE)

1. *My Strange Addiction* 2011.
2. Epstein 1994; Lindemann 2012, 2019.

3. Garfinkel 1964.

4. Becker 1963, 12.

5. Durkheim [1895] 2002.

6. Becker 1953.

7. Sutherland and Cressey 1966.

8. Hutcherson 2012.

9. *My Big Fat American Gypsy Wedding* 2012.

10. Merton 1938, 1968.

11. Merton 1938, 676.

12. Lewis 2008.

13. Goffman 1963, 2.

14. Goffman 1963, 3.

15. Goffman 1963, 3.

16. *Hoarding: Buried Alive* 2010.

17. Goffman 1963, 9.

18. Goffman 1963, 9.

19. *Lockdown* 2007.

20. Foucault 1990, 11.

21. Foucault 1995, 141.

22. Foucault 1995, 143.

23. Foucault 1995, 143–44.

24. Foucault 1995, 143.

25. Foucault 1995, 149.

26. Andreeva 2011.

27. Schneider 2019.

28. Pariona 2018.

29. Sawyer and Wagner 2019.

30. The Sentencing Project 2019.

31. Bureau of Justice Statistics 2016.

32. Tilly 1999, 257.

33. Tilly 1999.

34. Collins 2004, 158.

35. Bass 2001.

36. The Sentencing Project 2019.

37. Nellis 2016.

38. Harris 1999; Mitchell and Caudy 2015.

39. Everett and Wojtkiewicz 2002; Steffensmeier and Demuth 2000.

40. *Live PD* 2020.

41. Callanan and Rosenberger 2011; Eschholz et al. 2002.

42. Durkheim [1895] 2002.

43. Durkheim [1895] 2002.

44. Durkheim [1895] 2002.

45. Chemers 2016.

46. Chemers 2016.
47. Lundy, Ruth, and Park 2008; Papacharissi and Mendelson 2007.
48. Lemert 1999.
49. Lemert 1999, 387.
50. Nabi et al. 2006, 428.
51. Kilborn 1994.
52. Lundy, Ruth, and Park 2008, 215.
53. Hill 2015, 4.
54. Statista 2016.

CONCLUSION

1. Donald J. Trump (@realDonaldTrump), "Great meeting with @Kim Kardashian today, talked about prison reform and sentencing," Twitter, May 30, 2018, 6:59 p.m., https://twitter.com/realDonaldTrump /status/1001961235838103552 (account now suspended).
2. Edwards 2013, 3.
3. Biressi and Nunn 2005.
4. Adalian 2011.
5. *The Real World* 1992b.
6. Postman [1985] 2005, 4.
7. CNN 2011.
8. Walsh 2018.
9. Kraidy 2010, 3.
10. Anderson 2016.
11. Fallon 2018.
12. Gabler 1998, 10.
13. Kessler 2021.
14. Cloud 2018, x.
15. Kavka 2008, x.
16. Murray and Ouellette 2009, 7.
17. Corinthios 2019.
18. Aurthur and Wagmeister 2020.
19. Hauser 2020.
20. Andrejevic 2004, 2–3.
21. Hill 2012.
22. Hind and Shenton 2015, quoting Kim Kardashian.
23. Vandenbosch and Eggermont 2011.
24. Riddle and De Simone 2013, 237.
25. Riddle and De Simone 2013.
26. Leyva 2018, 1.
27. Fogel and Kovalenko 2013.
28. Fogel and Krausz 2013.
29. Ferris et al. 2007.

30. Ferris et al. 2007.
31. Stefanone and Lackaff 2009; Stefanone, Lackaff, and Rosen 2010.
32. Zurbriggen and Morgan 2006.
33. Crockett, Pruzinsky, and Persing 2007.
34. Domoff et al. 2012.
35. Riddle and De Simone 2013, 238, citing Gerbner 1969; see also Signorielli and Morgan 1996.
36. Dehnart 2018.
37. Elliott 2012, 144–45.
38. Press 2020.
39. Lofton 2017.

References

Abramovitch, Seth. 2018. "'Lines Got Blurred': Jeffrey Tambor and an Up-Close Look at Harassment Claims on 'Transparent.'" *Hollywood Reporter*, May 7. https://www.hollywoodreporter.com/features/lines-got-blurred-jeffrey-tambor-an-up-close-look-at-harassment-claims-transparent-1108939.

Abt, Vicki, and Leonard Muztazza. 1997. *Coming After Oprah: Cultural Fallout in the Age of the Television Talk Show*. Bowling Green, OH: Bowling Green University Popular Press.

Adalian, Josef. 2011. "Jonathan Murray on 25 Seasons of the Reality Hot-Tub Groundbreaker." *New York*, March 9. https://www.vulture.com/2011/03/the_real_world_last_vegas_jona.html.

Adelabu, Detris H. 2015. "Homes Without Walls Families Without Boundaries: How Family Participation in Reality Television Impacts Children's Development." In *Real Sister: Stereotypes, Respectability, and Black Women in Reality TV*, edited by J. Ward Ellis. New Brunswick, NJ: Rutgers University Press, 86–101.

Advocate.com editors. 2004. "Pride, Patriotism, and *Queer Eye*." *The Advocate*, June 8. https://www.advocate.com/news/2004/06/08/pride-patriotism-and-queer-eye.

Ahmed, Saifuddin, and Jörg Matthes. 2016. "Media Representation of Muslims and Islam from 2000 to 2015: A Meta-analysis." *International Communication Gazette* 79, no. 3: 219–244. doi: 10.1177/1748048516656305.

Allen, Kim, and Heather Mendick. 2013. "Keeping It Real? Social Class, Young People and 'Authenticity' in Reality TV." *Sociology* 47, no. 3: 460–476. doi: 10.1177/0038038512448563.

Allison, Donnetrice C. 2016. "Introduction: A Historical Overview." In *Black Women's Portrayals on Reality Television: The New Sapphire*, edited by Donnetrice C. Allison. New York: Lexington, ix–xxix.

Alvarez, Barbara. 2018. "15 Questionable Pics of Kate Gosselin." BabyGaga, January 16. https://www.babygaga.com/15-pics-of-kate-gosselin/.

Amato, Paul, Alan Booth, David Johnson, and Stacy Rogers. 2007. *Alone Together: How Marriage in America Is Changing.* Cambridge, MA: Harvard University Press.

America's Next Top Model. 2004. Season 3, episode 1, "The Girl with the Secret," UPN.

America's Next Top Model. 2005a. Season 4, episode 1, "The Girl Who Is a Lady Kat . . . Reow!," UPN.

America's Next Top Model. 2005b. Season 4, episode 7, "The Girl Who Sends Tyra Over the Edge," UPN.

Anderson, Deborah J., Melissa Binder, and Kate Krause. 2002. "The Motherhood Wage Penalty: Which Mothers Pay It and Why?" *American Economic Review* 92, no. 2: 354–358. https://www.jstor.org/stable/3083431.

Anderson, Meg. 2016. "Trump Often Uses the Campaign Spotlight to Promote His Own Brand." NPR, October 26. https://www.npr.org/2016/10/26/499441383/trump-often-uses-the-campaign-spotlight-to-promote-his-own-brand.

Anderson, Sarah. 2018. "Five Charts That Show Why We Need to Tackle Gender Justice and Poverty Together." Institute for Policy Studies, May 17. https://ips-dc.org/five-charts-show-need-tackle-gender-justice-poverty-together/.

Andreeva, Nellie. 2011. "Fox Cancels 'America's Most Wanted' as Series, John Walsh Is Shopping It Around." *Deadline*, May 16. https://deadline.com/2011/05/fox-cancels-americas-most-wanted-as-series-john-walsh-is-shopping-it-around-132461/.

Andrejevic, Mark. 2004. *Reality TV: The Work of Being Watched.* New York: Rowman & Littlefield.

Are You the One? 2019. Season 8, episode 1, "Come One, Come All, Part 1," MTV.

Arnovitz, Kevin. 2004. "Virtual Dictionary: A Guide to the Language of Reality TV." *Slate*, September 14. https://slate.com/news-and-politics/2004/09/a-reality-tv-lexicon.html.

Associated Press. 2018. "Kathy Griffin to Be Honored by West Hollywood for LGBTQ Activism." *USA Today*, June 5. https://www.usatoday.com/story/life/people/2018/06/05/kathy-griffin-honored-west-hollywood-lgbtq-activism/672139002/.

Aurthur, Kate. 2017. "'The Bachelorette' Ratings Are Falling Hard." *BuzzFeed News*, July 11. https://www.buzzfeednews.com/article/kateaurthur/the-bachelorette-ratings-are-falling-hard#.boggo9JZa.

Aurthur, Kate, and Elizabeth Wagmeister. 2020. "'Vanderpump Rules' Fires Stassi Schroeder and Kristen Doute for Racist Actions." *Van-

ity Fair, June 9. https://variety.com/2020/tv/news/stassi-schroeder-kristen-doute-fired-vanderpump-rules-1234629172/.

Avellar, Sarah, and Pamela J. Smock. 2003. "Has the Price of Motherhood Declined over Time? A Cross-Cohort Comparison of the Motherhood Wage Penalty." *Journal of Marriage and Family* 65, no. 3: 597–607. https://doi.org/10.1111/j.1741-3737.2003.00597.x.

The Bachelor. 2014. Season 18, episode 9, "Week 9: Saint Lucia," ABC.

The Bachelor. 2015. Season 19, episode 2, "Week 2: Tractor Race," ABC.

Bailey, Beth. 1989. *From Front Porch to Back Seat: Courtship in 20th-Century America*. Baltimore, MD: Johns Hopkins Press.

Bannon, Anne Louise. 2008. "19 Kids and Counting." Common Sense Media. Accessed January 30, 2021. https://www.commonsensemedia.org/tv-reviews/19-kids-and-counting.

Barber, Michael E., Linda A. Foley, and Russell Jones. 1999. "Evaluations of Aggressive Women: The Effects of Gender, Socioeconomic Status, and Level of Aggression." *Violence and Victims* 14, no. 4: 353–363. doi: 10.1891/0886-6708.14.4.353.

Bass, Sandra. 2001. "Policing Space, Policing Race: Social Control Imperatives and Police Discretionary Decisions." *Social Justice* 28, no. 1: 156–176. https://www.jstor.org/stable/29768062.

Baudrillard, Jean. 1983. *Simulations*. New York: Semiotexte.

Becker, Howard S. 1953. "Becoming a Marihuana User." *American Journal of Sociology* 59, no. 3: 235–242. https://www.journals.uchicago.edu/doi/pdf/10.1086/221326.

Becker, Howard. 1963. *Outsiders: Studies in the Sociology of Deviance*. New York: Free Press.

Bell, Christopher. 2010. *American Idolatry: Celebrity, Commodity and Reality Television*. Jefferson, NC: McFarland & Co.

Bennett, Kathleen. 1992. "Feminist Bisexuality: A Both/And Option for an Either/Or World." In *Closer to Home: Bisexuality and Feminism*, edited by Elizabeth Reba Weise. Seattle, WA: Seal Press, 205–231.

Bertrand, Marianne, and Sendhil Mullainathan. 2004. "Are Emily and Greg More Employable Than Lakisha and Jamal? A Field Experiment on Labor Market Discrimination." *American Economic Review* 94, no. 4: 991–1013. doi: 10.125s7/0002828042002561.

Bialik, Kristen. 2017. "Key Facts about Race and Marriage, 50 Years after *Loving v. Virginia*." Pew Research Center, June 12. http://www.pewresearch.org/fact-tank/2017/06/12/key-facts-about-race-and-marriage-50-years-after-loving-v-virginia/.

Bianchi, Suzanne M., Melissa A. Milkie, Liana C. Sayer, and John P. Robinson. 2000. "Is Anyone Doing the Housework? Trends in the Gender Division of Household Labor." *Social Forces* 79, no. 1: 191–228. https://doi.org/10.1093/sf/79.1.191.

Biegert, Mark. 2017. "Naked and Afraid: Who Taps Out More?" *Math Encounters Blog*, April 18. http://mathscinotes.com/2017/04/naked -and-afraid-who-taps-out-more-men-or-women/.

Bignell, Jonathan. 2005. *Big Brother: Reality TV in the Twenty-First Century*. New York: Palgrave.

Biressi, Anita, and Heather Nunn. 2005. *Reality TV: Realism and Revelation*. New York: Columbia University Press.

Bittman, Michael, and Judy Wajcman. 2000. "The Rush Hour: The Character of Leisure Time and Gender Equity." *Social Forces* 79, no. 1: 165–89. https://doi.org/10.1093/sf/79.1.165.

Blickley, Leigh. 2018. "10 Years Ago, Screenwriters Went on Strike and Changed Television Forever." *Huffington Post*, February 12. https://www .huffingtonpost.com/entry/10-years-ago-screenwriters-went-on-strike -and-changed-television-forever_us_5a7b3544e4b08dfc92ff2b32/.

Blistein, Joe. 2018. "Megyn Kelly Out at NBC After Blackface Comments." *Rolling Stone*, October 26. https://www.rollingstone.com/tv /tv-news/megyn-kelly-nbc-fired-blackface-747389/.

Bloomquist, Jennifer. 2015. "The Minstrel Legacy: African American English and the Historical Construction of 'Black' Identities in Entertainment." *Journal of African American Studies* 19, no. 4: 410–425. https://doi.org/10.1007/s12111-015-9313-1.

Bogle, Kathleen A. 2008. *Hooking Up: Sex, Dating, and Relationships on Campus*. New York: NYU Press.

Bourdieu, Pierre. 1984. *Distinction: A Social Critique of the Judgement of Taste*. London: Routledge & Kegan Paul.

———. 1986. "The Forms of Capital." In *Handbook of Theory*, edited by J. G. Richardson. New York: Greenwood, 241–258.

Boylorn, Robin M. 2008. "As Seen on TV: An Autoethnographic Reflection on Race and Reality Television." *Critical Studies in Media Communication* 25, no. 4: 413–433. https://doi.org/10.1080 /15295030802327758.

Breaking Amish. 2012. Season 1, episode 2, "What Have We Gotten Ourselves Into?," TLC.

Brown, Lauren. 2016. "7 Story Lines on *The Hills* That Were Actually Totally Fake." *Glamour*, May 24. https://www.glamour.com/story/7 -storylines-on-the-hills-that-were-actually-totally-fake.

Brown, Meaghen. 2017. "The Longer the Race, the Stronger We Get." *Outside*, April 11. https://www.outsideonline.com/2169856/longer -race-stronger-we-get.

Brown Givens, Sonja M., and Jennifer L. Monahan. 2005. "Priming Mammies, Jezebels, and Other Controlling Images: An Examination of the Influence of Mediated Stereotypes on Perceptions of an African American Woman." *Media Psychology* 7, no. 1: 87–106. https://doi.org/10.1207/S1532785XMEP0701_5.

Brückner, Hannah, Anne Martin, and Peter S. Bearman. 2004. "Ambivalence and Pregnancy: Adolescents' Attitudes, Contraceptive Use and Pregnancy." *Perspectives on Sexual and Reproductive Health* 36, no. 6: 248–257. https://doi.org/10.1111/j.1931-2393.2004.tb00029.x.

Budig, Michelle J., and Paula England. 2001. "The Wage Penalty for Motherhood." *American Sociological Review* 66, no. 2: 204–225. https://www.jstor.org/stable/2657415.

Bureau of Justice Statistics. 2016. "U.S. Correctional Population at Lowest Level since 2002." December 29. https://www.bjs.gov/content/pub/press/cpus15pr.cfm.

Bureau of Labor Statistics. 2019. "11. Employed Persons by Detailed Occupation, Sex, Race, and Hispanic or Latino Ethnicity." January 18. https://www.bls.gov/cps/cpsaat11.htm.

Butler, Judith. 1999. *Gender Trouble: Feminism and the Subversion of Identity.* New York: Routledge.

Byrne, Anne, and Deborah Carr. 2005. "Caught in the Cultural Lag: The Stigma of Singlehood." *Psychological Inquiry* 16, no. 2/3: 84–91. https://www.jstor.org/stable/20447267.

Callanan, Valerie J., and Jared S. Rosenberger. 2011. "Media and Public Perceptions of the Police: Examining the Impact of Race and Personal Experience." *Policing & Society* 21, no. 2: 167–189. https://doi.org/10.1080/10439463.2010.540655.

Callis, April Scarlette. 2013. "The Black Sheep of the Pink Flock: Labels, Stigma, and Bisexual Identity." *Journal of Bisexuality* 13, no. 1: 82–105. https://doi.org/10.1080/15299716.2013.755730.

Callis, April S. 2014. "Where Kinsey, Christ, and Tila Tequila Meet: Discourse and the Sexual (Non)-Binary." *Journal of Homosexuality* 61, no. 12: 1627–1648. https://doi.org/10.1080/00918369.2014.951208.

Calvert, Clay. 2000. *Voyeur Nation: Media, Privacy and Peering in Modern Culture.* Boulder, CO: Westview Press.

Campbell, Shannon B., Steven S. Giannino, Chrystal R. China, and Christopher S. Harris. 2008. "I Love New York: Does New York Love Me?" *Journal of International Women's Studies* 10, no. 2: 20–28. http://vc.bridgew.edu/jiws/vol10/iss2/3.

Carnevale, Anthony P., Megan L. Fasules, Michael C. Quinn, and Kathryn Peltier Campbell. 2019. *Born to Win, Schooled to Lose: Why Equally Talented Students Don't Get Equal Chances to Be All They Can Be.* Washington, DC: Georgetown University Center on Education and the Workforce. Accessed January 30, 2021. https://

1gyhoq479ufd3yna29x7ubjn-wpengine.netdna-ssl.com/wp-content /uploads/ES-Born_to_win-schooled_to_lose.pdf.

Casserly, Meghan. 2011. "Can Bethenny Crack a Billion?" *Forbes*, May 17. https://www.forbes.com/2011/05/17/celebrity-100–11-bethenny -frankel-skinnygirl-bravo-money-makers.html#33e45c01430e.

Cato, Mackenzie, and Francesca Renee Dillman Carpentier. 2010. "Conceptualizations of Female Empowerment and Enjoyment of Sexualized Characters in Reality Television." *Mass Communication and Society* 13, no. 3: 270–288. https://doi.org/10.1080/15205430903225589.

Celebrity Wife Swap. 2012. Season 1, episode 1, "Tracey Gold/Carnie Wilson," ABC.

The Challenge: Battle of the Exes. 2012. Season 22, episode 7, "Love and Marriage," MTV.

Chemers, Michael M. 2016. *Staging Stigma: A Critical Examination of the American Freak Show.* New York: Palgrave Macmillan.

Cherlin, Andrew. 2004. "The Deinstitutionalization of American Marriage." *Journal of Marriage and the Family* 66, no. 4: 848–861. https:// doi.org/10.1111/j.0022–2445.2004.00058.x.

Cherlin, Andrew J. 2009. *The Marriage-Go-Round: The State of Marriage and the Family in America Today.* New York: Knopf.

———. 2010. "Demographic Trends in the United States: A Review of Research in the 2000s." *Journal of Marriage and Family* 72, no. 3: 403–419. https://doi.org/10.1111/j.1741–3737.2010.00710.x.

Child Genius. 2015a. Season 1, episode 1, "I Am Not a Tiger Mommy," Lifetime.

Child Genius. 2015b. Season 1, episode 2, "Please Drink Some Water," Lifetime.

Chopped Junior. 2016, Season 2, episode 10, "The Big Stink," Food Network.

Chudnofsky, Lisa. 2013. "Heather B from the First Season of 'Real World': Where Is She Now?" *MTV News*, March 20. http://www.mtv .com/news/2384734/real-world-new-york-heather-b/.

Cillizza, Chris. 2019. "Elizabeth Warren's Native American Problem Just Got Even Worse." CNN, February 6. https://www.cnn.com/2019/02 /06/politics/elizabeth-warren-native-american/index.html.

Clark, Gregory. 2015. *The Son Also Rises: Surnames and the History of Social Mobility.* Princeton, NJ: Princeton University Press.

Cleveland, Jeanette N., Gwenith G. Fisher, and Katina B. Sawyer. 2015. "Work-Life Equality: The Importance of a Level Playing Field at Home." In *Gender and the Work-Family Experience*, edited by Maura J. Mills. New York: Springer, 177–199.

Cloud, Dana L. 2018. *Reality Bites: Rhetoric and the Circulation of Truth Claims in U.S. Political Culture.* Columbus: Ohio State University Press.

CNN. 2011. "McCain Invokes 'Snooki' Tweet, Warns of Twitter's Dangers."

Political Ticker, May 17. http://politicalticker.blogs.cnn.com/2011/05/17/mccain-invokes-snooki-tweet-warns-of-twitters-dangers/.

Coleman, Robin R. Means. 2014. *African American Viewers and the Black Situation Comedy: Situating Racial Humor.* New York: Routledge.

Colicchio, Tom. 2007. "Shave and a Haircut. Dim Wits." Bravo TV blog, January 17. http://www.bravotv.com/top-chef/Season-2/blogs/tom-colicchio/shave-and-a-haircut-dim-wits.

Collins, Patricia Hill. 1990. *Black Feminist Thought: Knowledge, Consciousness, and the Politics of Empowerment.* London: HarperCollins.

———. 2004. *Black Sexual Politics: African Americans, Gender, and the New Racism.* New York: Routledge.

Conley, Dalton. 2017. *You May Ask Yourself: An Introduction to Thinking Like a Sociologist.* New York: W. W. Norton & Co.

Cooley, Charles Horton. 1922. *Human Nature and the Social Order.* New York: Scribners.

Coontz, Stephanie. 2000. "Historical Perspectives on Family Studies." *Journal of Marriage and Family* 62, no. 2: 283–297. https://doi.org/10.1111/j.1741-3737.2000.00283.x.

———. 2005. *Marriage, a History: How Love Conquered Marriage.* New York: Viking.

Corinthios, Aurelie. 2019. "Kristin Cavallari Says 'Most' of Her Storyline on *The Hills* 'Wasn't Real.'" *People*, April 18. https://people.com/tv/kristin-cavallari-the-hills-fake-plotlines/.

Corner, John. 2002. "Performing the Real: Documentary Diversions." *Television & New Media* 3, no. 3: 255–269. https://doi.org/10.1177/152747640200300302.

Crenshaw, Kimberlé. 1989. "Demarginalizing the Intersection of Race and Sex: A Black Feminist Critique of Antidiscrimination Doctrine, Feminist Theory and Antiracist Politics." *University of Chicago Legal Forum* 1, no. 8: 139–167.

Crimesider staff. 2015. "Mom Accused of Leaving Kids at Food Court During Job Interview." CBS News, July 20. https://www.cbsnews.com/news/texas-mom-accused-of-leaving-kids-at-food-court-during-job-interview/.

Crockett, Richard J., Thomas Pruzinsky, and John A. Persing. 2007. "The Influence of Plastic Surgery 'Reality TV' on Cosmetic Surgery Patient Expectations and Decision Making." *Plastic and Reconstructive Surgery* 120, no. 1: 316–324. doi: 10.1097/01.prs.0000264339.67451.71.

Cummings, Dolan. 2002. *Reality TV: How Real Is Real?* London: Hodder & Stoughton.

Czerniawski, Amanda M. 2012. "Disciplining Corpulence: The Case of Plus-Size Fashion Models." *Journal of Contemporary Ethnography* 41, no. 2: 127–153. https://doi.org/10.1177/0891241611413579.

Dance Moms. 2012a. Season 2, episode 14, "The Battle Begins," Lifetime.

Dance Moms. 2012b. Season 2, episode 28, "Reunion: Off the Dance Floor, Part 2," Lifetime.

Davis, Allison P. 2017. "Regular, Degular, Shmegular Girl from the Bronx." *The Cut,* November 13. https://www.thecut.com/2017/11/cardi-b -was-made-to-be-this-famous.html.

Davis-Kean, Pamela E. 2005. "The Influence of Parent Education and Family Income on Child Achievement: The Indirect Role of Parental Expectations and the Home Environment." *Journal of Family Psychology* 19, no. 2: 294–304. doi: 10.1037/0893–3200.19.2.294.

Deadline team. 2013. "'Here Comes Honey Boo Boo' Breaks Ratings Records When Mama June Kinda Ties the Knot." *Deadline,* September 12. https://deadline.com/2013/09/here-comes-honey-boo-boo-breaks -ratings-records-when-mama-june-kinda-ties-the-knot-585985/.

Deery, June. 2004. "Reality TV as Advertainment." *Popular Communication* 2, no. 1: 1–20. https://doi.org/10.1207/s15405710pc0201_1.

———. 2012. *Consuming Reality: The Commercialization of Factual Entertainment.* New York: Palgrave Macmillan.

Dehnart, Andy. 2007. "VH1 Sets Another Record as 4.43 Million People Watched *I Love New York*'s Premiere." *RealityBlurred,* January 11. https://www.realityblurred.com/realitytv/2007/01/i-love-new-york -debut_ratings_record/.

———. 2018. "The Most-Popular Reality TV Shows of 2017." *RealityBlurred,* February 14. https://www.realityblurred.com/realitytv /2018/02/most-popular-reality-tv-shows-2017-ratings/.

De Moraes, Lisa, and David Bloom. 2014. "What TV Series Do Rich and Smart People Watch? You Might Be Surprised." *Deadline,* June 11. https://deadline.com/2014/06/tv-series-most-watched-rich-educated -viewers-787403/.

DiMaggio, Paul. 1987. "Classification in Art." *American Sociological Review* 52, no. 4: 440–455. https://www.jstor.org/stable/2095290.

Dodes, Rachel. 2018. "The Show Goes on for Arrested 'Housewife' LuAnn de Lesseps." *New York Times,* February 23. https://www.nytimes.com /2018/02/23/style/real-housewives-LuAnn-de-lesseps-arrest-cabaret .html.

Domoff, Sarah E., Nova G. Hinman, Afton M. Koball, Amy Storfer-Isser, Victoria L. Carhart, Kyoung D. Baik, and Robert A. Carels. 2012. "The Effects of Reality Television on Weight Bias: An Examination of *The Biggest Loser*." *Obesity* 20, no. 5: 993–998. doi: 10.1038/oby.2011.378.

Doyle, Sady. 2016. "America Loves Women Like Hillary Clinton—as Long as They're Not Asking for a Promotion." *Quartz,* February 25. https://qz.com/624346/america-loves-women-like-hillary-clinton -as-long-as-theyre-not-asking-for-a-promotion/.

Du Bois, W. E. B. 1903. *The Souls of Black Folk*. Paris: A. C. McClurg & Co.

Dubrofsky, Rachel E. 2006. *"The Bachelor*: Whiteness in the Harem." *Critical Studies in Media Communication* 23, no. 1: 39–56. https://doi.org/10.1080/07393180600570733.

Duck Dynasty. 2012. Season 1, episode 1, "Family Funny Business," A&E.

Duckett, Elena, Marcela Raffaelli, and Maryse H. Richards. 1989. "'Taking Care': Maintaining the Self and the Home in Early Adolescence." *Journal of Youth and Adolescence* 18, no. 6: 549–565. doi: 10.1007/BF02139073.

Duggar, Jill, Jinger Duggar, Jessa Duggar, and Jana Duggar. 2014. *Growing Up Duggar: It's All about Relationships*. New York: Howard Books.

Duh, Jane. 2017. "The 10 Worst Moms on TV Who Had No Business Having Kids." Betches, May 10. https://betches.com/ten-worst-tv-moms/.

Dunn, Christina. n.d. "Let's All Relax about Mommy Wine Culture." *Scary Mommy*. Accessed January 31, 2021. https://www.scarymommy.com/relax-mommy-wine-culture/.

Durkheim, Émile. [1897] 1951. *Suicide*, translated by John A. Spaulding and George Simpson. Glencoe, IL: Free Press.

———. [1901] 1982. *The Rules of the Sociological Method*, translated by W. D. Halls. New York: Free Press.

———. [1895] 2002. "The Normal and the Pathological." In *Constructions of Deviance: Social Power, Context, and Interaction*, edited by Patricia A. Adler and Peter Adler. Belmont, CA: Wadsworth Thomson Learning, 55–58.

Durrheim, Kevin, Michael Quayle, Kevin Whitehead, and Anita Kriel. 2005. "Denying Racism: Discursive Strategies Used by the South African Media." *Critical Arts* 19, no. 1–2: 167–186. doi:10.1080/02560040585310111.

Eagly, Alice H., Mona G. Makhijani, and Bruce G. Klonsky. 1992. "Gender and the Evaluation of Leaders: A Meta-analysis." *Psychological Bulletin* 111, no. 1: 3–22. https://doi.org/10.1037/0033–2909.111.1.3.

Eagly, Alice H., and Steven J. Karau. 2002. "Role Congruity Theory of Prejudice toward Female Leaders." *Psychological Review* 109, no. 3: 573–598. doi: 10.1037//0033–295X.109.3.573.

Eastwick, Paul W., and Eli J. Finkel. 2008. "Sex Differences in Mate Preferences Revisited: Do People Know What They Initially Desire in a Romantic Partner?" *Journal of Personality and Social Psychology* 94, no. 2: 245–264. https://doi.org/10.1037/0022–3514.94.2.245.

Edin, Kathryn, and Maria Kefalas. 2011. *Promises I Can Keep: Why Poor Women Put Motherhood before Marriage*. Berkeley: University of California Press.

Edwards, Leigh H. 2013. *The Triumph of Reality TV: The Revolution in American Television*. Santa Barbara, CA: Praeger.

Eliason, Michele J. 1997. "The Prevalence and Nature of Biphobia in Het-erosexual Undergraduate Students." *Archives of Sexual Behavior* 26, no. 3: 317–326. https://doi.org/10.1023/A:1024527032040.

Eliason, Mickey. 2000. "Bi-Negativity: The Stigma Facing Bisexual Men." *Journal of Bisexuality* 1, no. 2–3: 137–154. https://doi.org/10.1300 /J159v01n02_05.

Elliott, Deni. 2012. "Democracy and Discourse: How Reality TV Fosters Citizenship." In *The Ethics of Reality TV: A Philosophical Exam-ination*, edited by Wendy N. Wyatt and Kristie Bunton. New York: Continuum, 143–158.

England, Paula, and Reuben J. Thomas. 2006. "The Decline of the Date and the Rise of the College Hook Up." In *Family in Transition*, edited by Arlene Skolnick and Jerome Skolnick. Boston: Allyn & Bacon, 151–162.

Engstrom, Erika, and Beth Semic. 2003. "Portrayal of Religion in Real-ity TV Programming: Hegemony and the Contemporary American Wedding." *Journal of Media and Religion* 2, no. 3: 145–163. https:// doi.org/10.1207/S15328415JMR0203_02.

Epstein, Steven. 1994. "A Queer Encounter: Sociology and the Study of Sexuality." *Sociological Theory* 12, no. 2: 188–202. https://www.jstor .org/stable/201864.

Erickson, Angela C. 2018. "The Tangled Mess of Occupational Licens-ing." Cato Institute, September/October. https://www.cato.org/policy -report/septemberoctober-2018/tangled-mess-occupational-licensing.

Eschholz, Sarah, Brenda Sims Blackwell, Marc Gertz, and Ted Chiricos. 2002. "Race and Attitudes toward the Police: Assessing the Effects of Watching 'Reality' Police Programs." *Journal of Criminal Justice* 30, no. 4: 327–341. https://doi.org/10.1016/S0047-2352(02)00133-2.

Ettachfini, Leila. 2019. "15 Women Weigh In on This Year's Divisive Women's March." *Broadly*, January 17. https://broadly.vice.com /en_us/article/kzv4yy/15-women-weigh-in-on-this-years-divisive -womens-march.

Everett, Ronald S., and Roger A. Wojtkiewicz. 2002. "Difference, Dis-parity, and Race/Ethnic Bias in Federal Sentencing." *Journal of Quantitative Criminology* 18, no. 2: 189–211. https://doi.org/10.1023 /A:1015258732676.

Fair, Damien A., Alexander L. Cohen, Jonathan D. Power, Nico U. F. Dosen-bach, Jessica A. Church, Francis M. Miezin, Bradley L. Schlaggar, and Steven E. Petersen. 2009. "Functional Brain Networks Develop from a 'Local to Distributed' Organization." *PLoS Computational Biology* 5, no. 5: n.p. https://doi.org/10.1371/journal.pcbi.1000381.

Fallon, Claire. 2018. "Congrats to 'Bachelorette' Winner Brett Kava-naugh." *Huffington Post*, July 10. https://www.huffpost.com/entry

/bachelorette-brett-kavanaugh_n_5b4430d3e4b07aea75434957?4yj
=&guccounter=1.

Fein, Ellen, and Sherrie Schneider. 1995. *All the Rules: Time-Tested Secrets for Capturing the Heart of Mr. Right.* New York: Grand Central Publishing.

Fernandez, Celia. 2013. "55 Latinas Who Keep It Real on TV!" *Latina*, June 29. http://www.latina.com/entertainment/buzz/latina-reality-stars-who-keep-it-real.

Ferris, Amber L., Sandi W. Smith, Bradley S. Greenberg, and Stacy L. Smith. 2007. "The Content of Reality Dating Shows and Viewer Perceptions of Dating." *Journal of Communication* 57, no. 3: 490–510. https://doi.org/10.1111/j.1460-2466.2007.00354.x.

Fiore, Andrew T., and Judith S. Donath. 2005. *Homophily in Online Dating: When Do You Like Someone Like Yourself?* Cambridge, MA: MIT Media Laboratory. Accessed January 31, 2021. http://smg.media.mit.edu/papers/Fiore/fiore_donath_chi2005_short.pdf.

Flores, Antonio. 2017. "How the U.S. Hispanic Population Is Changing." Pew Research Center, September 18. http://www.pewresearch.org/fact-tank/2017/09/18/how-the-u-s-hispanic-population-is-changing/.

Fogel, Joshua, and Lyudmila Kovalenko. 2013. "Reality Television Shows Focusing on Sexual Relationships Are Associated with College Students Engaging in One-Night Stands." *Journal of Evidence-Based Psychotherapies* 13, no. 2: 321–331. https://search.proquest.com/scholarly-journals/reality-television-shows-focusing-on-sexual/docview/1470800730/se-2?accountid=12043/.

Fogel, Joshua, and Faye Krausz. 2013. "Watching Reality Television Beauty Shows Is Associated with Tanning Lamp Use and Outdoor Tanning among College Students." *Journal of the American Academy of Dermatology* 68, no. 5: 784–789. https://doi.org/10.1016/j.jaad.2012.09.055.

Foucault, Michel. 1990. *The History of Sexuality: An Introduction.* New York: Vintage Books.

———. 1995. *Discipline & Punish: The Birth of the Prison.* New York: Random House.

Framke, Caroline. 2018. "How RuPaul's Comments on Trans Women Led to a Drag Race Revolt—and a Rare Apology." *Vox*, March 6. https://www.vox.com/culture/2018/3/6/17085244/rupaul-trans-women-drag-queens-interview-controversy.

Framke, Caroline, and Alex Abad-Santos. 2015. "The Rise and Fall of *America's Next Top Model*, Explained in 8 Moments." *Vox*, December 5. https://www.vox.com/2015/12/5/9851546/americas-next-top-model-series-finale-best-moments.

France, Lisa Respers. 2017. "How 'The Real World's' First Season Sparked

Real Change." CNN, May 19. https://www.cnn.com/2017/05/19 /entertainment/real-world-25th-anniversary/index.html.

———. 2018. "Jon Gosselin Says He and Kate Are Still Fighting over Custody." CNN, December 13. https://www.cnn.com/2018/12/12 /entertainment/jon-kate-gosselin-custody/index.html.

Fredrickson, Barbara L., and Tomi-Ann Roberts. 1997. "Objectification Theory: Toward Understanding Women's Lived Experiences and Mental Health Risks." *Psychology of Women Quarterly* 21, no. 2: 173–206. https://doi.org/10.1111/j.1471–6402.1997.tb00108.x.

Fredrickson, Barbara L., Tomi-Ann Roberts, Stephanie M. Noll, Diane M. Quinn, and Jean M. Twenge. 1998. "That Swimsuit Becomes You: Sex Differences in Self-Objectification, Restrained Eating, and Math Performance." *Journal of Personality and Social Psychology* 75, no. 1: 269–284. https://doi.org/10.1037/0022–3514.75.1.269.

Gabler, Neal. 1998. *Life: The Movie.* New York: Vintage Books.

Gamson, Joshua. 1998. *Freaks Talk Back: Tabloid Talk Shows and Sexual Nonconformity.* Chicago: University of Chicago Press.

Garber, Marjorie B. 1995. *Vice Versa: Bisexuality and the Eroticism of Everyday Life.* New York: Simon & Schuster.

Gardner, Eriq. 2012. "'The Bachelor' Racial Discrimination Lawsuit Dismissed." *Hollywood Reporter*, October 15. https://www .hollywoodreporter.com/thr-esq/bachelor-racial-discrimination -lawsuit-dismissed-379100.

Garfinkel, Harold. 1964. "Studies of the Routine Grounds of Everyday Activities." *Social Problems* 11, no. 3: 225–250. https://doi.org/10 .2307/798722.

Garrity, Amanda. 2019. "What Is Simon Cowell's Net Worth?" *Good Housekeeping*, January 9. https://www.goodhousekeeping.com/life /entertainment/a20952987/simon-cowell-net-worth/.

Gates, Racquel. 2017. "What Snooki and Joseline Taught Me About Race, Motherhood, and Reality TV." *Los Angeles Review of Books*, October 21. https://lareviewofbooks.org/article/what-snooki-and-joseline -taught-me-about-race-motherhood-and-reality-tv/.

Gates, Racquel J. 2018. *Double Negative: The Black Image and Popular Culture.* Durham, NC: Duke University Press.

Geiger, Abigail, and Gretchen Livingston. 2018. "8 Facts about Love and Marriage in America." Pew Research Center, February 13. http:// www.pewresearch.org/fact-tank/2018/02/13/8-facts-about-love -and-marriage/.

Geiger, Wendy, Jake Harwood, and Mary Lee Hummert. 2006. "College Students' Multiple Stereotypes of Lesbians: A Cognitive Perspective." *Journal of Homosexuality* 51, no. 3: 165–182. https://doi.org/10 .1300/J082v51n03_08.

Gerbner, George. 1969. "Toward 'Cultural Indicators': The Analysis of Mass Mediated Message Systems." *AV Communication Review* 17, no. 2: 137–148. https://doi.org/10.1007/BF02769102.

Gerbner, George, Larry Gross, Michael Morgan, and Nancy Signorielli. 1986. "Living with Television: The Dynamics of the Cultivation Process." In *Perspectives on Media Effects*, edited by Jennings Bryant and Dolf Zillmann. Hillsdale, NJ: Lawrence Erlbaum Associates, 17–40.

Ghahremani, Tanya. 2012. "The 10 Worst Parents on Reality TV." Complex, January 10. https://www.complex.com/pop-culture/2012/01/10-worst-parents-on-reality-tv/11.

GLAAD. 2019. *2018–2019: Where We Are on TV*. GLAAD Media Institute. Accessed January 31, 2021. http://glaad.org/files/WWAT/WWAT_GLAAD_2018-2019.pdf.

Glasser, Carol L., Belinda Robnett, and Cynthia Feliciano. 2009. "Internet Daters' Body Type Preferences: Race–Ethnic and Gender Differences." *Sex Roles* 61, no. 1–2: 14–33. https://doi.org/10.1007/s11199-009-9604-x.

Goffman, Erving. 1959. *The Presentation of Self in Everyday Life*. Garden City, NY: Doubleday.

———. 1963. *Stigma: Notes on the Management of Spoiled Identity*. New York: Simon & Schuster.

———. [1961] 2017. *Asylums: Essays on the Social Situation of Mental Patients and Other Inmates*. New York: Routledge.

Gold, Marissa. 2015. "Your New Favorite Hangover Cure: Countess LuAnn's Eggs à la Française." *Glamour*, September 19. https://www.glamour.com/story/hangover-cure-eggs-a-la-francaise.

Gonzalez-Barrera, Ana, and Mark Hugo Lopez. 2015. "Is Being Hispanic a Matter of Race, Ethnicity, or Both?" Pew Research Center, June 15. https://www.pewresearch.org/fact-tank/2015/06/15/is-being-hispanic-a-matter-of-race-ethnicity-or-both/.

Goode, William J. 2006. "The Theoretical Importance of the Family." In *Family in Transition*, edited by Arlene Skolnick and Jerome Skolnick. Boston: Allyn & Bacon, 14–25.

Gopaldas, Ahir, and Anton Siebert. 2018. "Women over 40, Foreigners of Color, and Other Missing Persons in Globalizing Mediascapes: Understanding Marketing Images as Mirrors of Intersectionality." *Consumption Markets & Culture* 21, no. 4: 323–346. https://doi.org/10.1080/10253866.2018.1462170.

Greene, Theodore. 2014. "Gay Neighborhoods and the Rights of the Vicarious Citizen." *City & Community* 13, no. 2: 99–118. https://doi.org/10.1111/cico.12059.

Grindstaff, Laura. 2002. *The Money Shot: Trash, Class, and the Making of TV Talk Shows*. Chicago: University of Chicago Press.

Grobe, Christopher. 2017. *The Art of Confession: The Performance of Self from Robert Lowell to Reality TV*. New York: NYU Press.

Groom, Nichola. 2008. "Tori Spelling Relishes Role as Gay Icon." Reuters, April 16. https://www.reuters.com/article/us-spelling/tori-spelling -relishes-role-as-gay-icon-idUSN1440724920080416.

Grossman, Samantha. 2012. "American Idol's William Hung: Where Is He Now?" *Time*, January 19. http://newsfeed.time.com/2012/01/19 /american-idols-william-hung-where-is-he-now/print/.

Guttmacher Institute. 2019. "Sex and HIV Education." April 1. https://www .guttmacher.org/state-policy/explore/sex-and-hiv-education?gclid=C jwKCAjwqfDlBRBDEiwAigXUaNjkMiIDVB5hUrxdoxCKAnrBrmy- mukYopZ5COxfMmvIaXpmXWD_tAxoCJgAQAvD_BwE.

Hagi, Sarah. 2017. "*90 Day Fiancé* Is the Best Worst Show on Television." *The Cut*, October 20. https://www.thecut.com/2017/10/90-day -fiance-tlc-best-show.html.

Hamamoto, Darrell Y. 1994. *Monitored Peril: Asian Americans and the Politics of TV Representation*. Minneapolis: University of Minnesota Press.

Hamilton, Laura, Claudia Geist, and Brian Powell. 2011. "Marital Name Change as a Window into Gender Attitudes." *Gender & Society* 25, 2: 145–175. https://doi.org/10.1177/0891243211398653.

Harris, David A. 1999. "The Stories, the Statistics, and the Law: Why Driving While Black Matters." *Minnesota Law Review* 84, no. 2: 265–326. https://scholarship.law.umn.edu/cgi/viewcontent.cgi?article =2132&context=mlr.

Harris Insights & Analytics. 2014. "Doctors, Military Officers, Firefighters, and Scientists Seen as Among America's Most Prestigious Occupations." Harris Poll, September 10. https://theharrispoll.com /when-shown-a-list-of-occupations-and-asked-how-much-prestige -each-job-possesses-doctors-top-the-harris-polls-list-with-88-of-u-s -adults-considering-it-to-have-either-a-great-deal-of-prestige-45-2/.

Harris, Sheena. 2015. "Black Women: From Public Arena to Reality TV." In *Real Sister: Stereotypes, Respectability, and Black Women in Reality TV*, edited by Jervette Ward. New Brunswick, NJ: Rutgers University Press, 16–30.

Harris-Perry, Melissa V. 2011. *Sister Citizen: Shame, Stereotypes, and Black Women in America*. New Haven, CT: Yale University Press.

Hartmann, Heidi I. 1979. "The Unhappy Marriage of Marxism and Feminism: Towards a More Progressive Union." *Capital & Class* 3, no. 2: 1–33. https://doi.org/10.1177/030981687900800102.

Hauser, Christine. 2020. "'Survivor' and Other Reality Shows Will Feature More Diverse Casts, CBS Says." *New York Times*, November 11.

https://www.nytimes.com/2020/11/11/business/media/cbs-reality
-tv-diversity.html.

Hays, Sharon. 1996. *The Cultural Contradictions of Motherhood*. New Haven, CT: Yale University Press.

Hegewisch, Ariane, and Heidi Hartmann. 2019. "The Gender Wage Gap: 2018 Earnings Differences by Race and Ethnicity." Institute for Women's Policy Research, March 7. https://iwpr.org/publications /gender-wage-gap-2018/.

Heilman, Madeline E., Aaron S. Wallen, Daniella Fuchs, and Melinda M. Tamkins. 2004. "Penalties for Success: Reactions to Women Who Succeed at Male Gender-Typed Tasks." *Journal of Applied Psychology* 89, no. 3: 416–427. https://doi.org/10.1037/0021–9010.89.3.416.

Here Comes Honey Boo Boo. 2012. Season 1, episode 1, "This Is My Crazy Family," TLC.

Herek, Gregory M. 1984. "Beyond 'Homophobia': A Social Psychological Perspective on Attitudes toward Lesbians and Gay Men." *Journal of Homosexuality* 10, no. 1–2: 1–21. https://doi.org/10.1300 /J082v10n01_01.

Hill, Annette. 2015. *Reality TV: Key Ideas in Media & Cultural Studies*. New York: Routledge.

Hill, Kashmir. 2012. "How Target Figured Out a Teen Girl Was Pregnant Before Her Father Did." *Forbes*, February 16. https://www.forbes .com/sites/kashmirhill/2012/02/16/how-target-figured-out-a-teen -girl-was-pregnant-before-her-father-did/#185ad5cd6668.

Himberg, Julia. 2014. "Multicasting: Lesbian Programming and the Changing Landscape of Cable TV." *Television & New Media* 15, no. 4: 289–304. https://doi.org/10.1177/1527476412474351.

Hind, Katie, and Zoe Shenton. 2015. "Kim Kardashian: 'By Objectifying Myself as a Woman I Hold the Power.'" *Mirror*, July 1. https://www .mirror.co.uk/3am/celebrity-news/kim-kardashian-by-objectifying -myself-5979612.amp.

Hoarding: Buried Alive. 2010. Season 1, episode 2, "Beyond Embarrassment," TLC.

Holmes, Linda. 2018. "Under the Skin: Why That 'Arrested Development' Interview Is So Bad." NPR, May 24. https://www.npr.org/2018 /05/24/614009165/under-the-skin-why-that-arrested-development -interview-is-so-bad?fbclid=IwAR2GAQ7fNxPYKiH2XQcOmZY nHc3m961NN-GrKA4ukiG_Z8Sue8R2m09V2eg.

Holmes, Su, and Deborah Jermyn. 2004. *Understanding Reality Television*. New York: Routledge.

hooks, bell. 1981. *Ain't I a Woman: Black Women and Feminism*. Boston: South End Press.

Horton, Donald, and R. Richard Wohl. 1956. "Mass Communication and Para-social Interaction: Observations on Intimacy at a Distance." *Psychiatry* 19, no. 3: 215–229. https://doi.org/10.1080/00332747.1956 .11023049.

HRC staff. 2015. "Nine Times the Duggar Family Stood Against LGBT Equality." Human Rights Campaign, February 18. https://www .hrc.org/blog/nine-times-the-duggar-family-stood-against-lgbt -equality.

Huff, Richard M. 2006. *Reality Television*. Westport, CT: Praeger.

Hurtado, Fernando. 2018. "'The Riveras' on Being the Only Latino Family on American Reality TV." *Circa*, March 1. Retrieved from: https:// www.circa.com/story/2018/03/01/hollywood/the-riveras-on-being -the-only-american-reality-show-about-a-latino-family.

Hutcherson, Donald T. 2012. "Crime Pays: The Connection Between Time in Prison and Future Criminal Earnings." *Prison Journal*, 92, no. 3: 315–335. https://doi.org/10.1177/0032885512448607.

Ignatiev, Noel. 2012. *How the Irish Became White*. New York: Routledge.

I Love New York. 2007. Season 1, episode 1, "Do You Have Love for New York?," VH1.

Intersex Society of North America. 2008. "How Common Is Intersex?" Accessed January 31, 2021. http://www.isna.org/faq/frequency.

Jaffee, Sara, Avshalom Caspi, Terrie E. Moffitt, Jay Belsky, and Phil Silva. 2001. "Why Are Children Born to Teen Mothers at Risk for Adverse Outcomes in Young Adulthood? Results from a 20-Year Longitudinal Study." *Development and Psychopathology* 13, no. 2: 377–397. doi: 10.1017/S0954579401002103.

James, Sandy, Jody Herman, Susan Rankin, Mara Keisling, Lisa Mottet, and Ma'ayan Anafi. 2016. "The Report of the 2015 U.S. Transgender Survey." National Center for Transgender Equity. Accessed January 31, 2021. http://www.ustranssurvey.org/.

Jenkins, Sarah Tucker. 2017. "Spicy. Exotic. Creature. Representations of Racial and Ethnic Minorities on *RuPaul's Drag Race*." In *RuPaul's Drag Race and the Shifting Visibility of Drag Culture: The Boundaries of Reality TV*, edited by Niall Brennan and David Gudelunas. Cham, Switzerland: Palgrave Macmillan, 77–90.

Jennings, Rebecca. 2019. "The Controversy around Trump's Fast-Food Football Feast, Explained." *Vox*, January 30. https://www.vox.com /the-goods/2019/1/15/18183617/trump-clemson-mcdonalds-burger -king-wendys-dominos.

Jersey Shore: Family Vacation. 2018. Season 1, episode 14, "The Final Supper," MTV.

Johnson, Eric. 2016. "Kim Kardashian: Don't Like My Naked Selfies?

Don't Look at Them." *Recode*, June 6. https://www.recode.net/2016
/6/6/11864134/kim-kardashian-naked-selfies-podcast-kara-swisher.

Johnson, Rachel. 2016. "Rachel Johnson: Sorry Harry, but Your Beautiful Bolter Has Failed My Mum Test." *Daily Mail*, November 5. https://www.dailymail.co.uk/debate/article-3909362/RACHEL -JOHNSON-Sorry-Harry-beautiful-bolter-failed-Mum-Test.html.

Johnson, Steve. 2000. "'Survivor' Finale Posts Ratings Even Larger Than Show's Hype." *Chicago Tribune*, August 25. https://www.chicago tribune.com/news/ct-xpm-2000–08–25–0008250272-story.html.

Johnston, Josée, and Shyon Baumann. 2007. "Democracy versus Distinction: A Study of Omnivorousness in Gourmet Food Writing." *American Journal of Sociology* 113, no. 1: 165–204. https://doi.org /10.1086/518923.

Kane, Emily W. 2006. "'No Way My Boys Are Going to Be Like That!' Parents' Responses to Children's Gender Nonconformity." *Gender & Society* 20, no. 2: 149–176. https://doi.org/10.1177/0891243205284276.

Katz, Josh. 2016. "'Duck Dynasty' vs. 'Modern Family': 50 Maps of the U.S. Cultural Divide." *New York Times*, December 27. https://www .nytimes.com/interactive/2016/12/26/upshot/duck-dynasty-vs -modern-family-television-maps.html.

Kaufman, Amy. 2018. *Bachelor Nation: Inside the World of America's Favorite Guilty Pleasure.* New York: Dutton.

Kaufman, Seth. 2013. "What We Write About When We Write About Reality TV." *Huffington Post*, January 15. https://www.huffingtonpost .com/seth-kaufman/what-we-write-about-when-_b_2474548.html.

Kavka, Misha. 2008. *Reality Television, Affect and Intimacy: Reality Matters.* New York: Palgrave Macmillan.

———. 2012. *Reality TV.* Edinburgh, Scotland: Edinburgh University Press.

Kearney, Melissa S., and Phillip B. Levine. 2015. "Media Influences on Social Outcomes: The Impact of MTV's 16 and Pregnant on Teen Childbearing." *American Economic Review* 105, no. 12: 3597–3632. doi: 10.1257/aer.20140012.

Keeping Up with the Kardashians. 2007. Season 1, episode 1, "I'm Watching You," E!.

Kerr, Breena. 2019. "How MTV's 'Are You the One?' Is Changing Dating Shows." *Rolling Stone*, August 30. https://www.rollingstone.com/tv/tv -features/how-mtv-are-you-the-one-changing-dating-shows-877673/.

Kessler, Glenn. 2021. "Trump Made 30,573 False or Misleading Claims as President. Nearly Half Came in His Final Year." *Washington Post*, January 23. https://www.washingtonpost.com/politics/how-fact -checker-tracked-trump-claims/2021/01/23/ad04b69a-5c1d-11eb -a976-bad6431e03e2_story.html.

Kilborn, Richard. 1994. "'How Real Can You Get?' Recent Developments in 'Reality' Television." *European Journal of Communication* 9, no. 4: 421–439. https://doi.org/10.1177/0267323194009004003.

Kirby, Douglas, and Gina Lepore. 2007. Sexual Risk and Protective Factors: Factors Affecting Teen Sexual Behavior, Pregnancy, Childbearing and Sexually Transmitted Disease. Washington, DC: ETR Associates and the National Campaign to Prevent Teen and Unplanned Pregnancy, November 26. http://recapp.etr.org/recapp/documents/theories/RiskProtectiveFactors200712.pdf.

Kirschenman, Joleen, and Katherine Neckerman. 1991. "We'd Love to Hire Them, but . . . : The Meaning of Race for Employers." In *The Urban Underclass*, edited by Christopher Jencks and Paul E. Peterson. Washington, DC: Brookings Institution, 203–234.

Kochhar, Rakesh. 2018. "The American Middle Class Is Stable in Size, but Losing Ground Financially to Upper-Income Families." Pew Research Center, September 6. https://www.pewresearch.org/fact-tank/2018/09/06/the-american-middle-class-is-stable-in-size-but-losing-ground-financially-to-upper-income-families/.

Koppel, Ted. 2001. *ABC News Nightline*, June 14.

Kost, Kathryn, and Stanley Henshaw. 2014. *US Teenage Pregnancies, Births, and Abortions, 2010: National and State Trends by Age, Race, and Ethnicity*. New York: Guttmacher Institute.

Kraidy, Marwan. 2010. *Reality Television and Arab Politics: Contention in Public Life*. New York: Cambridge University Press.

Kraszewski, Jon. 2017. *Reality TV*. New York: Routledge.

Krueger, Joachim, Jutta Heckhausen, and Jutta Hundertmark. 1995. "Perceiving Middle-Aged Adults: Effects of Stereotype-Congruent and Incongruent Information." *Journals of Gerontology Series B: Psychological Sciences and Social Sciences* 50B, no. 2: 82–93. https://doi.org/10.1093/geronb/50B.2.P82.

Laqueur, Thomas. 1990. *Making Sex: Body and Gender from the Greeks to Freud*. Cambridge, MA: Harvard University Press.

Lareau, Annette. 2002. "Invisible Inequality: Social Class and Childrearing in Black Families and White Families." *American Sociological Review* 67, no. 5: 747–776. https://doi.org/10.2307/3088916.

Lawless, Jill, and Leanne Italie. 2020. "Questions of Racism Linger as Harry, Meghan Step Back." AP News, January 14. https://apnews.com/1420bd1ff04ac8f330bdd9cf9d061e52.

Leah, Rachel. 2018. "Former 'Transparent' Star Jeffrey Tambor Admits to Being 'Mean' but Denies Being a 'Predator.'" *Salon*, May 7. https://www.salon.com/2018/05/07/former-transparent-star-jeffrey-tambor-admits-to-being-mean-but-denies-being-a-predator/.

Lefebvre, Henri. [1991] 2014. "The Production of Space." In *The People,*

Place, and Space Reader, edited by Jen Jack Gieseking, William Mangold, Cindi Katz, Setha Low, and Susan Saegert. New York: Routledge, 289–293.

Lemert, Edwin M. 1999. "Primary and Secondary Deviation." In *Theories of Deviance*, 5th ed., edited Stuart H. Traub and Craig B. Little. Itasca, IL: F. E. Peacock, 380–390.

Lemons, J. Stanley. 1977. "Black Stereotypes as Reflected in Popular Culture, 1880–1920." *American Quarterly* 29, no. 1: 102–116. https://doi.org/10.2307/2712263.

Lena, Jennifer C. 2019. *Entitled: Discriminating Tastes and the Expansion of the Arts*. Princeton, NJ: Princeton University Press.

Lenig, Stuart. 2017. *The Bizarre World of Reality Television*. Santa Barbara, CA: Greenwood.

Levey Friedman, Hilary. 2013. *Playing to Win: Raising Kids in a Competitive Culture*. Berkeley: University of California Press.

Lévi-Strauss, Claude. [1949] 1994. "Kinship as Sexual Property Exchange." In *Four Sociological Traditions: Selected Readings*, edited by Randall Collins. New York: Oxford University Press, 227–243.

Lewis, Tania. 2008. *Smart Living: Lifestyle Media and Popular Expertise*. New York: Peter Lang.

Leyva, Rodolfo. 2018. "Experimental Insights into the Socio-cognitive Effects of Viewing Materialistic Media Messages on Welfare Support." *Media Psychology* 22, no. 4: 1–25. https://doi.org/10.1080/15213269.2018.1484769.

Lichter, S. Robert, and Daniel R. Amundson. 2018. "Distorted Reality: Hispanic Characters in TV Entertainment." In *Latin Looks: Images of Latinas and Latinos in the U.S. Media*, edited by Clara E. Rodriguez. New York: Routledge, 89–104.

Lin, Ken-Hou, and Jennifer Lundquist. 2013. "Mate Selection in Cyberspace: The Intersection of Race, Gender, and Education." *American Journal of Sociology* 119, no. 1: 183–215. https://doi.org/10.1086/673129.

Lindemann, Danielle J. 2012. *Dominatrix: Gender, Eroticism, and Control in the Dungeon*. Chicago: University of Chicago Press.

———. 2019. *Commuter Spouses: New Families in a Changing World*. Ithaca, NY: Cornell University Press.

Live PD. 2020. Season 4, episode 9, "02.29.20," A&E.

Lockdown. 2007. Season 1, episode 3, "Inside Maximum Security," National Geographic.

Lofton, Kathryn. 2017. *Consuming Religion*. Chicago: University of Chicago Press.

Longo, Gina Marie. 2018. "Keeping It in 'the Family': How Gender Norms Shape US Marriage Migration Politics." *Gender & Society* 32, no. 4: 469–492. https://doi.org/10.1177/0891243218777201.

López, Gustavo, Neil G. Ruiz, and Eileen Patten. 2017. "Key Facts about Asian Americans, a Diverse and Growing Population." Pew Research Center, September 8. https://www.pewresearch.org/fact-tank/2017/09/08/key-facts-about-asian-americans/.

López-Sintas, Jordi, and Tally Katz-Gerro. 2005. "From Exclusive to Inclusive Elitists and Further: Twenty Years of Omnivorousness and Cultural Diversity in Arts Participation in the USA." *Poetics* 33, nos. 5–6: 299–319. https://doi.org/10.1016/j.poetic.2005.10.004.

Lorber, Judith. 1994. *Paradoxes of Gender.* New Haven, CT: Yale University Press.

Love Is Blind. 2020. Season 1, episode 1, "Is Love Blind?," Netflix.

Lundy, Lisa K., Amanda M. Ruth, and Travis D. Park. 2008. "Simply Irresistible: Reality TV Consumption Patterns." *Communication Quarterly* 56, no. 2: 208–225. https://doi.org/10.1080/01463370802026828.

Maglio, Tony. 2018. "Summer 2018 TV Shows with the Richest and Poorest Viewers." *The Wrap,* June 28. https://www.thewrap.com/summer-2018-tv-shows-richest-poorest-viewers-photos/.

Mahajan, Deepa, Olivia White, Anu Madgavkar, and Mekala Krishnan. 2020. "Don't Let the Pandemic Set Back Gender Equality." *Harvard Business Review,* September 16. https://hbr.org/2020/09/dont-let-the-pandemic-set-back-gender-equality.

Married to Medicine. 2013. Season 1, episode 1, "A Taste of Your Own Medicine," Bravo.

Martins, Yolanda, Marika Tiggemann, and Alana Kirkbride. 2007. "Those Speedos Become Them: The Role of Self-Objectification in Gay and Heterosexual Men's Body Image." *Personality and Social Psychology Bulletin* 33, no. 5: 634–647. https://doi.org/10.1177/0146167206297403.

Marx, Karl. 1867. *Capital: A Critique of Political Economy,* translated by Samuel Moore and Edward Aveling. New York: International Publishers.

———. [1852] 1963. *The Eighteenth Brumaire of Louis Bonaparte.* New York: International Publishers.

———. [1852] 1994. "The Class Basis of Politics and Revolution." In *Four Sociological Traditions: Selected Readings,* edited by Randall Collins. New York: Oxford University Press, 17–35.

———. [1848] 1994. "History as Class Struggle." In *Four Sociological Traditions: Selected Readings,* edited by Randall Collins. New York: Oxford University Press, 3–12.

Marx, Karl, and Friedrich Engels. [1846] 1994. "Materialism and the Theory of Ideology." In *Four Sociological Traditions: Selected Readings,* edited by Randall Collins. New York: Oxford University Press, 13–17.

Massey, Douglas S., and Nancy A. Denton. 1993. *American Apartheid:*

Segregation and the Making of the Underclass. Cambridge, MA: Harvard University Press.

Mattingly, Marybeth J., and Suzanne M. Bianchi. 2003. "Gender Differences in the Quantity and Quality of Free Time: The U.S. Experience." *Social Forces* 81, no. 3: 999–1030. https://doi.org/10.1353/sof.2003.0036.

McBee, Matthew T. 2006. "A Descriptive Analysis of Referral Sources for Gifted Identification Screening by Race and Socioeconomic Status." *Journal of Secondary Gifted Education* 17, no. 2: 103–111. https://doi.org/10.4219/jsge-2006-686.

McCall, Leslie. 2005. "The Complexity of Intersectionality." *Signs* 30, no. 3: 1771–1800. https://doi.org/10.1086/426800.

McNearney, Allison. 2017. "Money Survey: 78% Still Think Men Should Pay for the First Date." *Money*, February 14. http://money.com/money/4668232/valentines-day-men-pay-first-date/.

Mead, George Herbert. [1934] 1994. "Thought as Internalized Conversation." In *Four Sociological Traditions: Selected Readings*, edited by Randall Collins. New York: Oxford University Press, 290–303.

Mejía, Zameena. 2018. "Kylie Jenner Reportedly Makes $1 Million per Paid Instagram Post—Here's How Much Other Top Influencers Get." CNBC.com, July 31. https://www.cnbc.com/2018/07/31/kylie-jenner-makes-1-million-per-paid-instagram-post-hopper-hq-says.html.

Merton, Robert K. 1938. "Social Structure and Anomie." *American Sociological Review* 3, no. 5: 672–682. https://doi.org/10.2307/2084686.

Merton, Robert. 1968. *Social Theory and Social Structure.* New York: Free Press.

Michael, Robert T., John H. Gagnon, Edward O. Laumann, and Gina Kolata. 1994. *Sex in America: A Definitive Survey.* Boston: Little, Brown & Co.

Mill, Roy, and Luke C. D. Stein. 2016. "Race, Skin Color, and Economic Outcomes in Early Twentieth-Century America." Arizona State University Mimeo. Accessed January 31, 2021. http://www.bu.edu/econ/files/2012/01/Mill_RaceSkinColorOutcomes.pdf.

The Millionaire Matchmaker. 2008. Season 1, episode 1, "Dave/ Harold," Bravo.

Mills, C. Wright. 1959. *The Sociological Imagination.* New York: Oxford University Press.

Mintz, Steven. 2010. "American Childhood as a Social and Cultural Construct." In *Families as They Really Are*, edited by Barbara J. Risman and Virginia E. Rutter. New York: W. W. Norton & Co., 56–67.

Mitchell, Ojmarrh, and Michael S. Caudy. 2015. "Examining Racial Disparities in Drug Arrests." *Justice Quarterly* 32, no. 2: 288–313. https://doi.org/10.1080/07418825.2012.761721.

Mitovich, Matt Webb. 2015. "TLC Cancels *19 Kids & Counting* in Wake of Josh Duggar Molestation Scandal." *TVLine*, July 16. https://tvline.com/2015/07/16/19-kids-and-counting-cancelled-josh-duggar-molestation-scandal/.

Montemurro, Beth. 2008. "Toward a Sociology of Reality Television." *Sociology Compass* 2, no. 1: 84–106. doi: 10.1111/j.1751–9020.2007.00064.x.

Moors, Amy C., Jes L. Matsick, Ali Ziegler, Jennifer D. Rubin, and Terri D. Conley. 2013. "Stigma Toward Individuals Engaged in Consensual Nonmonogamy: Robust and Worthy of Additional Research." *Analyses of Social Issues and Public Policy* 13, no. 1: 52–69. https://doi.org/10.1111/asap.12020.

Morrissey, Tracie Egan. 2010. "*The Real World*: Drunk Guy Throws Other Drunk Guy Off Two-Story Balcony." *Jezebel*, February 25. https://jezebel.com/the-real-world-drunk-guy-throws-other-drunk-guy-off-tw-5480482.

———. 2012. "Blackface Happened on MTV." *Jezebel*, March 8. https://jezebel.com/460838864.

Moss, Philip I., and Christopher Tilly. 2001. *Stories Employers Tell: Race, Skill, and Hiring in America*. New York: Russell Sage Foundation.

Muñoz, Jose Esteban. 1998. "Pedro Zamora's Real World of Counterpublicity: Performing an Ethics of the Self." In *Hispanisms and Homosexualities*, edited by Sylvia Molloy and Robert McKee Irwin. Durham, NC: Duke University Press, 175–196.

Murray, Susan. 2004. "'I Think We Need a New Name for It': The Meeting of Documentary and Reality TV." In *Reality TV: Remaking Television Culture*, edited by Susan Murray and Laurie Ouellette. New York: NYU Press, 40–56.

Murray, Susan, and Laurie Ouellette. 2009. "Introduction." In *Reality TV: Remaking Television Culture*, edited by Susan Murray and Laurie Ouellette. New York: NYU Press, 1–22.

My Big Fat American Gypsy Wedding. 2012. Season 1, episode 2, "14 and Looking for Mr. Right," TLC.

My Strange Addiction. 2010. Season 1, episode 2, "Thumb Sucker/Bodybuilder," TLC.

My Strange Addiction. 2011. Season 1, episode 7, "Eats Couch Cushion/Furry," TLC.

Nabi, Robin L., Carmen R. Stitt, Jeff Halford, and Keli L. Finnerty. 2006. "Emotional and Cognitive Predictors of the Enjoyment of Reality-Based and Fictional Television Programming: An Elaboration of the Uses and Gratifications Perspective." *Media Psychology* 8, no. 4: 421–447. https://doi.org/10.1207/s1532785xmep0804_5.

Naked and Afraid. 2013. Season 1, episode 1, "The Jungle Curse," Discovery.

Nellis, Ashley. 2016. *The Color of Justice: Racial and Ethnic Disparity in State Prisons*. Sentencing Project, June 14. https://www.sentencingproject.org/publications/color-of-justice-racial-and-ethnic-disparity-in-state-prisons/.

Nelson, Libby. 2016. "Hillary Clinton's Popularity Surges When Bad Things Happen to Her." *Vox*, July 11. https://www.vox.com/2016/7/11/12105960/hillary-clinton-popularity-poll-approval-ratings.

90 Day Fiancé: Happily Ever After? 2018. Season 3, episode 1, "Home Sweet Home?," TLC.

Nordyke, Kimberly. 2007. "It's Tequila with a Twist." *Hollywood Reporter*, December 20. https://www.hollywoodreporter.com/news/tequila-a-twist-157504.

Nussbaum, Emily. 2016. "Big Gulp: Drinking and Drama on 'Vanderpump Rules.'" *New Yorker*, May 16. https://www.newyorker.com/magazine/2016/05/23/drinking-and-drama-on-vanderpump-rules.

Obama, Michelle. 2018. *Becoming*. New York: Crown.

O'Connor, Clare. 2013. "Duck Dynasty's Brand Bonanza: How A&E (and Walmart) Turned Camo into $400 Million Merchandise Sales." *Forbes*, November 6. https://www.forbes.com/sites/clareoconnor/2013/11/06/duck-dynastys-brand-bonanza-how-ae-and-walmart-turned-camo-into-400-million-merchandise-sales/#2d08c6201714.

Orbe, Mark P. 1998. "Constructions of Reality on MTV's 'The Real World': An Analysis of the Restrictive Coding of Black Masculinity." *Southern Communication Journal* 64, no. 1: 32–47. https://doi.org/10.1080/10417949809373116.

Ouellette, Laurie, and James Hay. 2008. *Better Living Through Reality TV*. Oxford, UK: Blackwell Publishing.

Pager, Devah. 2003. "The Mark of a Criminal Record." *American Journal of Sociology* 108, no. 5: 937–975. https://doi.org/10.1086/374403.

Pager, Devah, and Diana Karafin. 2009. "Bayesian Bigot? Statistical Discrimination, Stereotypes, and Employer Decision Making." *Annals of the American Academy of Political and Social Science* 621, no. 1: 70–93. https://doi.org/10.1177/0002716208324628.

Palmer-Mehta, Valerie, and Alina Haliliuc. 2009. "'Flavor of Love' and the Rise of Neo-Minstrelsy on Reality Television." In *Pimps, Wimps, Studs, Thugs and Gentlemen: Essays on Media Images of Masculinity*, edited by Elwood Watson. Jefferson, NC: McFarland & Co., 85–105.

Papacharissi, Zizi, and Andrew L. Mendelson. 2007. "An Exploratory Study of Reality Appeal: Uses and Gratifications of Reality TV Shows." *Journal of Broadcasting & Electronic Media* 51, no. 2: 355–370. https://doi.org/10.1080/08838150701307152.

Pariona, Amber. 2018. "Incarceration Rates by Race, Ethnicity, and Gender in the U.S." *WorldAtlas*, February 28. https://www.worldatlas.com /articles/incarceration-rates-by-race-ethnicity-and-gender-in-the -u-s.html.

Park, Sung-Yeon, Mark A. Flynn, Alexandru Stana, David T. Morin, and Gi Woong Yun. 2015. "'Where Do I Belong, from Laguna Beach to Jersey Shore?': Portrayal of Minority Youth in MTV Docusoaps." *Howard Journal of Communications* 26, no. 4: 381–402. https://doi .org/10.1080/10646175.2015.1080636.

Parker, Stefanie. 2020. "How Many *Bachelor* Couples Are Married? Spoiler Alert: More Than You Think!" *Parade*, December 22. https:// parade.com/124942/parade/bachelor-couples-still-together/.

Parreñas, Rhacel Salazar. 2001. *Servants of Globalization: Women, Migration, and Domestic Work*. Stanford, CA: Stanford University Press.

PBS. n.d. "Lance Loud: A Death in an American Family." Accessed January 31, 2021. https://www.pbs.org/lanceloud/american/.

Pearce, Susan, Elizabeth Clifford, and Reena Tandon. 2011. *Immigration and Women: Understanding the American Experience*. New York: NYU Press.

Peterson, Richard A., and Roger M. Kern. 1996. "Changing Highbrow Taste: From Snob to Omnivore." *American Sociological Review* 61, no. 5: 900–907. https://doi.org/10.2307/2096460.

Peterson, Richard A., and Albert Simkus. 1992. "How Musical Tastes Mark Occupational Status Groups." In *Cultivating Differences: Symbolic Boundaries and the Making of Inequality*, edited by Michèle Lamont and Marcel Fournier. Chicago: Chicago University Press, 152–186.

Pew Research Center. 2015. "America's Changing Religious Landscape," May 12. http://www.pewforum.org/2015/05/12/americas-changing -religious-landscape/.

———. 2015. "Modern Immigration Wave Brings 59 Million to U.S., Driving Population Growth and Change Through 2065," September 28. https://www.pewhispanic.org/2015/09/28/modern-immigration -wave-brings-59-million-to-u-s-driving-population-growth-and -change-through-2065/.

———. 2017. "Fact Sheet: Changing Attitudes on Gay Marriage," June 26. https://www.pewforum.org/fact-sheet/changing-attitudes-on-gay -marriage/.

Phares, Vicky, Ari R. Steinberg, and J. Kevin Thompson. 2004. "Gender Differences in Peer and Parental Influences: Body Image Disturbance, Self-Worth, and Psychological Functioning in Preadolescent Children." *Journal of Youth and Adolescence* 33, no. 5: 421–429. https://doi.org/10.1023/B:JOYO.0000037634.18749.20.

Pickens, Therí A. 2014. "Shoving Aside the Politics of Respectability: Black Women, Reality TV, and the Ratchet Performance." *Women*

& *Performance: A Journal of Feminist Theory* 25, no. 1: 41–58. https://doi.org/10.1080/0740770X.2014.923172.

Plaugic, Lizzie. 2017. "Fyre Fest Reportedly Paid Kendall Jenner $250K for a Single Instagram Post." *The Verge*, May 4. https://www.theverge.com/2017/5/4/15547734/fyre-fest-kendall-jenner-instagram-sponsored-paid.

Poniewozik, James. 2012. "The Morning After: Honey Boo Boo Don't Care." *Time*, August 9. http://entertainment.time.com/2012/08/09/the-morning-after-honey-boo-boo-dont-care/.

Popenoe, David. 1993. "American Family Decline, 1960–1990: A Review and Appraisal." *Journal of Marriage and the Family* 55, no. 3: 527–542. https://doi.org/10.2307/353333.

Porter, Rick. 2019. "TV Ratings: 'AGT Champions' Premiere Tops Steady 'Bachelor.'" *Hollywood Reporter*, January 8. https://www.hollywoodreporter.com/live-feed/bachelor-agt-champions-tv-ratings-monday-jan-7-2019-1174479.

Postman, Neil. [1985] 2005. *Amusing Ourselves to Death: Public Discourse in the Age of Show Business.* New York: Penguin Books.

Pozner, Jennifer L. 2010. *Reality Bites Back: The Troubling Truth about Guilty Pleasure TV.* Berkeley, CA: Seal Press.

Praderio, Caroline. 2018. "A Woman Paused During a 106-Mile Ultra-Marathon to Breastfeed Her 3-Month-Old Son." *Insider*, September 12. https://www.thisisinsider.com/woman-breastfeeds-son-ultra-marathon-sophie-power-2018-9.

Press, Joy. 2020. "Reality TV's New Reality in the COVID Era." *Vanity Fair*, September 25. https://www.vanityfair.com/hollywood/2020/09/reality-tvs-new-reality-in-the-covid-era.

Project Runway. 2019a, Season 17, episode 1, "First Impressions," Bravo.

Project Runway. 2019b, Season 17, episode 6, "Power Play," Bravo.

Pullen, Christopher. 2006. "Gay Performativity and Reality Television: Alliances, Competition, and Discourse." In *The New Queer Aesthetic on Television*, edited by James R. Keller and Leslie Stratyner. Jefferson, NC: McFarland & Co., 160–176.

Punyanunt-Carter, Narissra Maria. 2010. "Parasocial Relationships in Dating and Makeover Reality Television." In *Fix Me Up: Essays on Television Dating and Makeover Shows*, edited by Judith Lancioni. Jefferson, NC: McFarland & Co., 68–78.

Quinn, Dave. 2017. "Bachelor Alum Leah Block Apologizes After Rachel Lindsay Calls Out Her Racially Insensitive Tweet." *People*, June 23. https://people.com/tv/leah-block-the-bachelorette-rachel-lindsay-racist-tweet/.

The Real Housewives of Atlanta. 2009. Season 2, episode 1, "New Attitude, Same ATL," Bravo.

The Real Housewives of Beverly Hills. 2011. Season 2, episode 5, "$25,000 Sunglasses?!," Bravo.

The Real Housewives of Beverly Hills. 2012. Season 2, episode 23, "Reunion: Part 3," Bravo.

The Real Housewives of New York City. 2008. Season 1, episode 1, "Meet the Wives," Bravo.

The Real Housewives of New York City. 2015a. Season 7, episode 13, "Sonja Island," Bravo.

The Real Housewives of New York City. 2015b. Season 7, episode 15, "Don't Be All, Like, Uncool," Bravo.

The Real Housewives of New York City. 2015c. Season 7, episode 20, "Reunion—Part 1," Bravo.

The Real Housewives of New York City. 2018. Season 10, episode 19, "Life Is a Cabaret," Bravo.

The Real Housewives of Orange County. 2011. Season 6, episode 12, "Fashion Victim," Bravo.

The Real World. 1992a. Season 1, episode 1, "This Is the True Story . . . ," MTV.

The Real World. 1992b. Season 1, episode 9, "Julie in a Homeless Shelter?," MTV.

The Real World. 1993. Season 2, episode 6, "Is David Going Home?," MTV.

The Real World. 2009a. Season 23, episode 1, "Looks Can Be D.C.–ving," MTV.

The Real World. 2009b. Season 23, episode 2, "Bipartisan Lovin'," MTV.

Richter, Nicole. 2011. "Ambiguous Bisexuality: The Case of *A Shot at Love with Tila Tequila.*" *Journal of Bisexuality* 11, no. 1: 121–141. https://doi.org/10.1080/15299716.2011.545316.

Riddle, Karyn, and J. J. De Simone. 2013. "A Snooki Effect? An Exploration of the Surveillance Subgenre of Reality TV and Viewers' Beliefs about the 'Real' Real World." *Psychology of Popular Media Culture* 2, no. 4: 237–250. doi: 10.1037/ppm0000005.

Riese. 2019. "Cast Full of Lesbians: 15 TV Shows That Put Queer Women First." *Autostraddle*, February 22. https://www.autostraddle.com/cast-full-of-lesbian-15-tv-shows-about-lesbian-bisexual-women-l-word-torch-449586/.

Risman, Barbara J. 2004. "Gender as a Social Structure: Theory Wrestling with Activism." *Gender & Society* 18, no. 4: 429–450. https://doi.org/10.1177/0891243204265349.

Rivers, Caryl, Rosalind C. Barnett, and Grace K. Baruch. 1979. *Beyond Sugar and Spice: How Women Grow, Learn, and Thrive.* New York: Ballantine Books.

Robehmed, Natalie. 2018. "How 20-Year-Old Kylie Jenner Built a $900

Million Fortune in Less Than 3 Years." *Forbes*, July 11. https://www
.forbes.com/sites/forbesdigitalcovers/2018/07/11/how-20-year-old
-kylie-jenner-built-a-900-million-fortune-in-less-than-3-years
/#19b21dd7aa62.

Roca, Teresa. 2017. "'90 Day Fiancé' Star Danielle Accuses Ex Mohamed
of Fraud & Stealing Money." *Radar Online*, October 2. https://
radaronline.com/exclusives/2017/10/90-day-fiance-star-danielle
-accuses-ex-mohamed-fraud-stealing-money/.

Rose, Randall L., and Stacy L. Wood. 2005. "Paradox and the Consumption of Authenticity through Reality Television." *Journal of Consumer Research* 32, no. 2: 284–296. https://doi.org/10.1086/432238.

Roth, April L. 2003. "Contrived Television Reality: *Survivor* as a Pseudo-
Event." In *Survivor Lessons: Essays on Communication and Reality
Television*, edited by Matthew J. Smith and Andrew F. Wood. Jeffer-
son, NC: McFarland & Co., 27–36.

Rouse, Wade. 2015. "*Real Housewives of New York* Recap: Who Brought
the Naked Man Home in the Turks & Caicos?" *People*, July 14.
https://people.com/tv/real-housewives-of-new-york-recap-luann
-de-lesseps-says-dont-be-all-uncool/.

Rubin, Gayle. 1975. "The Traffic in Women: Notes on the 'Political Economy' of Sex." In *Toward an Anthropology of Women*, edited by Rayna
R. Reiter. New York: Monthly Review Press, 157–210.

———. 1999. "Thinking Sex: Notes for a Radical Theory of the Politics
of Sexuality." In *Culture, Society and Sexuality: A Reader*, edited by
Richard Parker and Peter Aggleton. London: UCL Press, 143–178.

RuPaul's Drag Race. 2011. Season 3, episode 2, "Jocks in Frocks," Logo.

Ryan, Camille L., and Kurt Bauman. 2016. "Educational Attainment
in the United States: 2015." Census.gov. March. Accessed February 1, 2021. https://www.census.gov/content/dam/Census/library
/publications/2016/demo/p20-578.pdf.

Sakala, Leah. 2014. "Breaking Down Mass Incarceration in the 2010 Census: State-by-State Incarceration Rates by Race/Ethnicity." Prison
Policy Initiative, May 28. https://www.prisonpolicy.org/reports/rates
.html.

Sanders, Alan R., Eden R. Martin, Gary W. Beecham, S. Guo, K. Dawood,
G. Rieger, J. A. Badner, et al. 2015. "Genome-Wide Scan Demonstrates Significant Linkage for Male Sexual Orientation." *Psychological Medicine* 45, no. 7: 1379–1388. doi: 10.1017/S0033291714002451.

Sawyer, Wendy, and Peter Wagner. 2019. "Mass Incarceration: The Whole
Pie." Prison Policy Initiative, March 19. https://www.prisonpolicy
.org/reports/pie2019.html.

Schalet, Amy. 2006. "Raging Hormones, Regulated Love: Adolescent
Sexuality in the United States and the Netherlands." In *Family in*

Transition, edited by Arlene Skolnick and Jerome Skolnick. Boston: Allyn & Bacon, 129–134.

Schneider, Mac. 2019. "The Truth behind the TV Show *Cops*." *Vox*, May 3. https://www.vox.com/2019/5/3/18527391/truth-behind-tv-show-cops.

Schneider, Michael. 2018. "These Are the 100 Most-Watched TV Shows of the 2017–18 Season: Winners and Losers." *IndieWire*, May 25. https://www.indiewire.com/2018/05/most-watched-tv-shows-2017-2018-Season-roseanne-this-is-us-walking-dead-1201968306/.

Sentencing Project. 2019. "Criminal Justice Facts." Accessed February 1, 2021. https://www.sentencingproject.org/criminal-justice-facts/.

17 Kids and Counting. 2008. Season 1, episode 8, "Trading Places, Duggar Style," TLC.

Sexuality Information and Education Council of the United States. 2018. *A History of Federal Funding for Abstinence-Only-Until-Marriage Programs*. August. https://siecus.org/wp-content/uploads/2018/08/A-History-of-AOUM-Funding-Final-Draft.pdf.

A Shot at Love with Tila Tequila. 2007a. Season 1, episode 1, "Surprise! I Like Boys and Girls," MTV.

A Shot at Love with Tila Tequila. 2007b. Season 1, episode 2, "Can't We All Just Get Along?," MTV.

Signorielli, Nancy, and Michael Morgan. 1996. "Cultivation Analysis: Research and Practice." In *An Integrated Approach to Communication Theory and Research*, edited by Don W. Stacks and Michael B. Salwen. New York: Routledge, 111–126.

Simien, Justin. 2014. *Dear White People*. New York: Simon & Schuster.

Simmel, Georg. 1964. *The Sociology of Georg Simmel*, translated and edited by Kurt H. Wolff. New York: Free Press.

———. [1903] 1971. "The Metropolis and Mental Life." In *On Individuality and Social Forms*, edited by Donald N. Levine. Chicago: University of Chicago Press, 324–339.

Simon, Mallory, Sara Sidner, and Ralph Ellis. 2019. "Other Racist Photos Found in Northam's Medical School Yearbook." CNN, February 3. https://www.cnn.com/2019/02/03/politics/northams-medical-school-yearbook/index.html.

Sister Wives. 2010. Season 1, episode 1, "Meet Kody and the Wives," TLC.

Sister Wives. 2016. Season 10, episode 1, "Catfishing Fallout," TLC.

16 and Pregnant. 2010. Season 2, "Life After Labor Finale Special," MTV.

Skeggs, Beverley. 2009. "The Moral Economy of Person Production: The Class Relations of Self-Performance on 'Reality' Television." *Sociological Review* 57, no. 4: 626–644. https://doi.org/10.1111/j.1467–954X.2009.01865.x.

Skeggs, Bev, Nancy Thumim, and Helen Wood. 2008. "'Oh Goodness,

I Am Watching Reality TV': How Methods Make Class in Audience Research." *European Journal of Cultural Studies* 11, no. 1: 5–24. https://doi.org/10.1177/1367549407084961.

Smith-Shomade, Beretta E. 2002. *Shaded Lives: African-American Women and Television*. New Brunswick, NJ: Rutgers University Press.

Snapped. 2011. Season 6, episode 9, "Cynthia George," Oxygen.

Snooki & Jwoww: Moms with Attitude. 2019. Season 1, episode 13, "Snooki & JWoww's DNA Test Results Will Shock You," MTV YouTube.

Spector, Nicole. 2015. "Cosmopolitan Cover Calling Kardashians 'America's First Family' Sparks Backlash." *Today*, October 5. https://www.today.com/popculture/cosmopolitan-cover-calling-kardashians-americas-first-family-sparks-backlash-t48321.

Stanger-Hall, Kathrin F., and David W. Hall. 2011. "Abstinence-Only Education and Teen Pregnancy Rates: Why We Need Comprehensive Sex Education in the US." *PloS One* 6, no. 10: e24658. https://doi.org/10.1371/journal.pone.0024658.

Statista. 2016. "Which of the Following Genres of Reality TV Shows Do You Typically Watch?" Statista Research Department, September 25. https://www.statista.com/statistics/617828/popularity-reality-tv-genres-usa/.

———. 2019. "Popularity of Reality TV Genres in the U.S. 2016, by Gender." Statista Research Department, September 25. https://www.statista.com/statistics/623255/popularity-reality-tv-genres-gender-usa/.

Stefanone, Michael A., and Derek Lackaff. 2009. "Reality Television as a Model for Online Behavior: Blogging, Photo, and Video Sharing." *Journal of Computer-Mediated Communication* 14, no. 4: 964–987. https://doi.org/10.1111/j.1083-6101.2009.01477.x.

Stefanone, Michael A., Derek Lackaff, and Devan Rosen. 2010. "The Relationship between Traditional Mass Media and 'Social Media': Reality Television as a Model for Social Network Site Behavior." *Journal of Broadcasting & Electronic Media* 54, no. 3: 508–525. https://doi.org/10.1080/08838151.2010.498851.

Steffensmeier, Darrell, and Stephen Demuth. 2000. "Ethnicity and Sentencing Outcomes in US Federal Courts: Who Is Punished More Harshly?" *American Sociological Review* 65, no. 5: 705–729. https://doi.org/10.2307/2657543.

Stokes, Wendy. 2018. "Top 10 Richest Chefs in the World." *The Frisky*, November 11. https://thefrisky.com/top-10-richest-chefs-in-the-world/.

Students for Fair Admissions, Inc., v. President and Fellows of Harvard College. 2018. Civil Action No. 1:14-cv-14176-ADB. U.S. District Court for the District of Massachusetts, Boston Division. June 15. https://int.nyt.com/data/documenthelper/43-sffa-memo-for-summary-judgement/1a7a4880cb6a662b3b51/optimized/full.pdf#page=1.

Suggitt, Connie. 2018. "10 Record-Breaking Celebrity Achievements from 2018." *Guinness World Records*, December 21. http://www.guinnessworldrecords.com/news/2018/12/10-record-breaking-celebrity-achievements-from-2018-552082.

Suhr, Hiesun Cecilia. 2012. "Raising Popularity through Social Media: A Case Study of the Tila Tequila Brand." *International Journal of the Humanities* 9, no. 11: 9–22. https://doi.org/10.18848/1447-9508/CGP/v09i11/43371.

Supernanny. 2005. Season 1, episode 4, "The Wischmeyer Family," ABC.

Survivor. 2000a. Season 1, episode 3, "Quest for Food," CBS.

Survivor. 2000b. Season 1, episode 4, "Too Little, Too Late?," CBS.

Sutherland, Edwin H., and Donald R. Cressey. 1966. *Principles of Criminology.* Philadelphia: Lippincott.

Teeman, Tim. 2018. "'Real Housewife' LuAnn de Lesseps on Jail, Blackface, and Getting Groped by Russell Simmons." *Daily Beast*, April 6. https://www.thedailybeast.com/real-housewife-luann-de-lesseps-on-jail-blackface-and-getting-groped-by-russell-simmons.

Tejada, Chloe. 2017. "'Asian Bachelorette' Is the Reality Show We All Need Right Now." *Huffington Post*, August 3. https://www.huffingtonpost.ca/2017/08/03/asian-bachelorette_a_23063431/.

Terry-Humen, Elizabeth, Jennifer Manlove, and Kristin A. Moore. 2005. *Playing Catch-Up: How Children Born to Teen Mothers Fare.* Washington, DC: National Campaign to Prevent Teen Pregnancy. January. https://www.childtrends.org/wp-content/uploads/01/PlayingCatchUp.pdf.

Thomas, Mary E. 2005. "'I Think It's Just Natural': The Spatiality of Racial Segregation at a U.S. High School." *Environment and Planning A: Economy and Space.* 37, no. 7: 1233–1248. https://doi.org/10.1068/a37209.

Thomas, W. I., and Dorothy Swaine Thomas. 1928. *The Child in America: Behavior Problems and Programs.* New York: Knopf.

Thornton, Arland, and Linda Young-DeMarco. 2001. "Four Decades of Trends in Attitudes toward Family Issues in the United States: The 1960s through the 1990s." *Journal of Marriage and Family* 63, no. 4:1009–37. https://doi.org/10.1111/j.1741-3737.2001.01009.x.

Tilly, Charles. 1999. "The Trouble with Stories." In *The Social Worlds of Higher Education: Handbook for Teaching in a New Century,* edited by Ronald Aminzade and Bernice Pescosolido. Thousand Oaks, CA: Pine Forge Press, 256–270.

Toddlers & Tiaras. 2009a. Season 1, episode 2, "Miss Georgia Spirit," TLC.

Toddlers & Tiaras. 2009b. Season 2, episode 1, "Universal Royalty," TLC.

Toddlers & Tiaras. 2011a. Season 3, episode 11, "Universal Royalty, Texas," TLC.

Toddlers & Tiaras. 2011b. Season 4, episode 12, "Precious Moments Pageant," TLC.

Toddlers & Tiaras. 2012. Season 4, episode 19, "Precious Moments Pageant 2011," TLC.

Toffel, Hope. 1996. "Crazy Women, Unharmed Men, and Evil Children: Confronting the Myths About Battered People Who Kill Their Abusers, and the Argument for Extending Battering Syndrome Self-Defenses to All Victims of Domestic Violence." *Southern California Law Review* 70, no. 1: 337–380.

Toossi, Mitra, and Teresa L. Morisi. 2017. "Women in the Workforce before, during, and after the Great Recession." U.S. Bureau of Labor Statistics. July. https://www.bls.gov/spotlight/2017/women -in-the-workforce-before-during-and-after-the-great-recession /pdf/women-in-the-workforce-before-during-and-after-the-great -recession.pdf.

Top Chef. 2007. Season 2, episode 11, "Sense and Sensuality," Bravo.

Turner, Graeme. 2006. "The Mass Production of Celebrity: 'Celetoids,' Reality TV and the 'Demotic Turn.'" *International Journal of Cultural Studies* 9, no. 2: 153–165. https://doi.org/10.1177/1367877906064028.

Umstead, R. Thomas. 2013. "A&E's 'Duck Dynasty' Debut Draws 11.8 Million Viewers." *Next TV*, August 15. https://www.nexttv.com /news/ae-s-duck-dynasty-debut-draws-118-million-viewers -357791.

Undercover Boss. 2012. Season 3, episode 4, "Checkers & Rally's," CBS.

United States Bureau of Labor Statistics. 2008. "Table 1. Time Spent in Primary Activities (1) and the Percent of Married Mothers and Fathers Who Did the Activities on an Average Day by Employment Status and Age of Youngest Own Household Child, Average for the Combined Years 2003–06," May 8. http://www.bls.gov/news.release /atus2.t01.htm.

Valenzuela, Sebastián, Daniel Halpern, and James E. Katz. 2014. "Social Network Sites, Marriage Well-Being and Divorce: Survey and State-Level Evidence from the United States." *Computers in Human Behavior* 36: 94–101. https://doi.org/10.1016/j.chb.2014.03.034.

Vandenbosch, Laura, and Steven Eggermont. 2011. "*Temptation Island, The Bachelor, Joe Millionaire*: A Prospective Cohort Study on the Role of Romantically Themed Reality Television in Adolescents' Sexual Development." *Journal of Broadcasting & Electronic Media* 55, no. 4: 563–580. https://doi.org/10.1080/08838151.2011.620663.

Vaughn, Allison A., Stacy A. Teeters, Melody S. Sadler, and Sierra B.

Cronan. 2017. "Stereotypes, Emotions, and Behaviors toward Lesbians, Gay Men, Bisexual Women, and Bisexual men." *Journal of Homosexuality* 64, no. 13: 1890–1911. https://doi.org/10.1080/00918369 .2016.1273718.

Victory Institute. 2019. *Out for America 2019: A Census of Out LGBTQ Elected Officials Nationwide.* Accessed February 1, 2021. https:// victoryinstitute.org/wp-content/uploads/2019/06/Victory-Institute -Out-for-America-Report-2019.pdf.

Vincent, Clark E. 1951. "Trends in Infant Care Ideas." *Child Development* 22, no. 3: 199–209. https://doi.org/10.2307/1126306.

Wade, Lisa. 2017. *American Hookup: The New Culture of Sex on Campus.* New York: W. W. Norton & Co.

Wagner, Chandi. 2017. "School Segregation Then & Now: How to Move Toward a More Perfect Union." Center for Public Education, January. https://www.nsba.org/-/media/NSBA/File/cpe-school-segregation -then-and-now-report-january-2017.pdf.

Walsh, Paul. 2018. "Minnesota Rep Drafts Bill to Ban 'The Bachelor's' Arie from the State." *Star Tribune*, March 8. http://www.startribune .com/minnesota-rep-drafts-bill-to-ban-the-bachelor-from-the -state/476275923/.

Wang, Grace. 2010. "A Shot at Half-Exposure: Asian Americans in Reality TV Shows." *Television & New Media*, 11, no. 5: 404–427. https:// doi.org/10.1177/1527476410363482.

Wang, Wendy, and Kim Parker. 2014. "Record Share of Americans Have Never Married." Pew Research Center, September 24. https://www .pewsocialtrends.org/2014/09/24/record-share-of-americans-have -never-married/.

Warner, Kristen J. 2015. "They Gon' Think You Loud Regardless: Ratchetness, Reality Television, and Black Womanhood." *Camera Obscura: Feminism, Culture, and Media Studies* 30, no. 1: 129–153. https://doi .org/10.1215/02705346-2885475.

Weber, Brenda R. 2009. *Makeover TV: Selfhood, Citizenship, and Celebrity.* Durham, NC: Duke University Press.

Weber, Lindsey. 2016. "Why the Women Always Outperform the Men on 'Naked and Afraid.'" *Elle*, May 12. https://www.elle.com/culture /movies-tv/a36301/why-women-do-better-on-naked-and-afraid/.

Weber, Max. [1922] 1968. "The Distribution of Power within the Political Community: Class, Status, Party." In *Economy and Society: An Outline of Interpretive Sociology*, edited by Guenther Roth and Claus Wittich. New York: Bedminster Press, 926–940.

———. [1904] 2012. *The Protestant Ethic and the Spirit of Capitalism.* Translated by Stephen Kalberg. New York: Routledge.

Wegenstein, Bernadette, and Nora Ruck. 2011. "Physiognomy, Reality

Television and the Cosmetic Gaze." *Body & Society* 17, no. 4: 27–54. https://doi.org/10.1177/1357034X11410455.

West, Candace, and Don H. Zimmerman. 1987. "Doing Gender." *Gender & Society* 1, no. 2: 125–151. https://doi.org/10.1177/0891243287001002002.

West, Carolyn M. 2018. "Mammy, Sapphire, Jezebel, and the Bad Girls of Reality Television: Media Representations of Black Women." In *Lectures on the Psychology of Women*, 5th ed., edited by Joan Chrisler and Carla Golden. Long Grove, IL: Waveland, 139–158.

Weston, Kath. 1997. *Families We Choose: Lesbians, Gays, Kinship.* New York: Columbia University Press.

Whiting, Beatrice Blyth, and Carolyn Pope Edwards. 1988. *Children of Different Worlds.* Cambridge, MA: Harvard University Press.

Whiting, Jackie. 2013. "The Worst Parenting Moments from Reality TV Moms." College Humor, May 10. http://www.collegehumor .com/post/6888370/the-worst-parenting-moments-from-reality-tv -moms.

Whiting, Susan, Cloves Campbell, and Cheryl Pearson-McNeil. 2013. *Resilient, Receptive and Relevant: The African-American Consumer 2013 Report.* Nielsen Company, September. https://www.iab.com/wp -content/uploads/2015/08/Nielsen-African-American-Consumer -Report-Sept-2013.pdf.

Wilcox, W. Bradford, and Wendy Wang. 2017. *The Marriage Divide: How and Why Working Class Families Are More Fragile Today.* Washington, DC: American Enterprise Institute, September 25. https:// ifstudies.org/blog/the-marriage-divide-how-and-why-working -class-families-are-more-fragile-today.

Wilkerson, Isabel. 2020. *Caste: The Origins of Our Discontents.* New York: Random House.

Williams, Aaron, and Armand Emamdjomeh. 2018. "Segregation Map: America's Cities 50 Years after the Fair Housing Act." *Washington Post*, May 10. https://www.washingtonpost.com/graphics/2018 /national/segregation-us-cities/.

Wilson, John Paul, Kurt Hugenberg, and Nicholas O. Rule. 2017. "Racial Bias in Judgments of Physical Size and Formidability: From Size to Threat." *Journal of Personality and Social Psychology* 113, no. 1: 59–80. https://doi.org/10.1037/pspi0000092.

Wilson, William Julius. 1996. *When Work Disappears: The World of the New Urban Poor.* New York: Vintage Books.

Wirtz, Andrea L., Tonia C. Poteat, Mannat Malik, and Nancy Glass. 2020. "Gender-Based Violence against Transgender People in the United States: A Call for Research and Programming." *Trauma, Violence, & Abuse* 21, no. 2: 227–241. https://doi.org/10.1177/1524838018757749.

Wong, Y. Joel, Jesse Owen, Kimberly K. Tran, Dana L. Collins, and

Claire E. Higgins. 2012. "Asian American Male College Students' Perceptions of People's Stereotypes about Asian American Men." *Psychology of Men & Masculinity* 13, no. 1: 75–88. https://doi.org/10.1037/a0022800.

Yahr, Emily. 2014. "'Here Comes Honey Boo Boo' Canceled after Reports about Mama June's Connection with Convicted Child Molester." *Washington Post*, October 24. https://www.washingtonpost.com/news/arts-and-entertainment/wp/2014/10/24/here-comes-honey-boo-boo-canceled-after-reports-about-mama-junes-connection-with-convicted-child-molester/?noredirect=on&utm_term=.c91463afa5e2.

Yapalater, Lauren. 2016. "56 Things Built Under the Kardashian/Jenner Empire." *BuzzFeed*, June 6. https://www.buzzfeed.com/lyapalater/things-built-under-the-kardashianjenner-empire.

Zulkey, Claire. 2012. "*Here Comes Honey Boo Boo*—'It Is What It Is.'" *A.V. Club*, September 26. https://tv.avclub.com/here-comes-honey-boo-boo-it-is-what-it-is-1798174331.

Zurbriggen, Eileen, and Elizabeth M. Morgan. 2006. "Who Wants to Marry a Millionaire? Reality Dating Television Programs, Attitudes Toward Sex, and Sexual Behaviors." *Sex Roles* 54, no. 1–2: 1–17. doi:10.1007/s11199-005-8865-2.

Acknowledgments

Writing a book is a social act, and all of the following had important roles in bringing *True Story* to life:

Margo Fleming and the team at Brockman, who initially approached me about writing this book and without whom it wouldn't exist.

Colin Dickerman, for believing in this project, and Sean McDonald (and everyone at Farrar, Straus and Giroux), for picking it up and running with it.

The Sociology and Anthropology Department at Lehigh University, for the writing sabbatical and for all their continued support.

The students in my Sociology of Reality TV class, who keep my knowledge current—and make me feel like a fogy.

The friends and colleagues who've consumed and discussed various reality shows with me over the years—including, but not limited to, Ilana Keane, Jen Kondo, Danielle Nunez, Shaina Steinberg, and Allison Mickel. And the friends and colleagues who think these shows are trash but love me and support my work anyway.

Jessica Hickok. Obviously.

Keebler Fudge Stripes cookies.

The creators of these shows, the personalities who populate them, and the fans who watch and share their perspectives on social media and message boards.

My supportive husband, Hunter, who can now name at least four Real Housewives (though I'm pretty sure "Kim" was just a shot in the dark).

And my parents, Louise and Bruce, who always let me watch as much TV as I wanted, as long as I was getting good grades.

Index

abstinence: gender roles and double standard for, 50–51; virginity pledges for, 113–14

addiction, 233–34

advertainment, 13

agency and structure, 33–34

American Family, An, 8, 85, 101–102

American Idol: Asian Americans on, 179; popularity of, 3–4

America's Most Wanted, 243

America's Next Top Model, 19, 159, 161, 172–73

Andrejevic, Mark, 269

Angry Black Man stereotype, 163–65, 167

Apprentice, The, 148–49, 151, 166–67, 258, 268

archetypes, 11–12

Are You the One?, 64, 65, 214–15, 228–29

Asian Americans, 176–78, 179

autonomy, personal, 88–90

Baby Boom, 207

Bachelor, The: archetypes on, 11–12; class-action lawsuit against, 55; etiquette for 1950s heterosexual courtship on, 48; gender role expectations on, 47–50; gender roles and sexuality on, 50–51; hookup culture on, 52, 53; love and marriage regarding, 58–59; playfulness with contestant jobs on, 46; politics regarding, 255–56; popularity of, 46; psychological manipulation of contestants on, 18; racial issues with, 55–56, 57, 160; rose ceremony on, 45–46; *SNL* parody of, 55, 256; tractor racing on, 45; twosomes on, 47

Bachelorette, The, 150–51; gender role expectations on, 48; playfulness with contestant jobs on, 46; racial issues with, 56, 57, 160–61

Bad Girls Club, 20, 79, 251

Bad Moms, 99

Bailey, Beth, 48, 50

Beauty and the Geek, 211

Becker, Howard, 235, 236, 238

Big Brother, 35

Biggest Loser, The, 7

binge-watching, 20

bisexuality: gender in relation to, 221–22, 223–26; pride and secure in, 214, 230–31

blackface, 161–62

Black Lives Matter, 186

deviance (*cont.*)
235–36, 238; criminal justice
system for controlling, 241–46;
dealing with, 240–43; defining,
234–35; differential association
theory regarding, 236; drug
use and, 236; hierarchy,
250–53; love for, 243–46;
primary and secondary, 249;
reasons for, 235–38; reflection
on representation of, 253–54;
resonance with, 246–49;
responses to, 238–40; social
environments in relation to,
236–37; strain theory of, 237–38
differential association theory,
236
DiMaggio, Paul, 150
divide et impera, 74
divorce, 42
DIY celebrity, *see* do-it-yourself
celebrity
DNA tests, 183–84
documentaries, 250–51
doing gender, 189–91, 197
do-it-yourself (DIY) celebrity,
36–37, 238
double consciousness concept, 180
dramaturgical analysis, 35
Dr. Pimple Popper, 138
drug use, 236
Du Bois, W. E. B., 180
Duck Dynasty, 147–48, 149, 153
Durkheim, Émile, 28, 34, 79,
235–36, 246–47
dyads: definition of, 70; on *Naked
and Afraid*, 71–72; prevalence
of, 75; on *Survivor*, 70–71

edutainment, 250
elites: hierarchies of taste among,
139–42; omnivorousness of,
150–53

embodied capital, 136
employment, *see*
work/employment
Engels, Friedrich, 127,
217
ethnicity, 183
exchange value, 130–31
Expedition Robinson, 9

Fabulous Life of, The, 143
Facebook, 42
family: benefits of, 85–88;
caring support within, 85–86;
COVID-19 pandemic support
from, 86; expectations around,
103; individualism shift in,
88–90; personal autonomy
within, 88–90; reflection on
types of represented, 101–104;
sacredness of, 84–85; teaching
within, 85; *see also*
mothers/motherhood
fathers/fatherhood, 91
fin-syn rules, 9
Fire Island, 229
Flavor of Love, 165–66
Floyd, George, 185–86
formal sociology, 69
Foucault, Michel, 114–15, 215–17,
218, 228, 241, 242
Frankel, Bethenny, 151,
153
frankenbiting, 18
Friday Night Tykes, 192
Friends, 47
Frost, Jo, 98
full glitz pageants, 191–92

Gabler, Neal, 260
Garcia, Nina, 140–41
Garfinkel, Harold, 234–35
Gates, Racquel, 100, 232
gender: biological sex in relation

to, 190–96, 203; bisexuality in relation to, 221–22, 223–26; doing, 189–91, 197; homosexuality in relation to, 219–22; likeness of male and female, 196; male gaze and, 222–23; race stereotypes in relation to, 163–68; reflection on stereotyping, 210–13; sexual property in relation to, 200; as social construction, 190, 192, 212–13; as social fiction, 193; socialization of, 196–202; transgender, people, 54, 202–204; Trump administration on, 203
gender performance: on *Naked and Afraid*, 194–96; on *RuPaul's Drag Race*, 188–89, 193–94; on *Toddlers & Tiaras*, 191–92
gender roles: abstinence double standard and, 50–51; aggressive and mean behavior regarding, 207–10; *The Bachelor* portrayal of, 50–51; capitalism, marriage and, 198–99; couples, sexuality and, 50–55; couples and expectations of, 47–50; COVID-19, employment and, 199; etiquette for 1950s heterosexual courtship, 48; *The Girls Next Door* portrayal of, 54–55; hookup culture and, 52–53; regarding marriage and employment, 197–200, 201; *The Millionaire Matchmaker* portrayal of, 51; regarding women's transfer of domestic labor, 205–207
Gene Simmons Family Jewels, 91
Gerbner, George, 270–71
The Girls Next Door: gender roles

and sexuality on, 54–55; money and privilege on, 143
GLAAD advocacy group, 215
Goffman, Erving, 35, 239, 240, 246
gold, 131
Gold, Tracey, 97
gold diggers, 200
Goode, William J., 85–86
groups: commonalities across, 69; comparison of large and small, 75; dyad, 70–72, 75; focus on insufficiency of, 75–76; mastery over, 70, 76–77; in and out, 76; realness of competition shows regarding, 80–83; triad, 72–75, 82
groupthink: as mob mentality, 77; on *The Real Housewives*, 78–79; social current and, 79; on *Top Chef*, 77–78, 80; regarding *What Would You Do?*, 79–80

habitus, 117, 145–47
Harry (prince), 66
Hartmann, Heidi, 198–99, 200–201
Hatcher-Frazier, Holly, 179–80
Hays, Sharon, 92–93, 97
Hefner, Hugh, 54–55, 143
Hell's Kitchen, 208
Here Comes Honey Boo Boo, 6, 94, 109; body weight as focus on, 135–36, 137; popularity of, 133; Redneck Games on, 125, 135–36, 140
heteronormativity, 65, 115, 218, 225, 231
hierarchy: of acceptance, 21–22; deviance, 250–53; sexual, 63, 217–19; of taste, 139–42
Hills, The, 18, 20, 261
Hilton, Paris, 144
Hoarding, 239–40

rates in relation to, 159, 245; intensive mothering double standard and, 100–101; interracial couples and, 66; invisibility of, 173–78; Latinx people regarding, 174–76; mean judges' role regarding, 208–209; misrepresentation and under-representation of, 55–56, 102; police brutality and, 185–86; politics of representation and, 178–82; in post-Floyd era, 184–87; as social construction, 182–84; social space and, 158–63; technical robot stereotype regarding, 177–78; *see also* Black people; Black women

Ramsay, Gordon, 108, 208, 209–10

ratchet, 37, 132–33, 160, 167, 169, 175, 178, 251

realbooking, 42

Real Housewives, The, 6, 150, 151; de Lesseps of, 38–44, 161–62; finding connection with, 19–20; groupthink on, 78–79; as misnomer, 204; money and class mismatch on, 144–47; party planning argument escalation on, 156–58; politics regarding, 256

reality TV: as advertainment, 13; archetypes as lifeblood of, 11–12; binge-watching, 20; conservatism in relation to, 14–15; defining, 10; disclaimer as fan of, 19–23; documentaries compared to, 250–51; exploitation and COVID-19, 271; hierarchy of acceptance regarding, 21–22; insight and potential of, 23; learning from,

4–7; multiplatform approach of, 35–36; origins of, 7–9; parasocial relationships and, 12–13; politics and, 255–61; popularity explosion for, 3–4; producer intervention and, 18; reality of, 267–72; reasons for watching, 10–14; research hope, 272; research overview, 14–19; as social construction, 7; social media engagement with, 11; sociological lens on, 15–17; studies on, 7, 250, 269–70; surveillance culture and, 269; truths of ourselves exposed through, 262–67; voyeuristic pleasure from, 10–11; *see also specific topics*

Real L Word, The, 220

Real World, The: Angry Black Man portrayed on, 164–65; changes to, 31; characteristics emerging from, 8, 10; finding connection with, 19; LGBTQ people on, 30, 102, 202, 223–24, 230–31; politics regarding, 256–57; premiere episode of, 3, 19, 27; Sapphire stereotype portrayed on, 166; social difference at heart of, 30–31; structure and agency portrayed on, 34; urban environment adjustment in, 31–32

Redneck Games, 125, 135–36, 140

rejoicing third, *see tertius gaudens*

Richardson, Tiffany, 172–73

Richie, Nicole, 144

Risman, Barbara, 192

Riveras, The, 102

Rubin, Gayle, 63, 196, 218, 219, 228

Rules, The, 50

Run's House, 91

triads: complications within,
72–73; definition of, 72;
divide et impera in, 74; figures
important to, 82; prevalence of,
75; on *Survivor*, 73–74; *tertius
gaudens* in, 73, 74
Trump, Donald: *The Apprentice*
starring, 148–49, 151, 166–67,
258, 268; dynasty, 147–49; on
gender, 203; ideologies of, 263;
Kardashian, K., meeting with,
255; presidency of, 258–61,
268–69; presidential candidacy
of, 22, 149, 258; truth regarding
claims of, 260–61; U.S. Capitol
attack and, 259, 268
Turner, Graeme, 36
twosomes: dyad, 70–72, 75;
importance of specific, 66–67;
in society, 47

U2, 255
Undercover Boss, 127–29
unemployment, 28, 29
urban environments, 31–33
use value, 130–31

Vanderpump Rules, 150, 265
virginity pledges, 113–14
voyeuristic pleasure, 10–11

Walters, Barbara, 130
Warren, Elizabeth, 183–84
Weber, Brenda R., 138–39

Weber, Max: on capitalism, 142;
on class and work relationship,
129, 131
West, Candace, 189, 190–91,
192–93, 197
What Not to Wear, 138, 261–62
What Would You Do?, 79–80
*Who Wants to Marry a
Multi-Millionaire?*, 3
Wilson, Carnie, 97
women: as controllers of sex,
52; lesbians, 219–22; transfer
of domestic labor between,
205–207; *see also* Black women;
gender; gender roles
Wood, Eden, 105
work/employment: class in
relation to, 129–32; COVID-19,
gender roles and, 199;
COVID-19 and essential, 130,
134; gender roles and transfer
of women's domestic, 205–207;
marriage regarding gender
roles and, 197–200, 201; race
in relation to types of, 159;
Undercover Boss highlighting
division of, 127–29;
unemployment, 28, 29
Work Out, 218
Writers Guild of America strike, 9

Zamora, Pedro, 102, 230
Zimmerman, Don, 189, 190–91,
192–93, 197

Danielle J. Lindemann is an associate professor of sociology at Lehigh University who studies gender, sexuality, the family, and culture. She is the author of *Commuter Spouses: New Families in a Changing World* and *Dominatrix: Gender, Eroticism, and Control in the Dungeon*. Her research has been featured in media outlets such as *The New York Times*, *The Wall Street Journal*, *The Economist*, *The Atlantic*, *The Washington Post*, *Rolling Stone*, *Billboard*, and *The Chronicle of Higher Education*. She has spoken about her work on National Public Radio and has written op-eds for CNN.com, *Newsweek*, *Salon*, *Fortune*, and *Quartz*.